The Biggest Battles of the Pacific Theater: The History of the Decisive Campaigns that Led to Victory Over Japan in World War II

By Charles River Editors

A Japanese cruiser under attack during the Battle of Leyte Gulf

About Charles River Editors

Charles River Editors provides superior editing and original writing services across the digital publishing industry, with the expertise to create digital content for publishers across a vast range of subject matter. In addition to providing original digital content for third party publishers, we also republish civilization's greatest literary works, bringing them to new generations of readers via ebooks.

Sign up here to receive updates about free books as we publish them, and visit Our Kindle Author Page to browse today's free promotions and our most recently published Kindle titles.

Introduction

The light aircraft carrier *Princeton* on fire during the battle of Leyte Gulf

The Battle of Leyte Gulf

"Should we lose in the Philippines operations, even though the fleet should be left, the shipping lane to the south would be completely cut off so that the fleet, if it should come back to Japanese waters, could not obtain its fuel supply. If it should remain in southern waters, it could not receive supplies of ammunition and arms. There would be no sense in saving the fleet at the expense of the loss of the Philippines." – Soemu Toyoda, Combined Fleet Chief of the Imperial Japanese Navy

The waters of the Pacific Ocean – stretching deep blue under the tropical sun, or scourged by typhoons – provided World War II's most far-flung battlefield. Two of the world's premier mid 20th century maritime powers, the United States of American and the Empire of Japan, grappled for supremacy across that vast expanse.

Although not as well-remembered as D-Day or even the attack at Pearl Harbor that preceded it, the Battle of Midway was one of the most unique and important battles fought during World War II. In fact, the turning point in the Pacific theater took place between June 4-7, 1942 as a Japanese fleet moved a sizable fleet intending to occupy Midway Island and draw the American navy near. Instead, American aircraft flying from three aircraft carriers that had been away from Pearl Harbor in December 1941 got a bearing on the Japanese fleet and sunk four Japanese aircraft carriers, permanently crippling Japan's navy. The Battle of Midway was one of the first major naval battles in history where the enemy fleets never actually saw or came into contact with each other.

By the time the Battle of Midway was over, the defeat was so devastating that it was actually kept secret from all but the highest echelons of the Japanese government. Along with the loss of hundreds of aircraft and over 3,000 men killed, the four Japanese aircraft carriers lost, when compared to America's one lost carrier, was critical considering America's huge shipbuilding superiority. However, the Battle of Midway could also have easily turned out differently. Japan began the battle with more carriers, more and better aircraft, and more experienced crews than the Americans, and if the battle of the Coral Sea was any indication, the two sides had irrefutable proof of the dominance of the aircraft carrier in the Pacific. The implications of earlier clashes were now starkly underlined, and the fighting was now clearly about timing. The carrier fleets were incredibly powerful and crucially important, yet at the same time they were hugely vulnerable weapons systems. The protagonists at Midway were putting into practice a newly emerging naval doctrine, one which ultimately meted out a terrible punishment to the side that miscalculated. Carrier versus carrier combat had come of age.

The Guadalcanal Campaign, which ran from August 1942 to February 1943, was a bitter and protracted struggle that also happened to be a strange and transitional confrontation quite unlike any other in the long Pacific War. In conjunction with the American victory at the Battle of Midway, Guadalcanal represented the crucial moment when the balance of power in the Pacific tipped in favor of the Allies, but the idea that Guadalcanal would be such a significant battle would have come as a surprise to military strategists and planners on both sides.

Nonetheless, by the time the Guadalcanal campaign was underway, it was a confrontation that neither side actively sought, but that both sides came to believe they could not afford to lose. When Allied forces landed on the island, it was an effort to deny the Japanese the use of the island and other nearby islands, but the Japanese defenders fought bitterly in an effort to push them off the island, resulting in a rather unique battle that consisted mostly of a Japanese offensive against Americans that invaded amphibiously and dug in. While the Americans closed the campaign with a substantial material advantage, the American garrison on Guadalcanal was initially undermanned and terribly undersupplied.

Eventually, nearly 100,000 soldiers fought on the island, and the ferocity with which the

Japanese fought was a fitting prelude to campaigns like Iwo Jima and Okinawa. The campaign would include six separate naval battles, three large-scale land clashes, and almost daily skirmishing and shelling. Not surprisingly, the campaign exacted a heavy toll, with more than 60 ships sunk, more than 1200 aircraft destroyed, and more than 38,000 dead. While the Japanese and Americans engaged at sea and in the skies, of the 36,000 Japanese defenders on the ground, over 30,000 of them would be dead by the end of the Guadalcanal campaign, while the Americans lost about 7,000 killed.

By the end of the fighting, the Guadalcanal Campaign had unquestionably become a turning point in the Pacific War, representing both the last gasp of the Japanese offensive and the first stirrings of the American onslaught. In the wake of the Japanese defeat, Major General Kiyotake Kawaguchi asserted, "Guadalcanal is no longer merely a name of an island in Japanese military history. It is the name of the graveyard of the Japanese army."

By the spring of 1943, American military planners had begun to create a plan to dislodge Japan from east and southeast Asia. When Admiral Chester Nimitz was directed to capture an island in the Bonin group, Iwo Jima stood out for its importance in making progress against the mainland, with three airfields that would allow American air forces to attack the Japanese mainland. But the Japanese were also well aware of how important Iwo Jima was, and they fought desperately in bunkers and tunnels that required the Americans to carefully clear them out gradually. Less than 5% of the Japanese soldiers on Iwo Jima were taken alive, and American casualties were estimated at 26,000, with 6,800 killed or captured. A month later at Okinawa, which lasted from April-June, the Americans suffered an estimated 62,000 casualties, with 12,000 Americans killed or captured. These deadly campaigns came after widely-held predictions that taking these islands would amount to no more than a brief footnote in the overall theater. However, the national character of the Empire was equally misunderstood. Following the month of Iwo Jima, "commentator after commentator in the Anglo-American camp agreed that the Japanese were more despised than the Germans...uncommonly treacherous and savage...alluding to their remarkable tenacity...refused to give up any territory and incurred thousands of losses daily without any possibility of surrender."

Near the end of 1944, as Allied forces were pushing across the Pacific and edging ever closer to Japan, plans were drawn up to invade the Ryuku islands, the most prominent of them being Okinawa. Military planners anticipated that an amphibious campaign would last a week, but instead of facing 60,000 Japanese defenders as estimated, there were closer to 120,000 on the island at the beginning of the campaign in April 1945. The Battle of Okinawa was the largest amphibious operation in the Pacific theater, and it would last nearly 3 months and wind up being the fiercest in the Pacific theater during the war, with nearly 60,000 American casualties and over 100,000 Japanese soldiers killed. In addition, the battle resulted in an estimated 40,000-150,000 Japanese civilian casualties.

To do so, parts of the Philippines were considered main strategic points in the potential Allied attack in the Pacific. The end goal of the Allied plan was an invasion of the Japanese home islands, in which heavy aerial bombardment would precede a ground assault. In order for this to occur, Allied forces would have to occupy areas surrounding Japan, with China adding to Luzon (the largest island in the Philippines) and Formosa (a large island off the coast of China) to create a triangle from which they could launch their bombers.

Given the horrific nature of the combat put up by the Japanese, it's no surprise that the final campaigns had a profound psychological effect on the men who fought, but it also greatly influenced the thinking of military leaders who were planning subsequent campaigns, including a potential invasion of the Japanese mainland. The casualty tolls ultimately helped compel President Truman to use the atomic bombs on Hiroshima and Nagasaki in an effort to end the war before having to attempt such an invasion.

The Biggest Battles of the Pacific Theater: The History of the Decisive Campaigns that Led to Victory Over Japan in World War II analyzes the fighting between the Americans and Japanese across the Pacific. Along with pictures of important people, places, and events, you will learn about the biggest battles of the Pacific like never before.

The Biggest Battles of the Pacific Theater: The History of the Decisive Campaigns that Led to Victory Over Japan in World War II

The Philippines Campaign of 1941-1942

Before the Campaign

The conflict between Japan and the United States had roots going back as far as the late 19th and early 20th centuries when America gained control of Hawaii and the Philippines and became a player in Asia and the Pacific at the same time that Japan was beginning to impose its power in the region. America's "Open Door" proclamation of 1900 also created strains in the relationship because it was announced in part as an attempt to curb Japanese aggression toward China. Further upsetting Japan was the treatment of its citizens in the state of California, where many social commentators spoke of the dangers of the "yellow peril." Following the San Francisco earthquake of 1906, city officials banished almost all residents of Japanese ancestry out of the city. Anti-Japanese sentiment in the early twentieth century was not only contained in California, as the entire West Coast as well as Hawaii enacted local policies against the Japanese, for instance, prohibiting them from owning property in some areas and regulating where they could live.

In fact, Theodore Roosevelt became so concerned about the deteriorating relationship between the two countries that in 1913, he sent an American fleet on an across-the-world goodwill mission that included a stop in Japan in an attempt to repair the relationship. Much of the tension between Japan and the United States stemmed from Japan's belief that it had reached the level of a world power. They expected to be treated as such, and they reacted negatively to all perceived slights against both the country and its citizens.

In terms of Japanese interests in Asia, the focus of their territorial expansion in the 1920s and 1930s was China. They invaded Manchuria but soon found themselves in a war of attrition in mainland China. In order to cut off supply routes that were aiding the Chinese, Japan occupied French Indochina, which drew condemnation from the United States. In response to Japanese aggression, America, in the fall of 1940, placed a steel embargo on Japan, stopped oil sales to them, and also increased aid to Nationalist Chinese forces. Following the lead of the United States, Britain also placed an embargo on Japan, who was threatening their colonial territories of Malaya and Singapore.

These constraints to natural resources increased Japan's hunger to expand. Not only were they trying to assert their position as a world power equal to that of European colonial nations and the United States, they also wanted to gain resource independence. By the late-1930s, their expansionary goals privileged gaining territories that would provide them resources that would allow the Japanese imperial machinery to run smoothly and efficiently and without outside interference. Japanese imperial plans were divided between two groups that held influence in the government: one that wanted to focus the country's expansionary goals north, toward Russia, and a second group which believed that Japan needed to look to the south, where the Philippines, Hong Kong, the Malay Peninsula, Thailand, Burma and the Dutch East Indies would all constitute part of the Japanese Empire's future.

This second group was able to gain predominance among Japanese leaders, and when their imperial endeavors began in earnest with an invasion of China in 1937, the Japanese military saw their eventual path as moving toward the south, where they could implement a plan they called *Dai Nippon*, or Greater Japan.

As with Europe, the United States initially played a cautious game vis-à-vis their stance toward Japan. After all, America was a democratic continental power secure in her own borders and with a strong tradition of isolationism. This attitude was strengthened by her historic hostility towards empire. Why should American lives be shed in a conflict which seemed to be yet another example of the old empires fighting it out for real estate?

Once the Germans invaded the Soviet Union, the Japanese no longer needed to worry about their border with Russia, allowing them to focus exclusively on expanding across the Far East and various islands in the Pacific. But by then the Japanese leadership faced a difficult strategic dilemma. Their ambition to build a large Asian empire could not be realized without the defeat of China, and the Chinese war had descended into a quagmire. A Japanese victory in China remained just about plausible, but in order to secure one Japan needed to maintain a large army on the continent almost indefinitely. In short, the war was draining vast quantities of resources and had become attritional.

Perhaps fatefully, Japan was of the opinion that an attack on British targets in the Pacific would inevitably bring war with America. From a modern perspective this appears a questionable analysis, given America's strong isolationist sentiments. For Japan in 1941 though, there was a chain of logic which ran from a need to secure resources to the identification of targets in the Pacific to the need to confront America.

At the same time, President Roosevelt faced a dilemma too. Though he had won a fairly easy election in 1940, the key issue during the presidential election of 1940 had been the expanding war. Both mainstream candidates adopted an isolationist stance, with FDR promising that American boys "are not going to be sent to any foreign war". It was clear that majority opinion across the nation took the understandable view that the country could and should stay out of World War II. Roosevelt however, had a more nuanced personal opinion. He saw that it was not tenable for the United States to operate in a world system dominated by dictatorships. Sooner or later, these irrational and violent regimes would threaten America as well. That was a hard-nosed strategic and political insight.

Areas of Korea and China occupied by Japan in 1940

If anything, it seems far more accurate to assert that both sides misunderstood the others' position and thus unwittingly took steps that would lead to the attack on Pearl Harbor. Far from covering up evidence of an imminent Japanese attack, Roosevelt and the military planned accordingly for a Japanese attack in 1941, and one of the most obvious targets for potential Japanese expansion was the Philippines, where MacArthur was bedeviled by a bunch of logistical and manpower issues.

While the U.S. went about expanding its navy, the military went about putting plans in place to confront Japan in the Pacific. Plan Orange specifically addressed a possible war with Japan and had been evolving since before World War I.[1] It envisaged a strategic withdrawal to San Diego, while the U.S. Navy could be built up and strengthened, followed by a progressive counter-offensive. This was conservative but also realistic. It assumed short-term Japanese superiority and accepted that the Hawaiian Islands and Philippines would have to hang on - and possibly face invasion - in the absence of the main battle fleet. These were not concessions that were easy

---

[1] And its successor "Rainbow 5" factoring in British participation, followed by the "Plan Dog" memorandum and Roosevelt's "Europe First" policy, during early 1942.

to make politically, and MacArthur would vocally make the case for a stronger, more proper defense of the Philippines.

While that step was not forthcoming, Roosevelt did have the main Pacific fleet sent to Pearl Harbor, where it was meant as a deterrent to let Japan know the U.S. meant business. At the same time, however, stationing the Pacific fleet at Pearl Harbor meant the U.S. was potentially leaving the Philippines exposed, and American military planners were constantly in fear of a Japanese attack there in late 1941.

As a result of these decisions, there was a marked asymmetry in both perceptions and capabilities as Japan and the U.S. stared each other down from across the Pacific in mid-1941. The U.S. was not ready for a Pacific war and did not want war at all, and though it was making preparations it was in no position politically or militarily to jump to the defense of the European empires in Asia. At the same time, the oil embargo indicated they were not going to underwrite Japan's aggression against China either. Without those resources, and operating under the potentially mistaken belief that aggression against Allied possessions would draw the U.S. into the war, Japan came to view the U.S. as the key obstacle to its ambitions. Both sides recognized that Japan had at least a temporary naval supremacy in 1941, and to Japan's High Command this gave them what they viewed as a small window during which to deliver a decisive blow that might secure a permanent advantage. The tectonic plates of war were shifting.

It is against this backdrop that the idea for a crippling surprise attack against the U.S. fleet in Pearl Harbor was resurrected, planned in detail, and delivered to impressive effect. The extent to which the results of the attack were directly attributable to Japanese planning and tactical prowess is, however, more open to debate, because the idea of attacking Pearl Harbor was actually an old plan dating back nearly 15 years.

The U.S. still had a chance to connect dots on December 6, the day before the attack on Pearl Harbor was launched. At noon on that day, the Army intercepted and translated a message sent from Tokyo to their ambassador in Washington instructing him to receive an impending 14 part message that was to be considered a counterproposal to American negotiations, and he was instructed to deliver the message to Secretary of State Hull at 1:00 p.m. EST on December 7.

That timing was meant to allow the Japanese to launch the surprise attack before the Americans received the message, but there was another clue that the Japanese were preparing for war. The communication also instructed the Japanese embassy to destroy its cryptographic equipment after receiving the 14 part message, meaning that they would no longer need to encrypt outgoing communications back. Such a step would only be taken if the Japanese had no intention of maintaining the embassy or using it for communications, which was a very clear sign that they were ready for war.

Although the United States and its armed forces had prepared for the possibility of an attack, they had not anticipated that it would be at Pearl Harbor, so far away from Japan in the middle of the Pacific. The attacks on December 7, 1941 took American forces completely by surprise, inflicting massive damage to the Pacific fleet and nearly 3,000 American casualties. Several battleships were sunk in the attack.

MacArthur in the Philippines

General Douglas MacArthur's experience in the Philippines dated back to the 1920s, and he departed again for Manila in the summer of 1935 for a new challenge. Filipino leader Manuel Quezon wanted to employ a senior military advisor as the Philippines prepared for independence, and he trusted MacArthur, an old friend of his. Quezon was now the President of the Commonwealth of the Philippines, which was a transitional arrangement pending full independence. MacArthur's role was to design and build the new nation's armed forces.

MacArthur

The challenges facing MacArthur in his new job were daunting. He had to build armed forces from scratch on a shoestring budget, and the Philippines consists of thousands of islands with a coastline that is longer than America's. Internationally, Japan was now run by an aggressive military dictatorship and waging an atrocious war in China, and it also had bases on Kyushu and Formosa within easy striking distance of the main Philippine island of Luzon.

MacArthur's strategy was to build a small professional cadre able to draw on thousands of reservists in a time of crisis, similar to the American model he had devised years earlier. It would be organized into mini-divisions and supported by a tactical air force and small navy. For the latter, he successfully lobbied for the development and deployment of Patrol Torpedo (PT) boats.

MacArthur reckoned he had until mid-1942 to prepare for a potential Japanese attack, but he was beset with problems. There was inadequate support from America, and Quezon moved towards a policy of appeasement, lacking the political commitment needed for MacArthur's plan. On top of that, the Philippine troops had outdated equipment, there weren't enough of them, and linguistic problems precluded a homogenous force. Despite the difficulties, throughout this period MacArthur displayed an arrogance and optimism verging on the criminal. In several instances he deliberately misled the U.S. government on the Commonwealth's military readiness. In this, he was to be the architect of his own defeat.

Meanwhile, MacArthur's assistant, Dwight D. Eisenhower, could see where things were heading. The Philippines proved to be a trying place for Eisenhower, whose wife contracted an illness that nearly killed her there, and the cool Eisenhower clashed with the notoriously feisty MacArthur. Although Eisenhower claimed the falling out between the two was not as bad as has been suggested, his biographers have looked upon this time as a helpful experience that prepared Eisenhower to deal with the equally feisty British Prime Minister Winston Churchill and his initially disdainful commander Bernard Montgomery, who would at first openly question Eisenhower's abilities given his lack of combat service in World War I.

Disgruntled, Eisenhower found a posting back home, and MacArthur built a new team of officers to replace him. In mid-1937 MacArthur technically left the U.S. Army, but his relationship with his Philippine employers was at a low ebb too. It was not until July 1941, only five months before Japan's attack, that Roosevelt switched strategies and poured resources into the Philippine garrison. MacArthur was reappointed to the U.S. Army, promoted to Lieutenant General and given joint command of Commonwealth and U.S. forces. It would not be enough.

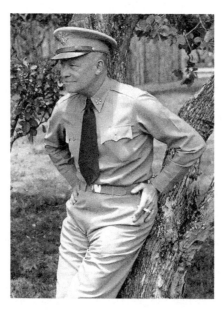

Eisenhower

Once Pearl Harbor had been attacked, it was apparent that the Philippines would also be targeted. In addition to the attack on Pearl Harbor, the Japanese attacked American possessions like the Midway Atoll, Wake, and Guam Islands. They also attacked the British colony of Hong Kong before invading the Malay Peninsula and taking Singapore. And finally, the government of Thailand surrendered to the Japanese without resisting thanks to pro-Japanese elements in the Thai government who convinced them of the futility of going to war with Japan.

Therefore, as Japan turned their attention to the Philippines, they had already had a number of successes in Asia, and their plans for enlarging the Japanese empire seemed to be progressing without problems. The invasion of the Philippines was to be carried out by General Masaharu Homma, who commanded a force of 43,000 men. Opposing this Japanese invasion force was MacArthur's forces, consisting of one division of 30,000 American soldiers along with 100,000 Filipino men, many of whom were reservists who had only received 8-10 weeks of training before the start of the conflict.

Homma

Prior to the beginning of World War II, American military planners had originally believed that the Philippines were not a defensible position against a potential Japanese invasion. Their initial war plans involved a limited defensive campaign that focused on protecting Manila Bay and denying the Japanese from using this vital port region. This plan was part of a larger American strategy against Japan called War Plan Orange (due to reasons of secrecy, Japan was designated nation Orange by American military commanders). In December 1941, as President Franklin Roosevelt began to favor a Europe-first strategy, War Plan Orange (WPO) was combined into a global strategy that the military command called RAINBOW (as it brought together the previous color plans designed for different regions of the world).

By 1941, the plan for the defense of the Philippines, which had been centered on holding out at Manila Bay for a period of six months and allowing an expeditionary force to dislodge the Japanese from the country, had been revised further. American military planners now believed that they could harass a Japanese invasion with a three-staged withdrawal to the Bataan Peninsula in a revised plan they designed WPO-3. The first stage involved a defense of landing positions, especially the beaches at Lingayen. Then, in the second phase, American and Filipino troops would begin an organized withdrawal to the Bataan peninsula. And finally, phase three involved American combat operations at Bataan, as well as several harbor islands such as Corregidor.

Nonetheless, the state of American and Philippine forces in the Philippines on the eve of the invasion was poor. The main body of troops came from the Philippine Army (PA), which was composed mainly of reservists, and their inexperience was compounded by the fact that the PA lacked modern weapons, equipment, and battle-tested officers. Even with the problems of the PA, MacArthur disagreed with American military planners and believed the Philippines could be defended, mainly by making up his troop strength through B-17 bombers and fighter planes. He believed that an increased aerial presence would allow him to better contest the beaches during the invasion, knock out artillery and mortar positions, and harass Japanese soldiers. MacArthur asked for and received clearance to obtain more aircraft to bolster his defenses, but these planes were not delivered in time to defend against the invasion.

As a result, the American army presence in the Philippines amounted to just 22,532 personnel in fighting condition on the eve of the invasion. Most of these troops were infantrymen, while another significant continent was made up of Philippine Scouts. The final piece of the American presence was the coastal defense artillery, which contained howitzers and mortars that could destroy enemy ships and also protect the vital waterways of the Manila and Subic Bays. American ground units were mixed with Philippine units, with the only exceptions being the 31st Infantry, which was composed entirely of American soldiers, and the 45th and 57th Infantry division, which, while made up of Filipino soldiers, had enlisted in the U.S. Army. The United States Navy's Asiatic Fleet, stationed at the Philippines, was under the command of Admiral Thomas C. Hart. These naval forces consisted of a handful of cruisers and World War I era destroyers, as well as a number of submarines. Like the ground troops in the Philippines, they were unprepared for combat operations in late 1941.

Hart

Unlike American forces in the Philippines, the Japanese had a strong presence in the region. The Japanese Southern Expeditionary Army, headquartered in French Indochina, was made up of four armies, as well as units that had gained valuable experience fighting in China and Manchuria. For the Japanese, the major problem they would face was not one of inadequate troop strength or experience but that they had to spread their forces out across the southern Pacific and could not concentrate just on the Philippines.

Disaster in the Air

On the morning of December 7, 1941, the Japanese began their attack with the bombing of Pearl Harbor. Due to the time zone difference, American military commanders in the Philippines were asleep, but Admiral Hart was notified at 0230 hours on December 8th, Manila time. Due to the split command between the navy and army, General MacArthur was not notified at the same time, so the army found out about the attack half an hour later when members of the Army Signal Corps intercepted commercial radio broadcasts about the attack.

Even with this delay in information, both army and navy units in the Philippines should have been notified of the situation and begun defensive measures against the inevitable Japanese attack. Instead, because of problems relaying orders, there was a scramble to assemble the necessary soldiers, aircraft and submarines, and get them in place to contest the eventual invasion of the Philippines.

The Japanese invasion of Luzon involved two phases. First, from December 8-21, the Japanese engaged in aerial bombardment of strategic targets in the Philippines. One of the most important was the attack on Clark Field, which was the main airbase for American planes and its fleet of B-17s. When word of the potential invasion reached American and Filipino military commanders, army air corps officers took a long time to decide to attack nearby Japanese airfields to preempt bombing runs against the Philippines. They finally settled on attacking Formosa, which was the closest Japanese base to them. They believed an American counterattack at Formosa would stall Japanese air power and delay their ability to mount the invasion.

Adding to this delay was the fact that once their targets had been selected, the commanding officer at Clark Field, General Lewis Brereton, needed MacArthur's approval before he could launch his planes. However, in order to contact MacArthur, he first needed to go through Brigadier General Richard Sutherland, MacArthur's chief of staff. Sutherland was notorious for being very protective of MacArthur, and when Brereton contacted him for approval of the mission, Sutherland replied that MacArthur was too busy. He told Brereton to prepare his bombers, but that Sutherland would give final approval for the mission only once MacArthur agreed. Further delays due to weather pushed the timeframe for the Formosa mission back, and by sunrise on December 8th, Japanese planes were already in the air and making their way to the Philippines while American bombers and their fighter escorts remained grounded.

By 9:00 a.m. that morning, radar stations began picking up Japanese bombers heading toward Luzon, but as American planes were still being scrambled, Clark Field was attacked by two waves of Japanese aircraft, which were easily able to destroy the American flying fortresses and fighter planes that sat in lines as they awaited fueling and loading. A group of 21 planes from nearby Nichols Field managed to get airborne, but they were greatly outnumbered and easily shot down by Japanese pilots. MacArthur's Far Eastern Air Force lost most of its strength - nearly 100 planes, largely destroyed on the ground, in a matter of hours. In this short time frame Japan secured complete air superiority over the islands. Hesitation and bad luck had played their part, but the fact was that the defenders had not deployed sufficient fighters on Luzon. Unescorted B-17's were likely to have achieved precisely nothing against their supposed target, the Imperial Japanese Navy at Formosa. Crucially, the Americans were entirely unaware that Japan's superior A4M Zero fighter could operate out and back from Formosa without refueling.

Photo # SC-130991   Cavite Navy Yard burning after Japanese air raid, 10 December 1941

Pictures of Cavite Navy Yard on fire after Japanese air raids

Japanese forces were also able to score important naval victories in the Pacific against a number of countries. In an engagement off the coast of Malaya, Japanese forces destroyed the British battleships *Prince of Wales* and *Repulse*. American planes managed to sink the Japanese battleship *Haruna*, but Japanese attacks against the main American naval base at Cavite, as well as a secondary base at Olongapo in Subic Bay in the Philippines, destroyed their ability to resupply and support the Asiatic fleet, thus rendering the navy unable to play a significant role in attempting to repel the upcoming Japanese landings at Luzon.

Ultimately, Admiral Hart was subsequently ordered to move his fleet south, away from the Philippines, in order to avoid losing the main American naval presence remaining in the region. Thus, with the Japanese pressing a decisive advantage from the air, Hart evacuated most of his navy, except for the submarines, from the Philippines. The submarines were no match for Japan's navy, leaving MacArthur and his forces even more under siege. This decision enraged MacArthur, who exploded on Hart and asked him, "What in the world is the matter with your submarines?" MacArthur would later accuse Hart of cowardice to Secretary of War Henry Stimson, while Hart angrily shot back that MacArthur was " inclined to cut my throat and perhaps the Navy in general."

The Japanese Landings

A map indicating the Japanese invasion points on Luzon

On December 10, General Homma ordered landings at Aparri and Vigan, thus beginning ground operations in the Philippines. The Aparri invasion was carried out by the Tanaka

Detachment of 2,000 soldiers, whose orders were to take Aparri and then seize its airfield, thus extending the range of Japanese aerial superiority. The Tanaka Detachment faced little opposition as it landed, created a beachhead, and then took control of the airfield.

A second Japanese landing at Vigan involved the Kanno Detachment, which again was composed of 2,000 soldiers. However, since the Americans were alerted to the landing at Aparri, the Vigan landing was attacked by some of the remaining B-17 bombers and P-40 fighters that had avoided destruction at Clark Field. American planes destroyed one minesweeper and two transport ships, forcing the Vigan attack force to pull back, but the next day, the Kanno Detachment again attempted to land. This time, they went ashore four miles to the south of their previous location, where they were able to gain a foothold and secure the town of Laoag and its airfield.

A third invasion force landed in southeastern Luzon, where 2,500 men secured the town of Legaspi and its railroad line by December 12. The Japanese then shifted their attention further south, where they launched an attack on the southern island of Mindanao with a force of 5,000 soldiers. The Japanese secured the airfield at Davao, which allowed their planes to reach as far as Borneo, as well as adding to their air superiority over southern Luzon. These initial attacks, which secured important airfields in and around Luzon, had the effect of isolating the island. Any attempts by the United States to reinforce their troops in the Philippines would be both dangerous and costly, making such an attempt from Hawaii or the West Coast of the United States extremely unlikely.

After this initial phase of the Japanese attack, American and Filipino ground forces prepared for the inevitable large-scale assault on their positions. MacArthur had at his disposal a force that on paper looked capable of opposing the Japanese land invasion, but it actually stood very little chance of holding out against the more experienced and better-equipped Japanese soldiers. Furthermore, while American pre-war plans called for the forces in the Philippines to resist until reinforcements arrived, the attack on Pearl Harbor and subsequent fears of Japanese attacks on the West Coast, which meant preparing coastal regions of Hawaii, Alaska, Washington, Oregon and California (as well as defending the Panama Canal), meant that aiding the Philippines was not a priority for military officials in the nation's capital.

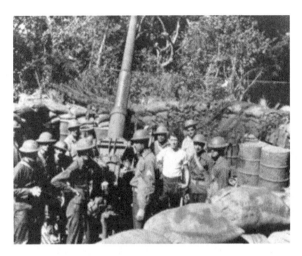

Army artillery forces on the Philippines

Even with the Japanese taking up strong positions in the Pacific to utilize their air and naval power, Mac Arthur believed that a convoy headed by an aircraft carrier could break through and reach the Philippines. While MacArthur lobbied his superiors in Washington to attempt such a mission, military leaders understood that the Pacific Fleet could not risk testing that theory and losing a carrier. MacArthur also called for American allies to attack the Japanese, in hopes that the Chinese could begin a major offensive while the Soviets invaded Manchuria. This was not feasible, however, as the Europe-first strategy agreed upon by the Allies meant that the Americans, British and Soviets put the war in the Pacific on the backburner.

By December 22, the Japanese had switched tactics, moving from a focus on capturing air fields and aerial bombardment toward a major ground invasion. On the 22nd, 80 transport ships were sighted near the Lingayen Gulf on the west coast of the Philippines. The transports deposited the Japanese 48th Division, basically unopposed, at landing areas at Agoo, Caba, and Bauang. Helping the 48th Division, the Tanaka Detachment, which had earlier taken Aparri, moved south toward the landing area. The Japanese attack on Luzon through Lingayen targeted a drive toward Manila, which they hoped to quickly capture as part of their initial 50 day plan for conquering the Philippines.

A picture of Homma coming ashore at Lingayen

In most areas, Japanese landing forces were met by Filipino units. At Bauang, Filipino soldiers utilized .30 and .50 caliber machine guns to cause heavy casualties to some Japanese units. Elsewhere, however, a lack of artillery meant that Filipino soldiers could not mount an effective defense against the Japanese landings. Overall, the Japanese were able to effectively establish beachheads and then began driving inland at speeds that the American and Filipino forces were unprepared to oppose.

Military commanders believed that Lingayen would be a crucial site for a potential invasion because that location offered a direct route to Manila, the capital city. Due to its strategic importance, MacArthur had the 11th Division and Philippine Scouts' 26th Cavalry defend the Lingayen Gulf near San Fernando. He also sent the 71st Division to Lingayen from its original location at Mindanao. The 71st was tasked with stopped Japanese troops from moving south to link up with any invasion forces that landed at different locations on Luzon. North of San Fernando, Philippine Army units were positioned to contest two highways: Route 3 and Route 5. MacArthur also set two National Guard tank battalions in reserve to support the defense; due to his lack of tanks and armored cars, these units were in short supply and needed to be held back so that they could quickly move to invasion locations to shore up defenses.

MacArthur's main ground strategy did not depend on tanks or even American units. Instead,

MacArthur banked on his Philippine Army divisions to oppose the Japanese. He believed that members of the Philippine Army would be motivated by the fact that they were defending their homeland, and also that they would have an advantage in knowing the geography of the areas that they would be fighting in. However, thanks to the inexperience of the Philippine Army, their sheer numbers hid the fact that they would have a hard time standing up to the battle-tested veterans of the Japanese army, and as the Japanese moved inland, they quickly pushed the Filipino forces opposing them backwards. MacArthur became increasingly concerned that these units were being routed.

General Homma did in fact plan for his main invasion force to land at Lingayen. Homma committed the Japanese 48th Division, his best troops, to land at this location, where they would gain a foothold and then drive toward Manila for a quick end to the campaign. The invasion force that landed at Lingayen included 76 army and 9 navy transports, as well as additional naval vessels that had been diverted from the Malaya campaign against the British to protect the landing ships. With most of his fleet moving south, Admiral Hart sent six submarines to contest the landing party, but the submarines only managed to sink one transport vessel and a cargo ship. Unfortunately for Admiral Hart's Asiatic Fleet, many of the torpedoes that they were equipped with in the early part of the war had faulty detonators, so even when striking a target, they did not explode on impact.

Between December 22 and December 28, the Japanese landed over 43,000 men at Lingayen. In addition to the 48th Division, Homma landed additional units at Agoo, Caba, and Bauang, and they were all tasked with fighting their way toward Lingayen, where they would link up with the 48th Division. Like the Philippine Army units, the Americans also were unable to mount a serious defense, but they were able to offer some resistance with naval and air units. For example, an Australian-based B-17 force which was returning from a mission at Davao attacked a group of escort ships while a number of P-40s also attacked Japanese naval vessels. Both groups of planes, while contesting the seas, were unable to stop Japanese landing parties from coming ashore.

The speed with which the Japanese moved forced McArthur to commit additional forces to North Luzon in order to keep his troops there from being overrun. General Jonathan Wainwright sent units from the 11th Division, the 26th Cavalry, and Company C of the 192nd Tank Battalion to engage the enemy near Agoo. Even with the reinforcements, the American-Filipino forces continued to be forced backwards, and American tanks came under heavy fire from both Japanese tanks and bombers. The 26th Cavalry was one of the few units who did not retreat in the face of Japanese attacks as they held the town of Binalonan on December 24, which allowed retreating Philippine Army units to move south without being engaged by Japanese soldiers. When they finally abandoned the town, they had lost roughly 50% of their troop strength.

Wainwright and MacArthur

It was at this point that MacArthur decided to stop trying to protect the beaches and instead implement phase two of WPO-3, which called for an orderly retreat into the Bataan Peninsula. As part of the plan, American and Filipino forces created four defensive lines to provide a screen against the Japanese drive toward Manila. The resistance against the Japanese at these four defensive lines would give the defenders the time to implement the fifth and last defensive line, which would provide more heavy resistance. The engagement at the fifth line would then give the remaining American and Filipino units in the field the time to make their way to Bataan.

However, the swiftness of the Japanese invasion surprised not only military commanders, but also many Philippine leaders. As President Manuel Luis Quezon recalled, "Before noon of December 12, 1941, I received a telephone call from General MacArthur to inform me that he was sending his aide-de-camp, Lieutenant Colonel Huff, to see me on a very important and urgent matter. I told the General I would see his aide immediately. I was in my house situated on the cliffs overlooking the Mariquina River. When Colonel Huff arrived, he told me that General

MacArthur wanted me to be read on four hours' notice to go with him to [the American fortress at] Corregidor. I was shocked. I never imagined that I would ever have to take refuge on Corregidor."

Thus, Quezon and a few other important governmental officials were evacuated from Manila to the island of Corregidor on December 24, 1941. Prior to leaving, Quezon informed the remaining members of the government that in a joint decision with General MacArthur, they had decided to declare Manila an open city so as to save the city's residents from the aerial bombardment and land invasion that was sure to come from the Japanese. By declaring Manila an open city, Quezon and MacArthur hoped to save Manila's civilian population from the death and destruction of the invasion.

A picture of Japanese soldiers moving toward Manila

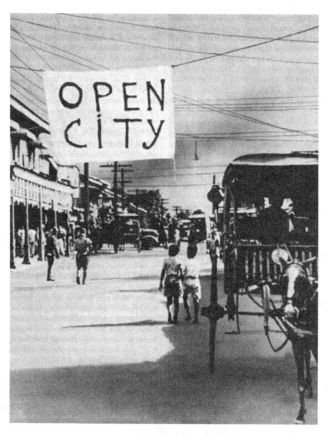

A picture of Manila on December 26

With the retreat of the American-Filipino forces toward Bataan, this meant that Manila would be left undefended. In implementing WPO-3, MacArthur understood that he would be unable to hold the capital city, but he also understood that attempting to defend it, which the Japanese believed would occur, would mean that his entire ground force could be destroyed in one engagement. At the same time, a siege and subsequent battle in Manila could mean the deaths of hundreds or thousands of civilians. Nonetheless, as a USAFFE communiqué reported, "Until Manila was declared an open city, the Japanese did not attempt to attack civilian installations from the air, but as soon as the army withdrew, including anti-aircraft protection, they immediately raided, hitting all types of civilian premises including bridges, convent, the cathedral, business houses and residences."

Even with these attacks, as the Japanese advance guard reached Manila, government officials tried to create a stable, peaceful environment by telling civilians that they would not be attacked unless they provoked the Japanese. As Jorge B. Vargas, who was appointed mayor of Manila upon the evacuation of Quezon, stated, "Manila is an open city. Let us be calm and proceed with our daily task and give the enemy no excuse to misunderstand our position." At the same time, the civilian government ordered all civilians to turn in their firearms and also disarmed the police force.

Japanese troops took advantage of the chaos that had accompanied their arrival to declare martial law, and they began to treat residents of the city in a hostile manner. Japanese soldiers acted aggressively toward civilians, often with little provocation. Looters were shot, while those accused of misdemeanor crimes were often tied to a post and forced to stand in a public location for long periods of time. Some civilians were attacked for little or no reason, and those who failed to bow to passing Japanese soldiers were subjected to being slapped in the face.

The Japanese military in Manila also engaged in widespread confiscation. Military officials took hotels, offices, and residential houses, and even schools such as the University of the Philippines were confiscated for Japanese military use. Japanese soldiers also confiscated cars and trucks from city residents, and they looted warehouses and stores for supplies like rice, sugar, and canned food. In essence, while MacArthur believed he was helping the residents of Manila avoid atrocities at the hands of the Japanese, they were in fact treated in a hostile manner as the Japanese occupied the city.

Bataan

The 4ᵗʰ Marines in January 1942

Filipino scouts on horseback move past a tank in early 1942

For American and Filipino troops on Luzon, MacArthur decided that a withdrawal to the Bataan peninsula would give them the best chance at holding out while waiting for reinforcements to arrive from across the Pacific. The Bataan peninsula gave MacArthur a relatively defensible position in which he could reform his lines and conserve resources as best he could. Indeed, American and Philippine troops would eventually hold out at Bataan for five months before they were forced to surrender in the face of heavy Japanese attacks.

However, since MacArthur had originally planned on defending the beaches of Luzon and had rejected any idea of retreat, he had moved many of the supplies up to the front line. Now, as his forces were retreating, many were unable to bring the supplies back with them. For example, at Cabanatuan, American units positioned there were forced to leave 50 million bushels of rice, which was the equivalent of a five-year supply, and naturally, the loss of supplies in the retreat would have devastating consequences later on in the campaign. At the same time, military planners had based their strategy on a much smaller force than would end up arriving at the Bataan peninsula. Part of this was because extra air and naval units that were stranded on Luzon joined in the retreat, as well as civilians who joined the ranks of retreating soldiers while trying to get away from the Japanese invaders.

As the retreat was under way, General Wainwright was given the task of attempting one last stalling maneuver to provide extra time for the retreating soldiers. Between December 24 and

December 31, Wainwright and his PA divisions (the 11th, 21st, and 91st), along with the 26th Cavalry Regiment and the American Provisional Tank Group, stalled the advancing Japanese 48th Division by creating roadblocks and using the tank group's 75mm guns to inflict damage on the advancing Japanese infantry units.

For Homma and his Japanese strategists, prior to MacArthur's declaration of Manila as an open city, their single-minded goal was to drive to the capital and capture it, but when the Americans made the announcement on December 26th that they would not be defending the city, Homma realized that he would have to change his plans. The decisive battle over Manila that the Japanese had envisioned would not occur, and instead, he would need to defeat the American-Filipino forces at Bataan.

For the two retreating wings of the American-Philippine ground troops, the North and South Luzon Forces, the goal was to reach Bataan at the same time. If one group moved too quickly for the other, half of the ground forces on Luzon could be isolated by the Japanese and destroyed. Therefore, in early January 1942, the two groups moved in tandem as they made their way toward the end goal of Bataan. Japanese forces, after realizing that the final engagement would not occur at Manila, began following American and Filipino troops toward Bataan. The Japanese 48th Division, Homma's best, inflicted heavy damage against the 11th and 21st Divisions, who were ordered to hold the strategic point of Layac, and the ensuing engagements, involving tanks and artillery, inflicted heavy casualties on both sides. The 11th and 21st Divisions held their position under intense pressure from the Japanese, which allowed the straggling units from the North Luzon Force to find their way to Bataan. As this was occurring, the South Luzon Force also made its way to Bataan and also completed the crucial task of blowing up two bridges at the Pampanga River.

The Bataan peninsula had been chosen as the withdrawal point because of its natural barriers against attack. The area was only about 25 miles long and 15 miles wide, and in its center were mountains. The rest of the peninsula was mainly jungle, which provided cover for defenders. It only had two main roads running north and south, which meant that attackers would have trouble pushing into the interior of the region.

However, despite the natural protection that Bataan offered, the major problem that the American and Filipino troops there had was one of supplies. While low levels of food would mean that the soldiers would have to immediately go on half rations, they also lacked adequate supplies of weapons, ammunition and medicine. The original WPO-3 plan called for the soldiers at Bataan to hold out for six months before they could be reinforced for a push out against the Japanese, and even though many officers knew that reinforcements were not forthcoming, they continued to tell their troops that reinforcements were on their way in an attempt to keep morale up.

MacArthur split his American forces at Bataan into two groups. Wainwright commanded what was called I Philippine Corps, which involved 22,500 men stationed along the western portion of the peninsula. I Corps was made up of four divisions: the 1st, 31st, 71st, and 91st Divisions, along with the 26th Cavalry Regiment. Meanwhile, George Parker oversaw II Philippine Corps, consisting of 25,000 soldiers who were stationed along the eastern portion. II Corps was also made up of four divisions: the 11th, 21st, 41st, and 51st, along with the 57th Infantry Regiment.

Parker

A map of Japanese landing points and American lines

There were three main defensive positions at Bataan. The I Corps and II Corps defended a main position between Mount Silanganan and Mount Natib. The I Corps was in charge of the region between the South China Sea and Mount Silanganan, which amounted to roughly four miles, and this position was called the Mauban Line. The II Corps then covered a region from Mount Natib's foothills to the shores of Manila Bay, which was called the Abucay Line. Mount Natib sat between the two, but because MacArthur believed the terrain of Natib was so formidable that nobody could cross it, he left a gap there between I Corps and II Corps. As it turned out, it would be in the gaps at Mount Natib that the Japanese would be able to make an attack on the American-Filipino positions.

MacArthur also created a second battle line, which ran from Bagac across the peninsula to Orion. This line was based on the WPO-3 plan and was supposed to be the last chance for the defenders to hold Bataan. Finally, an area on the coast near the Mariveles Mountains was a potential site for a Japanese amphibious landing, so MacArthur positioned the Philippine Constabulary, 4th Marines, and air force and naval personnel there. The overall strategy to defend Bataan involved using the terrain advantage to hold off the Japanese for as long as possible in the hopes that the war would eventually swing in America's favor and reinforcements would help them break out.

Japanese soldiers using flamethrowers against the Orion-Bagac line

For ground forces at Bataan, soldiers' diets were very poor. They were often given roughly 8 ounces of rice a day, along with a piece of fish or meat every few days. The usual meal consisted of thin rice porridge that was eaten twice a day. Due to the lack of food, many soldiers suffered from starvation and diseases associated with malnutrition. Along with the soldiers at Bataan were roughly 15,000 civilians, including government officials and ordinary Filipinos trying to get away from the Japanese invasion. The civilians were split into four camps in the interior of the Bataan peninsula, but the military had not planned on these extra mouths to feed, and the civilian presence further taxed their food supplies. American military commanders were also afraid that some civilians might be spying for the Japanese. They therefore posted sentries that restricted movements into and out of the civilian camps, and furthered the hardships that these civilians suffered.

For civilians, food was a major problem; most were not able to bring any food with them, so they counted on the army to provide them with their meals. Rationing for civilians was quite cruel, as they had to subsist on meager portions of rice, with one can of salmon also being given to every 20 persons per day. As one survivor of Bataan recalled, "Women and children would risk going as near as possible to the front to beg for food…During chow, one could see the most pitiable scene of famished women and children waiting at the bank of the river for soldiers to go there to wash their mess kits. Given a grain of rice left in the kit would be enough reason for from ten to twenty people to fight for its possession."

Another major problem for civilians was a lack of medicine. Along with the soldiers, civilians suffered from a variety of diseases such as malaria, dysentery, and malnutrition. Some unscrupulous physicians who were among the civilians sold the medicine that they acquired from the army for high fees. Military commanders eventually figured out that that this black market in medicine was developing and decided to stop giving medicine to the civilian population. Death was therefore a constant occurrence among the civilians: "There was a case of a family of a soldier composed of a mother and five children ranging from eight months to seven years. Somehow, the soldier, a sergeant, who was in the firing line, managed to get a pass to visit his family. Upon arrival in the camp, he saw only one member of his family alive – the eight-month-old child was being cared for by another family. The other members died of hunger and disease." (Buenafe, p. 100).

The Japanese made their initial foray into the Bataan peninsula by moving down the East Road with three infantry regiments: the 9th, 141st and 142nd, along with the 7th Tank Regiment. They tried to break through against the II Corps, and they also formed regimental combat teams which were tasked with supporting the main attacking troops and trying to push through gaps in the defensive lines that were opened up by artillery fire. As this was occurring, the 65th Brigade was ordered to move across the foothills of Mount Natib to the eastern coastal plain. Finally, the 122nd Regiment was ordered to move south along the west coast of Bataan, where they would have to cut their way through the dense jungle on that side of the peninsula. Once they reached Bagac, they would move eastward across the peninsula along the main east-west road at Bataan.

Along the foothills of Mount Natib, the Japanese 65th Brigade attacked the 51st Division near Abucay Hacienda. The 51st had been part of the South Luzon Force that had fought fiercely during the Japanese landings at Lamon Bay but had failed to stop the advance of the Japanese 16th Division. Ironically, the 51st was placed at the foothills of Natib because it was supposed to be a spot that would not see much action due to the presence of the mountain. This would supposedly allow the 51st a chance to rest after having been engaged in heavy fighting with the enemy for the past week. Nearby was the 41st Division, which held the center of that section of the line, and the 57th Infantry, a new regiment that would be fighting as a unit for the first time.

On January 9, the Japanese 65th Brigade began its attack on the Abucay Line when two Japanese regimental combat teams broke through defensive positions under heavy artillery fire. These advance Japanese units skirmished with Philippine Scouts, who were eventually able to force them out of the gaps that the Japanese artillery had created. As this was occurring, the

Japanese 122nd Infantry made its way west toward Olongapo, where they took a coastal defense position and then the town of Olongapo itself. On the night of January 11, the 65th Brigade went on a series of night attacks as they attempted to break through positions manned by Philippine Army units. The Filipino soldiers inflicted heavy casualties on the Japanese, and no territory was gained in the attacks.

The 65th also launched attacks against the center and western sections of the Abucay Line. In the center, Japanese soldiers pushed the 41st Division backward, but the defenders held the line and no penetration was made. Along the western section, the battle-weary 51st Division faced a series of assaults, and they were only able to hold on against them because reserve forces were committed to the area and helped the 51st to hold the line. Japanese artillery and air attacks against this section softened the defenses up, and eventually the Japanese found a gap between the 41st and 51st Divisions. On January 15, they began pushing the 51st Division back away from the Abucay Line. The Americans had already committed all their reserves earmarked for that area, and with no more ability to reinforce the section, they had to give way.

American commanders, understanding the danger that the II Corps position was in with the breaching of the western wing of the line, ordered a counterattack by the 51st Division with support from the 21st Division. This maneuver began to force the Japanese back in its early stages on the morning of the 16th, but when the Japanese 9th Regiment began an enveloping action to isolate the advancing soldiers, they stopped the momentum of the counterattack and opened a new breach in the line.

As this was occurring, the I Corps also faced attacks from advancing Japanese troops, but MacArthur had to focus his attention on the action surrounding II Corps, where a breakthrough was most at risk of occurring. MacArthur ordered the Philippine Division and the rest of the reserves to plug the gaps that had been created in the 51st Division. Meanwhile, Japanese troops under General Nara advanced as far as Abucay Hacienda, where they were met by the American 31st Infantry Regiment and the 45th Infantry Regiment. These two regiments tried to hold, but were overcome by the Japanese assault. The Japanese troops then continued their advance where they engaged more Philippine units. As this was occurring, Homma, believing that he possessed the advantage, made preparations for a large-scale assault on January 22nd that was designed to break through the Philippine Division and therefore the Abucay Line.

Japanese soldiers advancing in Bataan

MacArthur and his commanders understood that the Japanese were in a strong, central position from which they could move through the Mount Natib foothills and breach the defenses. Wainwright, however, was still convinced that Natib was too formidable an obstacle, and that the Japanese could not reach his I Corps from that location. Unfortunately, Japanese forces did in fact traverse the terrain of Mount Natib and Homma sent additional troops in the form of the 16th Division's 20th Infantry Regiment, along with artillery and antitank units and the Kimura Detachment that had been previously operating near Davao. Thus, as the Japanese planned their assault on the II Corps along the eastern section of the American-Philippine defenses, they also began an attack on the I Corps in the west.

On January 18, the Kimura Detachment began their attack against the 1st Regular Division at the Mauban Line. The Kimura soldiers were able to break through the Mauban Line, while other units moved in from the southwest and drove a wedge into the defense. By January 21, the Japanese had broken through the line and had isolated groups of American and Filipino soldiers, forcing them to retreat.

At the Abucay Line, the Japanese offensive of January 22 opened with heavy artillery fire to soften up the American and Filipino defenses, and Japanese bombers unloaded on artillery positions that attempted to fire back. After hours of fierce fighting, the American and Filipino troops stationed at Abucay Hacienda were finally dislodged from that location and forced to retreat. As MacArthur received reports about the intense pressure placed upon his soldiers and the new gaps that were opening up in the line, he decided to abandon their positions and withdraw into the interior.

The Japanese also planned an amphibious assault on the naval base at Mariveles, which would open up Corregidor to attack. Taking Mariveles would additionally block the communications and supply routes for the American-Filipino forces. To execute this plan, the 1st and 2nd Battalions of the Japanese 20th Infantry Regiment were tasked with landing at inlets near Mariveles and then fighting their way over cliffs overlooking the sea. As if that wasn't enough, units would have no reinforcements until the main force was able to overcome the American-Filipino defensive line.

The Japanese landing forces faced difficulties almost from the beginning. Choppy seas caused problems, as did American patrol boats, which sunk two of the landing craft. The Japanese also had problems with their maps, which were not detailed enough to provide navigational help, and their landing boats ended up four miles south of their target point. A second group landed even further away, a full seven miles from their destination.

Meanwhile, the defense forces at Mariveles were made up of airmen, marines, sailors, and Philippine Constabulary forces, but most of these men had very little infantry training. Naval lookouts observed a landing group of 300 Japanese soldiers and sent a portion of this mixed force out to attack them. The mixed force was unable to stop their advance, so MacArthur had to send regular infantry units to Mariveles to help out. Meanwhile, a group of 600 Japanese soldiers had been able to dig in at Quinauan Point, and another mixed force was sent to engage them. Again, these units were unable to dislodge the Japanese soldiers, even as more reinforcements were sent in, including tanks.

Finally, on January 29, the mixed forces, with reinforcements sent from the main line, defeated the smaller Japanese group of 300 soldiers, but at Quinauan Point, the mixed force had even more trouble against the Japanese. The tide only turned when the American-Filipino forces began using tank and infantry operations against the Japanese. With his invasion units under heavy duress, Homma finally ordered an amphibious rescue operation, but this too was unsuccessful, with only 34 soldiers surviving the attempt.

As the amphibious operation against Mariveles was ongoing, the Japanese continued their attacks against the defenses at the Bagac-Orion Line. Since the I and II Corps were in retreat, Japanese commanders tried to press their advantage through night attacks. At first they were unable to make a breakthrough, but on January 28, they were able to breach the line in two places defended by Philippine Army units. As the Japanese attempted to move through the gaps in the line, MacArthur ordered a counterattack, which stopped the Japanese advance but was unable to push forward. By early February, after days of heavy fighting, the Japanese realized that the Bagac-Orion line had reached a stalemate, so Homma withdrew his forces. Understanding that his men were fatigued and that he had suffered high casualty rates throughout his divisions in the Bataan Peninsula, Homma decided to wait for reinforcements to bolster his troop-strength before delivering the all-out assault that would end the campaign.

The End of Bataan

All told, the Japanese army in Luzon had suffered 6,700 casualties, with more than 12,000 out of action due to sickness and disease. Homma asked Tokyo for reinforcements, but there would be delays in getting new troops to the Philippines in a timely manner. For example, the 4th Division had to be transferred from Shanghai to Bataan. Also, siege artillery based in Malaya and Hong Kong were sent as well, but it would take until early April for the bulk of these forces to reach Bataan, so there was a lull in fighting as the sides disengaged.

With the pause, some American commanders wanted to go on the offensive to retake the Mauban-Abucay line and push the Japanese further back. Although this plan was discussed, it was ultimately rejected, and in fact, the pause in fighting ended up hurting the American-Filipino forces because they were continually weakened by the lack of food and medicine.

Back in Washington, Roosevelt and his military planners by this point had concluded that the Philippines were basically lost, and they believed that keeping MacArthur, who had become a national hero, in the Philippines was extremely dangerous in case he was captured or killed. Roosevelt therefore ordered MacArthur to leave his command and travel to Australia. One of the reasons MacArthur had become so indispensable is that he had devoted much energy during the siege to his own self-promotion. A series of bombastic and often wildly inaccurate bulletins issued from his command were lapped up by the American press. Exacerbating the situation, MacArthur had accepted $500,000 from Quezon in back pay during the siege, which may also explain why MacArthur backed a proposal by Quezon to grant the Philippines immediate independence so that she could become a neutral state. Roosevelt rejected the proposal out of hand, and for MacArthur it was another example of playing politics, a dangerous habit.

Regardless, MacArthur, who had been commanding his forces from the stronghold at Corregidor, left the island on March 12th. with his family and several staff members. MacArthur made Wainwright the new commander and ordered him to continue to fight until he no longer had the ability to resist. Just before boarding the vessel that would take him away from the Philippines, MacArthur made a promise to his troops and to the people of the Philippines that he would return in the future.

MacArthur's arrival in Australia brought a new command, and America's highest award: the Medal of Honor. The inscription on the Medal read, "For conspicuous leadership in preparing the Philippine Islands to resist conquest, for gallantry and intrepidity above and beyond the call of duty in action against invading Japanese forces, and for the heroic conduct of defensive and offensive operations on the Bataan Peninsula. He mobilized, trained, and led an army which has received world acclaim for its gallant defense against a tremendous superiority of enemy forces in men and arms. His utter disregard of personal danger under heavy fire and aerial bombardment, his calm judgment in each crisis, inspired his troops, galvanized the spirit of resistance of the Filipino people, and confirmed the faith of the American people in their Armed Forces."

If anything, the medal was political because it was important to present the idea of a valiant defense and a heroic commander, and it certainly masked some of the poor decisions MacArthur had made during the campaign. But in fairness, MacArthur dedicated it to his troops, and besides, much stronger claims for the very same award could be made for his personal bravery both during World War I and at Vera Cruz. By winning the award, MacArthur and his father became the first father-son duo to both be awarded the Medal of Honor.

Meanwhile, the remaining soldiers at Bataan had the continued problems of lack of supplies, increasing casualties, and with MacArthur gone, the morale among the troops began to plummet. Additionally, by March 24, the first wave of Japanese reinforcements began to arrive. Japanese commanders placed their new artillery along the eastern part of Bataan and began shelling American-Filipino fortifications. The Japanese also began a new attack involving 11,000 men that took place near Mount Samat. Wainwright still had nearly 80,000 men at his disposal, but these men were mostly sick or wounded.

Japanese forces began their renewed attack against the Bagac-Orion Line on the morning of April 3 with a six-hour artillery barrage designed to soften up defensive positions. As one Filipino officer recalled, "The Japanese concentrated their artillery fire on an area about a kilometer wide by two kilometers deep... The Japanese big guns poured an unceasing stream of shell on that small area. A Filipino officer recalled having personally seen at least 17 flashes of fire – denoting at least 17 enemy batteries visible to the naked eye. " (Buenafe, p. 105). The area along the Bagac-Orion Line that had been hit "was so thoroughly and intensively shelled that, afterwards, it resembled no man's land, for the former green vegetation and trees of the jungle had been burned to crisp and only the charred stumps and trunks of trees remained in mute testimony to the severity of the barrage. It was said that out of the battalion of around 450 men and officers trapped in that area, only 150 were able to crawl out of their foxholes and dugouts to make a feeble attempt of resisting the advancing enemy." (Buenafe, p. 106).

After the barrage, Japanese then concentrated artillery and air attacks on the area near Mount Samat. Japanese troops were quickly able to move around the Philippine Army positions that had been targeted in the barrage and then began moving southward. These Japanese soldiers pushed the Philippine Army units back, and even with reinforcements sent into the area, they were unable to hold their original positions along the Bagac-Orion Line. As one American officer wrote, "[W]hen counter-attacks were ordered to relieve the dire situation there, they failed due to complete physical exhaustion of our troops." (Buenafe, p. 108).

Continued artillery and air attacks against II Corps forced them back further and further, and by April 8, American and Filipino troops began retreating to Cabcaben and Mariveles. Wainwright committed all his reserves to the fight at this point, and with no more troops to reinforce the crumbling defenses, Homma believed that he could strike the decisive blow with more one assault on their lines. Homma sent the 4th Division to attack Mariveles, and at the same time, the 16th Division would pursue the retreating troops, again toward Mariveles. As this was occurring, the 65th Brigade would move to the west to cut off I Corps from II Corps.

On April 9, the Japanese began their final assault, and American and Filipino soldiers were overwhelmed by concentrated artillery fire and fresh Japanese units thrown into the battle. The attackers reached Mariveles on that day, and American commanders understood that with II Corps in complete disarray and with all reinforcements having already been committed to the field, there was no way to stand up against the Japanese onslaught. Later that day, the American-Philippine forces on the Bataan peninsula surrendered to the Japanese.

Allied leaders discussing surrender terms at Bataan

Japanese soldiers celebrating victory after the Battle of Bataan

Even after the surrender came on April 9, the Allies intended to use Bataan as a rallying cry. That night, the Voice of Freedom broadcast struck a defiant tone:

"Bataan has fallen. The Philippine-American troops on this war-ravaged and bloodstained peninsula have laid down their arms. With heads bloody but unbowed, they have yielded to the superior force and numbers of the enemy.

The world will long remember the epic struggle that Filipino and American soldiers put up in the jungle fastness and along the rugged coast of Bataan. They have stood up uncomplaining under the constant and grueling fire of the enemy for more than three months. Besieged on land and blockaded by sea, cut off from all sources of help in the Philippines and in America, the intrepid fighters have done all that human endurance could bear.

For what sustained them through all these months of incessant battle was a force that was more than merely physical. It was the force of an unconquerable faith—something in the heart and soul that physical hardship and adversity could not destroy! It was the thought of native land and all that it holds most dear, the thought of freedom and dignity and pride in these most priceless of all our human prerogatives.

The adversary, in the pride of his power and triumph, will credit our troops with nothing less than the courage and fortitude that his own troops have shown in battle. Our men have fought a brave and bitterly contested struggle. All the world will testify to the most superhuman endurance with which they stood up until the last in the face of overwhelming odds.

But the decision had to come. Men fighting under the banner of unshakable faith are made of something more than flesh, but they are not made of impervious steel. The flesh must yield at last, endurance melts away, and the end of the battle must come.

Bataan has fallen, but the spirit that made it stand—a beacon to all the liberty-loving peoples of the world—cannot fall!"

Allied soldiers listening to the broadcast

The End of the Campaign

With the fall of Bataan, Japanese forces concentrated their efforts on Corregidor. There were over 11,000 American and Filipino troops on the island, and by including survivors who came to the island from Bataan, the number of troops stood at about 15,000. In order to take Corregidor, the Japanese would have to use an amphibious assault, and it took time to create a plan and move troops into place to execute it. Therefore, the assault did not begin until April 29. Prior to this, artillery and air bombardment targeted Corregidor's defenses, and these attacks knocked out many of the artillery positions that would have defended the coasts from invasion.

Corregidor was the best fortified of the islands in Manila Bay, which had relatively good defenses in case of invasion. This was in contrast to the preparations at Bataan, which were poor, and this lack of preparation played an important role in the problems American and Filipino troops had in defending positions there. In fact, in both 1933 and 1937, American commanders in the Philippines had suggested fortifying the Bataan peninsula, but instead the 500 square mile peninsula remained undeveloped in the years prior to the Japanese invasion.

Map showing the Japanese landing points

The Japanese plan for Corregidor involved sending two landing parties of one regiment each. The first landing would take place on May 5 on the northern part of the island, while the second landing would occur on May 6 (this was because there were not enough boats to execute the landings simultaneously). Homma estimated that the invasion would take about a day before they captured the island.

The May 5 landing encountered problems, as American and Filipino troops saw the landing craft coming and fired their 75mm guns at the boats, inflicting heavy losses as well as destroying 31 boats. Even after sustaining such casualties during the landing, however, the Japanese troops who were able to make it on to Corregidor advanced and captured an artillery battery before coming upon a 500 man mixed unit of sailors, soldiers and Marines who tried to halt their progress. This mixed unit was unable to stop the advance of the Japanese landing party, who along with three tanks were too powerful for the Corregidor defense forces. By the afternoon of May 5, the Japanese had killed between 600 and 800 soldiers and had wounded another 1,000 men. Many of the men who made up the American and Filipino mixed forces were not trained as infantrymen, and although they tried to defend the beaches as best they could, they were overmatched by Japanese infantry units.

A mortar battery at Corregidor

The pressure the Japanese invasion placed on the soldiers at Corregidor, along with the fall of Bataan, had the effect of destroying morale. As the invasion of Corregidor continued, American and Filipino troops began to sense the coming defeat. As one officer wrote, "Wainwright might indeed boast to the world that Corregidor 'can and shall be held.' But the growing demoralization ate away the substance of the words. Only the hope of victory can made endurable the horrible sufferings of war, and in Corregidor there was no hope of victory. There was no future paradise to soften the rigors of the present; for Corregidor there was no future but defeat, no reality but the uncertain present." (Buenafe, p. 112).

At this point, Wainwright decided that he had no way of stopping the Japanese advance, and when they took the Malinta Tunnel, the main underground fortification shielding soldiers from artillery and air bombardment, he decided that it was time to surrender there. With the end of the Philippines operations nearing, Homma turned his attention to the southern Philippines, where he still had engagements ongoing at Mindanao and areas in the south of Luzon. In order to complete this last phase of the invasion, Homma once more had to request reinforcements. Military leaders sent units from the 18th Division, 5th Division, and 14th Army for this last portion of the campaign.

The first step was conquering the Visayan Islands, which sat between Luzon and Mindanao. MacArthur had originally placed five Philippine Army divisions at the Visayan Islands but had removed two divisions to help in the fighting on Luzon. The remaining forces lacked artillery, and the soldiers that made up the three divisions, like all Filipino soldiers, were quite raw and lacked proper equipment.

Philippine Army forces first saw Japanese movements at Visayan on April 9, when reports of a 4,800 man invasion force were sent to Philippine Army leaders. This invasion force was met by 6,500 Philippine Army soldiers, but they were unable to hold their positions, and the key city of Cebu fell the next day. They later lost a second key point at Cantabaco, and by April 12, Philippine Army forces had retreated into the north, where they organized a guerilla campaign against the Japanese that lasted for about a month.

On April 16, a Japanese force of 4,000 men was dispatched to take Panay. American and Filipino forces tried to slow the Japanese advance by destroying bridges and roads before engaging in guerilla warfare, but even with this resistance, the Japanese quickly took the island four days later.

The final phase of the campaign was the invasion of the island of Mindanao. Japanese forces launched two amphibious invasions of Mindanao, and by May 3rd, they had gained a foothold and had begun to move inland. The American commanders at Mindanao, seeing the speed with which Japanese soldiers were pushing inland, ordered a retreat into the interior of the island, which would give them more of a terrain advantage due to the mountains in that region. By May 9, the American-Filipino forces had been decisively defeated.

When American commanders at Bataan had surrendered their forces there, Homma believed the campaign was over, so he was angered when American and Filipino forces on Corregidor and the southern Philippines continued fighting. When Wainwright, on Corregidor, released command of Mindanao-Visayan to his subordinates there on May 6 and then attempted to surrender Corregidor, Homma would not accept Wainwright's surrender unless all American-

Filipino forces surrendered. Thus, Wainwright ordered all forces to surrender in a radio broadcast on May 7th.

This led to a conflict between Wainwright, MacArthur (who was now stationed in Australia), and the commander of Mindanao-Visayan, General William Sharp. MacArthur had ordered Sharp to ignore Wainwright's command and to continue fighting, arguing that Wainwright had become "temporarily unbalanced." Since Sharp was disobeying his orders, Wainwright was forced to remove Sharp as commander and then order his forces at Mindanao and Visayan to surrender. Some soldiers on Visayan disagreed with Wainwright's command and began a guerilla campaign against the Japanese. Other groups of soldiers around the Philippines also refused Wainwright's orders and escaped into the jungles, but by June 9, all organized resistance had ended.

The Bataan Death March

The route of the Bataan Death March

Back at Bataan, when the joint American and Filipino force surrendered, they encountered various reactions by victorious Japanese soldiers. As the prisoners were being prepared for transport away from Bataan and into internment camps in the interior of Luzon, some Japanese soldiers began to take personal effects off of their new prisoners. As 2d. Lt. Kermit Lay recalled, "They pulled us into a rice paddy and began shaking us down. There were about 100 of us so it took time to get to all of us. Everyone had pulled their pockets wrong side out and laid all their things out in front. They were taking jewelry and doing a lot of slapping. I laid out my New Testament. In the Bible I had some pesos and a ten-yen note my first sergeant had given me. There was a captain in front of me and I whispered to him whether I should leave the Jap money out. He said, 'Well, I guess so. They said to lay everything out.' Something told me there was trouble, though. I don't know how it came to me, I guess the Good Lord was on my side, but when I could I reached down and picked up that ten-yen note, folded it up real small and tucked it in right behind my belt. After the shakedown, the Japs took an officer and two enlisted men behind a rice stack and shot them. We got to inquiring why they'd been shot. The men who had been next to them said they had Japanese souvenirs and money." (Knox, p. 116).

Japanese soldiers guarding POWs after the battle

Japanese mistreatment of American and Filipino prisoners was an outgrowth of the more general brutality of the Japanese military system. As Sgt. Ralph Levenberg recalled of an exchange between a Japanese soldier and a superior officer involving Levenberg's tinted glasses:

"I had a pair of specially made tinted rimless glasses. I got pulled out of the line by this Jap guard who wanted my glasses. When he pulled them off I tried to motion to him that he wouldn't be able to see much out of them, but he kept grunting and making it very clear that he was bound and determined to have a pair of American sunglasses. About then came along the tallest Jap I'd ever seen in my life. A lieutenant. He yelled, and this little guard froze at attention. The lieutenant came over and returned the glasses to me and indicated I should put them away. Then he turned on this private who was still at complete attention. The officer removed a small sword sheath from his belt and began beating this guard in the face with it, murmuring Japanese comments to him the whole time. That guard never wavered until he dropped completely unconscious. His face was just absolutely like he'd been run over with a tractor. I got back in line and kept my glasses in my pocket." (Knox, p. 116).

On the other hand, some American prisoners were initially treated relatively well by their Japanese captors. Capt. Loyd Mills of the 57th Infantry, Philippine Scouts remembered, "At one stop a Japanese sergeant, who spoke beautiful Oxford-type English, came up to me. He wasn't one of our guards, but happened to be around. 'You are going to find a lot of bad Japanese and you are going to find a lot of good ones. Please don't think that all the Japanese are alike as far as the treatment you are going to receive.' Then he opened up a can of sardines, and with some rice, gave them to me and the men around me. It was the first real food I'd had in days." (Knox, p. 117). As that account suggests, while the experience of the Bataan death march was generally one of extreme brutality and suffering at the hands of Japanese soldiers, not all of them participated in the mistreatment of American and Filipino prisoners of war.

The first groups marched out of the Bataan peninsula were fortunate to the extent that they did not face the same level of brutality as later groups, but even for individuals who did not necessarily face physical danger, rumors swirled about atrocities that the Japanese committed. Cpl. Wayne Lewis, for example, spoke of the psychological effects of Japanese treatment:

"The day after I surrendered they put me in a group and started us marching up the road. And I was on these damn crutches. They were too short. They were rubbing the hell out of my sides because they didn't come up to my armpits. Rumor had it that the Japs were checking the numbers in the group, and if at the next check point the numbers didn't match, they'd kill people to even the count. They we heard [a rumor that] for every guy missing at the next check point they were shooting ten guys.

By the time I got to Kilometer Post 147 I knew I wasn't going to make it. I started lagging behind. I couldn't keep up. What was scaring me was that I figured they were going to kill me. I was at the rear of the column by then, and a bolt in one of the lousy crutches began to get loose.

When we got near Hospital No.2, where I started from, I saw this guy wandering out of the jungle. He must have had malaria because he wasn't wounded. He was out of his head, but he had two good legs. So I told the sergeant who was staying with me to take this guy in my place. 'I'm going back to the hospital.' So I hit the jungle and managed to crawl back to Hospital No.2, where I stayed until Corregidor was whipped." (Knox, p. 125).

While the rumors may have been unfounded, there was no question that the marching prisoners quickly came to understand the dangers posed by some of the Japanese guards. Captain William Dyess wrote about the death march in 1943 and recalled the first murder he witnessed:

"The victim, an air force captain, was being searched by a three-star private. Standing by was a Jap commissioned officer, hand on sword hilt. These men were nothing like the toothy, bespectacled runts whose photographs are familiar to most newspaper readers. They were cruel of face, stalwart, and tall.

The private a little squirt, was going through the captain's pockets. All at once he stopped and sucked in his breath with .a hissing sound. He had found some Jap yen.

He held these out, ducking his head and sucking in his breath to attract notice. The big Jap looked at the money. Without a word he grabbed the captain by the shoulder and shoved him down to his knees. He pulled the sword out of the scabbard and raised it high over his head, holding it with both hands. The private skipped to one side.

Before we could grasp what was happening, the black-faced giant had swung his sword. I remember how the sun flashed on it. There was a swish and a kind of chopping thud, like a cleaver going through beef.

The captain's head seemed to jump off his shoulders. It hit the ground in front of him and went rolling crazily from side to side between the lines of prisoners.

The body fell forward. I have seen wounds, but never such a gush of blood as this. The heart continued to pump for a few seconds and at each beat there was another great spurt of blood. The white dust around our feet was turned into crimson mud. I saw the hands were opening and closing spasmodically. Then I looked away.

When I looked again the big Jap had put up his sword and was strolling off. The runt who had found the yen was putting them into his pocket. He helped himself to the captain's possessions.

This was the first murder. . ."

One of the main problems for prisoners being marched into the interior was a lack of water.

The Japanese for the most part did not allow prisoners to get water, so they could go long periods of time without being able to drink any. Capt. Mark Wohlfeld told of one incident in which American soldiers were finally allowed to drink out of a "buffalo wallow" during one stop: "Some of our young guys started asking the Japs whether they could have a drink of water. I looked to my right and saw a buffalo wallow about fifty yards off the road. It looked like green scum. The guards started to laugh and said, "O.K., O.K." So all these kids, eighteen- or nineteen-year-old enlisted men, ran for the water and began drowning each other trying to get a drink. The Japs thought it was hilarious. I noticed at the end of the scum some others drinking through handkerchiefs, thinking that would filter the bacteria out. Finally, a Japanese officer came along and began shouting at the men in the water. There must have been fifty of them, and they scattered and ran back for the road. That wasn't the end of it. This officer found some Jap soldiers who had been watching us and ordered them to pull out of the line any Americans who had water stains on their uniforms. When we marched out, after a short while we heard shooting behind us." (Knox, p. 128).

Sgt. Charles Cook also told of the issue of water. Due to the heat and humidity on Luzon, lack of water was a major problem not just physically but also psychologically as prisoners marched for hours on end with little or no water: "You didn't dare stop to get water. They'd bayonet you if you tried. I'll never forget or forgive them. Dag blast it, somebody gave orders to water their horses. Why not us? I know one time I broke ranks to fill my canteen with water. I heard this Jap holler. He was running up to me. So I ran through the back of the barrio, jumping fences and scattering chickens. I came back to the column and just mixed in with the men. The guard never found me." (Knox, p. 132).

Pvt. Leon Beck talked about the way the Japanese would use water to taunt prisoners: "They'd halt us at these big artesian wells. There'd be a four-inch pipe coming up out of the ground which was connected to a well, and the water would be flowing full force out of it. There were hundreds of these wells all over Bataan. They'd halt us intentionally in front of these wells so we could see the water and they wouldn't let us have any. Anyone who would make a break for the water would be shot or bayoneted. Then they were left there. Finally it got so bad further along the road that you never got away from the stench of death." (Knox, p. 134).

Since the march from Bataan to San Fernando took about five days, many prisoners inevitably began to straggle, and not surprisingly, the Japanese showed them little mercy. Captain Dyess noted:

> "The hours dragged by and, as we knew they must. The drop-outs began. It seemed that a great many of the prisoners reached the end of their endurance at about the same time. They went down by twos and threes. Usually, they made an effort to rise. I never can forget their groans and strangled breathing as they tried to get up. Some succeeded. Others lay lifelessly where they had fallen.

I observed that the Jap guards paid no attention to these. I wondered why. The explanation wasn't long in coming. There was a sharp crackle of pistol and rifle fire behind us.

Skulking along, a hundred yards behind our contingent, came a 'clean-up squad' of murdering Jap buzzards. Their helpless victims, sprawled darkly against the white, of the road, were easy targets.

As members of the murder squad stooped over each huddled form, there would be an orange flash in the darkness and a sharp report. The bodies were left where they lay, that other prisoners coming behind us might see them.

Our Japanese guards enjoyed the spectacle in silence for a time. Eventually, one of them who spoke English felt he should add a little spice to the entertainment.

'Sleepee?' he asked. 'You want sleep? Just lie down on road. You get good long sleep!'

On through the night we were followed by orange flashes and thudding sounds."

Picture of dead prisoners along the march

For those who weren't fortunate enough to escape but were still lucky enough to be alive, the march brought them to the town of San Fernando, where they were kept in pens in preparation for being loaded onto trains and taken to internment camps. However, the experience within these pens was not much better than it had been during the march. Prisoners continued to lack water and food and were exposed to the hot sun during the day. Many suffered from starvation and disease. Cpl. Hubert Gater's group was placed in a pen late one day and then removed early the next morning. Gater recalled:

> "Sometime after dark the Japs brought some cans of rice to the enclosure gate. A five-gallon can for each hundred men. These cans were not full. Who cared? Those close to the gate were fed. There was not enough to go around. There was no crowding or pushing. A friend helped a friend. Many didn't care. Besides being tired, many were in the last stage of malaria. Just to be left alone in the grass or dirt to rest, sleep, or die…

> It was a long night….Morning came. Malaria, dysentery, and complete exhaustion was taking over. We discovered many in the field were dead. Some perhaps the day before that we hadn't noticed. Men with dysentery lay in their own filth. The sound of men moaning and gasping came from every direction. As the sun came up, so did the odor and the flies.

> Later I talked to men at Camp O'Donnell who were behind us and arrived at San Fernando a day or two later. The dead had not been buried. The same terrible odor had doubled, and the sick and dying almost filled the area." (Knox, p. 148).

When the trains arrived to take prisoners away from San Fernando, they were loaded into hot boxcars with roughly 100 men in each. As Hubert Gater described of his experience on the train-ride, "We jammed in – standing room only. Into the oven we went and, protest be damned, the doors were closed. The three hours that followed are almost indescribable. Men fainting with no place to fall. Those with dysentery had no control of themselves. As the car swayed, the urine, the sweat, and the vomit rolled three inches deep back and forth around and in our shoes. Very little complaining." (Knox, p. 151).

While Gater mentioned men in his boxcar passing out from lack of air, Pfc. Jack Brady described prisoners who actually died while on the train ride: "It seems to me that once in a while our train would stop, and the Jap guards would open the doors so we could get some fresh air. Then is when we'd get the dead ones out. If we could, we'd lift the corpses and pass them over to the door." (Knox, p. 151).

After taking the train, the prisoners arrived at Camp O'Donnell, which the Japanese would use as an internment camp for American and Filipino prisoners of war. Camp O'Donnell was a partially completed American airfield located near the town of Capas, but the barracks at the camp were turned into a makeshift hospital, and the only supplies on hand for the prisoners were those that American and Filipino soldiers had carried with them on the march out of Bataan.

Unfortunately, the prisoners of war at Camp O'Donnell would not be covered by the 1929 agreement on treatment of prisoners of war that had been convened at Geneva, Switzerland. This agreement defined the term "prisoners of war" and also demanded that they would be humanely treated. Japan, however, had failed to ratify the agreement, in part because the Japanese representative to the conference, Isaburo Yoshida, asserted "that real improvement in the condition of prisoners depends, in the final analysis, on the humanitarian sentiments and good will of the belligerents." (Knox, p.154).

Furthermore, Japanese military personnel believed anyone who surrendered was a traitor to their country and deserved harsh treatment. In the Japanese military mindset, there was no room for surrender, but if one failed to fight to the death, they could commit suicide as an alternative. The concept that no soldier should be taken prisoner helps explain treatment of Filipino and American prisoners at the hands of the Japanese in the Philippines.

Life at Camp O'Donnell was harsh, and many men there suffered from disease and other maladies. For those who could still function, there were a number of tasks that needed to be done on a daily basis. As Pfc. Jack Brady recalled:

> "Unfortunately, there was no such thing as being laid up for a while at O'Donnell. There were people in much worse shape than I. Water had to be hauled, people had to be buried, wood needed to be brought in – all kinds of things needed doing. So in O'Donnell, if you could move, you did something.
>
> The place was organized very simply. You picked where you wanted to lie down and that became yours. Officers or senior noncoms selected the men for work details. Those men selected, of course, weren't that many. Most of the men couldn't, or didn't, move. The first detail I went on was where I loaded wood onto trucks and carts for use in the camp. We needed wood to make the fire to boil the water to cook the rice in.
>
> We had to have a water detail too, because the only source in the camp of reasonably good water came from one pipe. The rest of the water had to come from the river. If it wasn't boiled before it was used, it would kill you. It would take a while, but you'd die. The stuff had more germs in it than it had water. We carried the water to the camp in fifty-gallon drums. It took eight men to carry each drum – four men carried and four men rested. Because there was a constant need for water, this was a day-long detail. As soon as you made one trip, you'd go back for

another." (Knox, p. 161).

Not surprisingly, things weren't much better in terms of food. Prisoner Gustavo Ingles explained, "Well, our ration [was] given on the cover of the meat can, so if you put rice there and then you use a piece of wood to keep it flat, that was our ration.... So, you can find worms together with the boiled rice. At first we were throwing that away until one of the American prisoners found out that we were throwing it away. He said, 'Give it to us because we need it.' At first we didn't mind, and he told us that, 'We can't understand it, why you're throwing it away, that is protein.' So, I told him, 'Now that we know, we won't give it to you any more...' It was no more about the chemistry, about what to eat, which we didn't understand by that time. What we understand is only what entered the mouth, that's it's purely rice. Sometimes they put salt so that it would taste different."

As bad as conditions were for American prisoners, it was worse for the Filipinos. Their death rates were much higher than those for the Americans, and on top of that, they received even more brutal treatment than that given to the Americans. Sgt. Knox remembered the large numbers of Filipino dead: "The Filipinos were dying like flies. Carried in a tent-half buttoned up to form a tube, their bodies went by in an endless column. It never ended. Day and night the bodies were carried to the cemetery. I was kind of stunned by the death rate." (Knox, p. 164).

Death was a constant at Camp O'Donnell, and while some men succumbed to disease and other ailments, others just gave up. As the stories show, survival was as much about mental toughness and a will to live as it was about overcoming injury and disease. Those who failed to take things one day at a time instead looked at the long-term implications of imprisonment often lost the will to survive. This was a situation that Pfc. Wilburn Snyder spoke of in one of his interviews: "Not everyone that died died because they gave up, but many did. I spent much of my time trying to get two of my buddies to eat. That was the big problem. Many just said, 'Well, phooey, what's the use?'" (Knox, p. 167). Cpl. Gater spoke of a similar situation: " The theory of self-survival would bother me many times. Not only for myself, but for others. Can a man will himself to die in a two or three-week period? Mahatma Gandhi could go on a thirty-day hunger strike and survive. Some of our men seemed able to give up and die in three weeks or less." (Knox, p. 168).

One of the best ways to ensure survival was to make friends or get into a group in which the members could aid each other and pool their resources. Resource pooling involved a number of activities that provided larger opportunities for trading goods and services by creating networks with other individuals and groups and caring for members during periods of illness or injury. As Capt. Lloyd Mills discussed, "You tried to keep alive. Luckily for me I got into a group. That was the only way to survive. Generally, groups were made up of guys out of the same outfit. We tried to help each other. Someone would steal or swap for quinine. When one of us would get a malaria attack, the other guy would help out. I had a friend. We'd come over on the same boat.

He was out of the 31st Infantry. One night he came down to my area shouting for me. He said, 'You've got to get me over to the hospital.' He was really hurting; he had an internal obstruction. I told him, 'No, don't go over there.' He said that if I didn't do something for him, he'd die right there. I took him over to the hospital and found the doctor. Before I left he gave me his billfold to keep for him. They operated. He never came back. Anyway, back in his billfold there was a 100-peso bill. With it I was able to buy some stuff which I spread around in my group." (Knox, p. 207).

By the end of April 1942, about 9,300 Americans and 48,000 Filipinos had arrived at Camp O'Donnell. During the march from Bataan to the arrival at Camp O'Donnell, historians estimate the number of deaths were between 5,000-10,000 Filipinos and 600-700 Americans.

The Aftermath of the Campaign

The Philippines campaign gave Washington important experience in confronting the Japanese. Pre-war strategies for the Pacific theater did not accurately reflect the resources or capabilities of American forces in the region. The American-Philippine force had delayed the invasion by turning a planned 50 day campaign by the Japanese into a 6 month battle, but military leaders in Washington believed that even had the Philippine Army been properly trained and equipped, their isolation relative to the placement of the rest of the American forces around the world meant that they would have eventually capitulated to the Japanese invasion.

The Philippines pre-war plan, WPO-3, was flawed, as the idea that ground forces in the Philippines would hold on until reinforcements from across the Pacific arrived were obsolete the moment the Japanese attack on Pearl Harbor began. The physical damage to the Pacific Fleet that the Japanese attack caused, along with the psychological effects of Japan's capabilities of attacking Hawaii (and perhaps even the West Coast), meant that reinforcing the Philippines was not possible. Additionally, MacArthur began his defense by rejecting WPO-3, instead moving vital supplies and manpower in an all-out push to contest Japanese landing points. Without an overall strategy, the Philippines defense suffered. At the same time, the army and navy had different aims and did not communicate properly with one another. Admiral Hart had orders to move his fleet south in order to protect it from Japanese naval and air units, but this had the effect of damaging MacArthur's prospects of contesting the Philippines' beaches where he would only have ground forces and no significant naval presence to help.

The loss of aircraft in the pre-invasion Japanese bombings of Luzon was also a huge blow against American and Filipino forces. MacArthur had been counting on air support from his B-17 bombers to help American and Filipino ground units, and with the loss of a significant amount of his aircraft prior to the invasion, the Japanese would have air superiority for the entirety of the invasion, which they used to devastating effect over the course of the six month campaign. As at Pearl Harbor, the Philippines campaign showed military planners in Washington how vital airplanes would be in the war.

Finally, by dispersing his ground forces to defend the entirety of the Philippines instead of immediately implementing WPO-3 to gather his troops at Bataan, MacArthur caused huge logistical problems and allowed the Japanese to encounter small groups of opposing troops instead of gathering all his forces together for a more concerted defense. Had his forces been able to move vital supplies to Bataan from the beginning, they could have put up a much stronger defense and would have stopped much of the suffering that American and Filipino troops experienced in the defense of Bataan later in the campaign.

Even with these mistakes in military strategy and execution, the fact of the matter was that the defense of the Philippines was a doomed task, and there was almost no way for MacArthur to hold off the Japanese invasion. Roosevelt's agreement to a Europe-first policy also meant that the Philippines were a secondary concern to military planners in Washington, so MacArthur's requests for additional troops and supplies would not be met. In fact, MacArthur's vocal statements about reinforcements, as well as his attempts to push American allies to attack Japanese forces in Asia, created conflicts within the army, and many military officials began to view MacArthur as a loose cannon that needed to be handled cautiously.

For the Japanese, the successful conclusion of the Philippines campaign was an important victory over the United States that showed their military prowess against a world power. However, looking more closely at their victory, the majority of the forces they faced were Philippine Army soldiers who were undertrained and poorly equipped. General Homma had also badly miscalculated in believing that MacArthur would try to defend Manila and that a decisive engagement would occur quickly in the campaign around the capital city. Instead, the decisive engagement occurred on the Bataan peninsula, and the American-Filipino defense at Bataan created major delays for Japanese expansion and especially forced them to commit more troops to the Philippines than they had wanted.

All told, the length of the Philippines campaign would have ripple effects in their ability to operate in other regions across the Pacific. Conquering the Philippines gave the Japanese a key piece to their plan of a Greater East Asia Co-prosperity Sphere, and it also gave the Japanese a resource-rich territory that would help them toward their goal of building an imperial network that would allow them to have a degree of resource self-sufficiency. On the other hand, the additional time they spent concentrating on the Philippines would hurt them just a few months later in the Pacific, especially after the decisive Battle of Midway proved to be a turning point in the war.

Coral Sea

Strategic Background

Despite Americans constructing a makeshift defense, the Philippines were clearly lost by March. On the night of March 12, 1942, MacArthur, his family and closest advisors were smuggled out of Corregidor on PT boats. From there they surged across the black ocean to Mindanao and were picked up by American B-17 bombers. They stealthily flew to northern Australia, a dangerous flight over Japanese-held territory, during which MacArthur casually remarked to General Sutherland, "It was close; but that's the way it is in war. You win or lose, live or die, and the difference is just an eyelash." It was at Adelaide on March 18 that MacArthur met the assembled press and told them, "I came through and I shall return."

For a time, Japanese strategists could contemplate a contingency plan even if the U.S. proved ready to fight. If they couldn't knock America out with one opening blow, perhaps they could sap her will to fight by presenting the Southern Resource Area as a fait accompli. This would be followed by a series of further blows against the U.S. Navy, designed to push her well behind in the race to catch up with Japan's naval strength. Having crippled the American fleet and secured her Resource Area, Japan could assert that she had no further imperial ambitions, and a chastened America might concede the point rather than face years of attritional warfare across the Pacific. It was another variation of the original plan, but again it relied on a misunderstanding of America's will to fight. Having failed to knock the USA out after Pearl Harbor, and in the light of America's ultimate ability to field far more units than Japan could ever dream of, it was all she had.

For those thinking along these lines, the opening months of the Pacific War provided some solace. Japan's thinly spread but highly effective forces swept south and west, securing those areas she deemed to be vital to her future. The tiny British garrison in Hong Kong was easily snuffed out, and far more importantly, Japan sank two British battleships off Malaya, landed an army there and moved down the peninsula. In doing so she subdued independent Thailand almost en passant. In Britain's worst ever military defeat, her army of 130,000 surrendered at Singapore in February 1942. Japan also moved into Burma and within four months was threatening the border with British India. At the same time, the Philippines was attacked, with most of America's Far Eastern Airforce destroyed on the ground during the first few hours. Although MacArthur's besieged army would cling on to the Bataan peninsula until May, Manila and the rest of the country were secured by the end of January 1942.

Meanwhile, Japanese invasion forces had also conquered the Dutch East Indies, thereby securing an enclave on the northern coast of New Guinea which threatened to expose the defence of Australia. Indeed, in February, Japanese aircraft bombed Darwin. Japan also grabbed the Solomon Islands, a British protectorate screening the northeast coast of Australia. To complete the picture, the American holdings of Wake and Guam fell, leaving the island of Midway as the most westerly American base in the central Pacific. Even French Indo-China was effectively in Japanese hands, because the Vichy government had acquiesced to Japanese military occupation in December 1941.

A glance at the map in April 1942 would therefore show a huge expanse of the Pacific region now controlled by Japan. In less than four months, Japan had humiliated American and Allied forces, and her land acquisitions were matched by naval success. The attack on Pearl Harbor had neutralized most of the battleships in the U.S. Pacific Fleet, and in addition to the loss of the battleships *Prince of Wales* and *Repulse* off Malaya, the British lost the aircraft carrier *Hermes* to Japanese aircraft in April when they raided deep into the Indian Ocean. This caused the British to pull their Pacific Fleet right back to Mombasa in East Africa. The Americans, Dutch and Australians had lost further vessels as well, notably at the battle of the Java Sea in February.

As a result, when the summer of 1942 started, the only significant naval threat remaining to Japan in the Pacific was what remained of the American Pacific Fleet following the attack on Pearl Harbor, and some of those battleships had been pulled back to San Francisco. This fact was not known by Japan, but given their superiority in battleships, the Japanese were not overly concerned about the remnants of the American fleet either way. What had remained untouched by the attack on Pearl Harbor were the American carriers; if these could be destroyed, then Japan would have secured all of her objectives. At that stage, perhaps, there might be a further opportunity to press the Allies for some kind of peace treaty, cementing Japan's new empire into place.

The Japanese flagship carrier *Akagi* in April 1942

In May however, things began to go wrong.

Operation Mo

Norman Einstein's map of the Coral Sea

The Battle of the Coral Sea resulted from an IJN operation codenamed Operation Mo, aimed at simultaneously taking Port Moresby on the southeast coast of New Guinea and bombing the important airfields at Charters Towers and Townsville in northeast Australia. The Japanese high command hoped to cut off Australia's lines of communication with the United States through this operation.

The Japanese abandoned the notion of invading Australia as impractical at the start of 1942, but they still hoped to isolate the Commonwealth nation, and if the Japanese acquired Port

Moresby, they could also loose land-based bombers against military targets and cities in Australia. By these methods, Prime Minister Tojo Hideki hoped to force Australia out of the war. The ethnically English nation "Down Under" provided hard-fighting soldiers to the Allies and excellent submarine bases to the Americans.

Tojo

Typically for the IJN, the Japanese prepared an excessively intricate plan for Operation Mo. The Japanese chose Port Moresby as the main target in part because of numerous night bombing raids launched from there against important IJN facilities at Rabaul, and in part because it enabled attacks on Australia proper. At the same time, the Japanese scheme relied on perfect coordination between five completely separate forces to succeed. The South Seas Force plan called for the "Tulagi Invasion Force" to leave Rabaul on April 29th. The Moresby Escort Fleet left Truk on April 29th also, while the Moresby Main Force would leave Truk on April 30th. The Moresby Carrier Force would depart Truk on May 1st, and the Moresby Invasion Force sortie from Rabaul on May 4th. The 25th Air Flotilla provided air support.

Among the unit movement orders issued by Combined Fleet HQ, the Carrier Force received Secret South Seas Fleet Operational Order Number 13, which described the maneuvers to be used (and used the designation "x" for the day of the projected landings at Port Moresby) and read in part:

"Sortie from Truk towards the Solomon Islands on about day x–10 through waters to the north-east, and then continue to provide direct support for the Tulagi invasion operation. On day x–5 (the day after the start of reconnaissance flying boat patrols from Tulagi) enter the Coral Sea from the east of the Solomon Islands, begin to provide direct support to the Moresby Invasion Force as required, according to the following strategies.

"a. When a powerful naval force is detected, first attack and destroy[...]

"c. Up until day x+5 after the successful landing at Port Moresby, continue preparations for the appearance of a powerful enemy naval force in the area of the Coral Sea within range of Japanese airbases." (Bullard, 2007, 58).

The orders went on to state that while strong American naval forces probably would not be present, the English Royal Navy might scrape together a force of destroyers and a few light and heavy cruisers to harass the Port Moresby landings. The route given for the Japanese carriers caused them to enter the Coral Sea from the east, between San Cristobal (now Makira) in the Solomon Islands and Espiritu Santo in the New Hebrides archipelago.

The Japanese aimed for surprise with this route, rather than entering the Coral Sea from the north as the Allies probably expected. The Japanese carriers would screen the invasion force while steaming towards Australia, launching a surprise attack against Townsville and Charters Towers airfields. Since these airfields lay well beyond Japanese land-based aircraft range from the nearest Imperial airfields, their aircraft complements – the Japanese hoped – would prove vulnerable to a sudden, massive carrier strike.

Vice Admiral Inoue Shigeyoshi held overall command over the South Seas Force (Japanese 4th Fleet), remaining at Rabaul to attempt coordination of the armada's numerous branches. Meanwhile, Rear Admiral Takagi Takeo held command over the Moresby Carrier Force. Eventually killed in action at the Battle of Saipan in 1944, Rear Admiral Takagi led a force centered around the two major fleet carriers *Shokaku* and *Zuikaku* in the Coral Sea. Vessels of the *Shokaku* class represented the finest aircraft carriers in the Pacific until the 1943 advent of the superior USN *Essex*-class. However, since Takagi lacked any background in carrier warfare, he commanded the escorting cruisers and destroyers, delegating full control over the *Shokaku* and *Zuikaku* to Rear Admiral Hara Chuichi. Hara, an exceptionally tall, beefy man by the standards of the short, slender Japanese of the mid-20th century, received the nickname "King Kong," both for his large physique and for his hard-charging energy.

Inoue

Takeo

Hara

Optimism characterized the Japanese mood at all levels as the Port Moresby expedition sailed in late April and early May. As the official Japanese military records state, the officers and men showed themselves "in high spirits for adventure." (Bullard, 2007, 61). The Americans, meanwhile, set about preparing to offer them more adventure than they bargained for.

Operation Mo relied heavily on the element of surprise to achieve its objectives, and the Japanese failed to realize they had lost that crucial element thanks to the skilled U.S. Navy code-breakers, and the prickly, independent-minded, outspoken young captain Joseph Rochefort in particular. Rochefort managed to tease a workable outline of the Operation Mo plans out of fragmentary, cryptic intercepts of Japanese signals and orders. This knack ensured his position as one of the chief Pacific code-breakers despite his tendency to speak his mind forcefully to high-ranking officers. Another code-breaker, Thomas Dyer, explained Rochefort's singular skill and the crucial effect it had on the Pacific war, noting that it "was his ability – to make a silk purse out of a sow's ear. […] The early messages about Coral Sea were perfectly capable of being read in a totally different way than the correct way. Knowledge of the character of the Japanese and this, that, and the other, enabled him to get the right meaning." (Carson, 2011, 269).

Rochefort

Rochefort correctly identified a mystifying codename, RZP, as referring to Port Moresby, though Admiral Chester Nimitz still doubted if this represented the actual Japanese objective. More certainly the voluminous radio chatter pointed to a massive buildup at Rabaul and Truk. On April 17th, Rochefort and the other code-breakers finally convinced Nimitz, a vigorous and effective leader who became one of America's small constellation of five-star admirals, that the Japanese thunderhead gathering at Rabaul would sweep south, not east. Nimitz signaled his intention to move forces into the Coral Sea to his superior Admiral Ernest J. King, C-in-C US Fleet.

The fierce, secretive, energetic King, whom President Franklin D. Roosevelt quipped probably "shaved with a blowtorch" (Toll, 2012, 166), concurred with Nimitz's (and Rochefort's) analysis, guessing quite closely when the Japanese planned to launch the invasion. He also backed Nimitz's decision to send carriers into the Coral Sea.

Thus, to counter the Japanese threat, Nimitz dispatched two task forces into the ocean bounded by Australia, Papua New Guinea, and the Solomon Islands. American doctrine still used one aircraft carrier as the core of a separate task force at this point in the war (the Coral Sea engagement would permanently change that idea), but Nimitz combined two such task forces. He ordered Task Force 17, based on *USS Yorktown* with Rear Admiral Frank "Jack" Fletcher commanding, and Task Force 11, centered on *USS Lexington,* under Rear Admiral Aubrey "Jake" Fitch, to rendezvous quickly and counter the Japanese threat. Frank Fletcher received overall command.

Nimitz

Fletcher

Nimitz sent the following orders to Fletcher: "An enemy offensive in New Guinea dash Solomon area is at present indicated for first week of May probable primary objective Moresby. May eventually include three or four carriers [and] about 80 heavy bombers and same number of fighters at New Guinea and New Britain air bases. Your task [is to] assist checking further advance by enemy in above area by seizing favorable opportunities to destroy ships, shipping, and aircraft." (Lundstrom, 2006, 132).

These orders strongly resembled those usually issued by the German Wehrmacht but far less common in other military establishments of the era. The German army provided an objective but left the method of achieving it entirely to the initiative of the commander on the scene, which, given the high professionalism of the Wehrmacht, often produced excellent results. Nimitz followed the same procedure with Fletcher, allowing the admiral leeway in how to achieve his objectives, though in this case with a mixed outcome.

The two American carriers and their escorting destroyers and cruisers met at the rendezvous coordinates codenamed Point Buttercup at dawn on May 1st. On the same day, the Japanese action, excited at the prospect of finally launching a counterstrike at the "Japs" who had enjoyed unbroken successes until then.

Fletcher sent no escorting fighters with the strike forces launched, instead keeping the fighters orbiting the *Yorktown* as a combat air patrol (CAP). The ship sent out three waves – Scouting Five, made up of 13 SBD-3 dive bombers under William Burch, Bombing Five, comprising 15 SBD-3s under Wallace Short, and Torpedo Five, 12 TBD-1 torpedo bombers under Joseph Taylor. The formations flew due north over Guadalcanal at 17,000 feet, passing through heavy rain squalls and gusty winds above the island's jungle-covered mountains. The meteorological conditions made flying difficult, but it also hid the Americans from Japanese scouting aircraft.

The American strike waves broke out into clear sunlight past Guadalcanal, with a cumulus cloud deck at 6,000 feet. At 8:20 AM, Burch's Bombing Five launched the first attack on the Japanese ships at Tulagi.

With steam already up, the Japanese vessels got underway immediately, abandoning the harbor in an effort to escape the American attacks, but this tactic only offered partial success. For hours, the American pilots hunted the Japanese ships, shuttling back and forth over Guadalcanal to rearm and refuel, then flying out to attack again. In the manner of the pilots of every nation, they claimed to have populated the ocean richly with Japanese cruisers, battleships, and other heavy warships, when in fact they only faced a pair of destroyers and a mix of light minelayers and transports. They also claimed they sank far more vessels than the handful the Japanese actually lost. David Berry, piloting a 1,000-lb bomb equipped SBD-3, described a successful attack on a Japanese "gunboat," which was actually a small minelayer, probably *Wa #1* or *Wa #2*: "Sam [Adams] dove and missed. […] I was next. I missed, too. […] When I pulled out, I looked back and saw a bomb hit. I think it was Rawley's. […] When the smoke and debris subsided, there were a few crates in the water – a big reddish-brown splotch – but no ship. Rawley's bomb blew that gunboat into a thousand pieces, and she just disappeared." (Ludlum, 2006, 72).

Admiral Shima himself experienced a close call during the repeated American attacks. An SBD-3 dove at his ship, the large minelayer *Okinoshima,* with murderous intent. However, the USN pilot dove straight into a cumulus cloud, which momentarily confused him. He released his 1,000-lb bomb slightly too soon, and it plunged into the water very close to the minelayer rather than punching through its deck. Nevertheless, the shock sufficed to scramble or damage machinery throughout the *Okinoshima,* and other ships later took Shima's flagship under tow for Truk to receive repairs.

The *Okinoshima*

The Japanese floatplanes took to the air to attack the less maneuverable SBD-3s. In response, Fletcher released a quartet of Grumman F4F Wildcat fighters. The rugged, high-speed Wildcats, living up to their name, tore the floatplanes to shreds, shooting down three to crash in the thick jungles of Guadalcanal. The F4F Wildcats then pounced on the second Japanese destroyer *Yuzuki*, riddling the vessel with .50 caliber machine gun bullets from stem to stern as it tried to escape. Nine crew and the captain, Hirota Tachibana, died in the hail of half-inch diameter slugs, and the ship soon trailed a long banner of leaking fuel oil over the sea surface as it limped towards distant Rabaul.

Lost in the clouds, one TBD Devastator torpedo bomber and two F4F Wildcats ran out of fuel, forcing their crews to land – the TBD ditching in the ocean, the F4Fs landing on the Guadalcanal beach. The two F4F pilots, Scott McCuskey and J.P. Adams, met a group of friendly natives, who showed them to a fresh stream and brought them coconuts to eat, while the two Americans rigged an improvised tent from a parachute. That evening, the destroyer USS *Hammann* managed a rescue of the men despite violent surf. Meanwhile, the destroyer USS *Perkins* searched for the crew of the TBD, including Lieutenant Leonard Emil Ewoldt, but could not find them. However, the Americans found and rescued Ewoldt later. The Lieutenant received the Navy Cross for his participation in the Tulagi attack and lived to the age of 87 years in Hartley, Iowa.

The attack on Tulagi by American carrier-based aircraft, clearly identified by sharp-eyed observers among the Japanese, surprised the IJN. This could only mean that, contrary to their previous faulty intelligence, at least one USN aircraft carrier, and probably more, had entered the Coral Sea. Borne high on a tide of victories up to this point, the Japanese Combined Fleet HQ issued a statement expressing their aggressive satisfaction with this turn of events: "Having confidence in the strength of the 5th Air Flotilla, it will be possible to catch and destroy the enemy aircraft carriers that have eluded us since the beginning of the war. In addition to bringing us great joy, this will inform the enemy appropriately of our strength. The South Seas Fleet has yearned for suitable hard fighting, given that there was a good chance of receiving raids from enemy carriers up until the completion of the Port Moresby operation." (Bullard, 2007, 61).

The Americans aboard *Yorktown,* including Fletcher, celebrated what they believed represented a great victory. Prudently, however, Fletcher retreated south during the early hours of May 5th, slipping away into the storms and squalls along the cold front. Now that they had been suddenly alerted to the presence of at least one American carrier in the Coral Sea, the Moresby Carrier Force started hunting for the USN ships. The Japanese, eager for battle, remained confident that they would soon send their enemies to a grave in the black, crushing depths a mile and a half under the Coral Sea's rolling swell.

Searching for the Enemy, May 5-6

On the morning of May 5th, the triumphant *Yorktown* and its escorts emerged from beneath the cold front clouds into brilliant sunlight sparkling on the wave crests of the dark ocean, and a bit later, the ships of Task Force 17 rejoined *Lexington* and Task Force 11. Rear Admiral Aubrey Fitch flew over to the *Yorktown* to talk with Fletcher, finding the carrier's crew in an exultant mood after their success at Tulagi, greatly inflated by the pilots' description of the ships they sank as light and heavy cruisers.

Fletcher, believing himself safe for the moment, sent out numerous scouting aircraft missions. He also ordered the ships to continue refueling from the fast oiler *Neosho.* Fletcher's emphasis on frequent refueling proved wise, as it helped greatly to maintain the overall mobility of his ships, and the *Neosho* would soon suffer ruinous damage at the hands of Japanese pilots, further confirming Fletcher's choice in fueling when able.

The Australian vessels of Task Force 44 commanded by Rear Admiral John Crace joined the other two task forces at the rendezvous area designated Point Corn. Lieutenant Commander Paul Stroop, a staff officer aboard the *Lexington,* later recalled Crace's opinions about the shared mission: "I remember quite distinctly the first communication that we had from our Royal Navy friend, Admiral Crace, had to do with his evaluation of the importance of the Coral Sea area. [...] he said that he considered this area of the greatest importance and our combined forces should do everything they could to keep the Japanese from coming in to the Coral Sea area." (Wooldridge, 1993, 37).

In the meantime, the Moresby Carrier Force under Admiral Takagi approached the vicinity of Tulagi, sending aircraft and ships to investigate the situation. Like Fletcher, Takagi had focused on refueling his carriers and their escorts for prolonged maneuvering on the Coral Sea, but ordered the refueling operation broken off when heard of the American attack at Tulagi, hoping to catch a carrier unawares.

The Carrier Force discovered Admiral Shima had aborted the operation after losing both his destroyers and various minelayers, plus most of the six F1M2 floatplanes. The *Kikuzuki* lay on the beach, soon to slide off at high tide and sink in the coastal shallows. The USN later towed it to Purvis Bay, where its stripped, rusting hulk remains.

Shima had embarked all of the expedition's men and sent them to join the Port Moreby invasion force, judging the Tulagi venture too damaged and too exposed to the Americans to continue. The Port Moresby invasion force had left Rabaul and sailed south into the Coral Sea on May 5th. The light carrier *Shoho* rejoined this armada after having provided initial air cover to the Tulagi landing.

The Japanese sent out their Type 97 Kawanishi H6K flying boats, four-engine twin-tailed aircraft with a then-remarkable range of 4,112 miles, which made them capable of staying in the air for 24 hours at cruising speed. They also appeared quite large to carrier crews, accustomed to such craft as the F4F Wildcat, 28 feet long with a 38 foot wingspan; a Kawanishi measured 84 feet long with a 131 foot wingspan, carrying a crew of 9 men.

An H6K

Towards the evening of May 5th, one such Kawanishi approached the *Lexington* above a layer of stratus clouds, hidden from the ships below. However, Lieutenant Commander James Flatley, part of the *Yorktown's* F4F combat air patrol 12 miles from his home carrier, spotted the large

Japanese aircraft and moved to attack, as Stanley Johnston, aboard the *Lexington*, reported: "We could see neither Flatley nor the Jap, both being above the cloud level. At this point the *Lexington*'s fighter director Lieut. 'Red' Gill broke in to ask Flatley: 'Where is the Kawanishi?' 'Wait a minute, and I'll show him to you,' Flatley replied. [...] Then suddenly there was a glow in the clouds like a ball of fire. It increased and then there popped out of the vapor a huge plane, spinning madly and burning like a torch [...] It hit the water [...] and instantly exploded. There was a big flash of flame and then nothing but a huge pillar of black smoke." (Johnston, 1942, 158).

The Japanese crew either sent no radio message about the carriers prior to their deaths, or else they did so but failed to reach Admiral Takagi. Radio communications in the Coral Sea proved problematic for both sides at around this time, possibly due in part to the unsettled weather. Nevertheless, the canny Japanese noted the Kawanishi's failure to return and correctly guessed that the American carriers could be found in the patrol area assigned to that particular aircraft.

On the night of May 5th and the early morning hours of the 6th, Fletcher sailed his armada south, refueling while in motion from the fast oilers built for precisely this purpose, such as the *Neosho*. The men on the *Neosho* carried out their duties with great professionalism, though the oiler suffered battering by large waves and some of its crew endured injuries when massive seas poured over its decks. Photographs from the Coral Sea show men clinging desperately to the rails while much of the ship's structure around them is hidden in masses of raging foam.

The *Neosho*

Admiral Takagi also turned his thoughts to topping off his detachment's oil bunkers once it became clear that the Americans did not choose to lurk near Tulagi. The Moresby Carrier Force sailed west into the Coral Sea, meeting a Japanese fleet oiler 180 miles westward from Guadalcanal on the morning of May 6th.

The American code-breakers continued to monitor and interpret Japanese signals traffic. On the night of May 5th to 6th, they intercepted a fragmentary radio signal they believed had ordered Takagi's carrier to move towards Australia and launch airstrikes against the airfields there. In this case, the usually reliable Joseph Rochefort, star of the *Hypo* decoding unit, botched his job badly. Inoue, in fact, had ordered Takagi to ignore Australia, giving him a seek-and-destroy mission against the American carrier group.

Based on this faulty data, Fletcher reversed course during the night, heading back northwest to find the Japanese carriers. In the meantime, more flying boats reported the approximate American position. On the afternoon of May 6th, Takagi sailed south with those ships that had refueled in search of the Americans. The hostile forces now moved forward on a near-collision course, with neither certain of the other's location.

Admiral Fitch summarized the American analysis of the situation on the 6th: "Naval units, including one carrier and the invasion fleet were reported converging on Deboyne Island. It was expected that the enemy would use Jomard Entrance to enter the Coral Sea. Two more CVs, probably Carrier Division Five, were reported in the vicinity of Bougainville Island, on May 6 [...] Carrier Division Five [was expected to] run southward from the vicinity of Bougainville and might be within striking distance on the morning of May 7." (Lundstrom, 2006, 157).

This statement shows how deeply the fog of war had hidden the Japanese location from Fletcher and his crews. Fitch placed the Japanese carriers 500 miles distant, but at the moment when he made this analysis, their actual location lay just 170 miles away and closing.

Luckily for Fletcher and the American Task Force as a whole, the Japanese received equally faulty information in the afternoon. A Kawanishi crew mistakenly reported the American forces as sailing south at the time they were actually heading northwest. Thus, Rear Admiral Hara "King Kong" Chuichi took the carriers south in pursuit.

On the night of May 6th and the early morning hours of the 7th, Fletcher's Task Force 17 (the umbrella designation for the combined forces of the original Task Forces 17, 11, and 44) and Hara's carriers passed within 70 miles of one another without realizing the proximity of their enemies. The Japanese moved past on the east, chasing Fletcher south, while Fletcher sailed by on the west chasing the Japanese north.

Fitch, aboard the *Yorktown*, ordered the SBDs armed with one 500-lb bomb and a pair of 100-lb bombs in place of the standard 1,000-lb bomb on the evening of the 6th. Fortunately for the SBD-3 Dauntless pilots, Commander Henry "Hap" Arnold, the ship's air officer, had already had his crews arm the SBDs with the larger, more effective ordnance. Not wishing to give away the position of his ship by sending the men out to change the bomb loads using flashlights for illumination, the beams of which might be seen for some distance over the dusk-wrapped ocean surface, Captain Elliot Buckmaster, the *Yorktown's* skipper, countermanded Fitch's order, and his decision stood.

One other important development occurred on May 6th. Fletcher formed a separate task unit, Task Force 17.3, under the Australian Rear Admiral John Crace, to speed ahead to the Louisiade Archipelago and dispute the Jomard Passage with the Port Moresby Invasion Force. Crace's command included three cruisers and three destroyers. Simultaneously, Fletcher detached the fast oiler *Neosho* and sent the doughty vessel south – towards safety, as he then believed. He detached the destroyer USS *Sims* to escort the valuable refueling ship, though the extra protection seemed almost superfluous.

May 7

At dawn on May 7th, the Moresby Invasion Force, including the light carrier *Shoho*, moved into the Jomard Passage, the channel between Papua New Guinea on the north and the Louisiade Archipelago to the south, connecting the Solomon Sea and the Coral Sea. As the sun rose in a clear sky over the invasion force and *Shoho* moved into the vicinity of Misima Island, Captain Izawa Ishinosuke sent out scouts in a search pattern southward, looking for American aircraft carriers. 115 miles south of the Louisades, and sailing north under clear skies, Rear Admiral Crace's three cruisers and three destroyers kept a sharp lookout for the invasion force. Further south still, the mass of Fletcher's Task Force 17 sailed northwest, at a slower speed.

At daybreak, a cold front from the south dominated the weather at Fletcher's location. A thick layer of cumulus clouds covered the sky, with rain squalls trailing to the ocean surface at intervals. A cool wind blew in gusts, raising a choppy sea.

With visibility limited to around 10 miles, the Americans hoped to obtain cover from Japanese airstrikes. Since they still believed the Japanese carriers lay to their north, this would give them an advantage, as clear skies and unlimited visibility prevailed northward. Staff officer Lieutenant Commander Paul Stroop, aboard the *Lexington*, described the American actions as morning broke over the roughened surface of the Coral Sea: "The battle plan was quite standard. It was something that we had used in peacetime maneuvers. We simply drew a limiting circle in the direction of the area of interest and assigned planes to go out on radii so that at the outer end of their search they would be twice visual distance apart. In other words, the objective was to cover the outer limits of your search sector completely. This was visual search, using the scouting planes, which went out about 175 miles." (Wooldridge, 1993, 37).

The stout, cylindrical shapes of the SBD dive bomber scouts buzzed off the decks of both carriers and skimmed away under the gray and white canopy of densely packed cumulus clouds, buffeted by wind gusts. Meanwhile, 200 miles east, the Japanese fleet carriers launched their own scouting aircraft, many directed southward, where Takagi believed the American carrier force might be found. On the decks of both American and Japanese carriers, dive bombers, fighters, and torpedo bombers idled, their engines rumbling and propellers turning slowly, awaiting news of potential targets.

The actions of the American and Japanese forces – and their mistakes – continued to mirror one another eerily. At 8:15 AM, Lieutenant John Nielsen flew north of Misima Island and spotted two cruisers and two destroyers of the Port Moresby Invasion Force. He signaled this fact to Task Force 17 and turned for home. However, the signaling device used included a mechanical fault unknown to Nielson. This switched the codes for ship types one position, so that the signal he sent actually reported two aircraft carriers and two cruisers. Fletcher, receiving this signal, believed Nielsen had located Takagi's 5th Carrier Division, moving in advance of the Moresby Invasion Force – a not unreasonable assumption. Thus, the Americans sailed north to close the distance and bring the two putative targets within range of their carrier craft.

At 9:15 AM, Fitch judged the contact now close enough and loosed the full aerial might of Task Force 17 against the reported carriers. This force consisted of 53 SBD-3 Dauntless dive bombers, 22 TBD-1 Devastator torpedo bombers, and 8 F4F fighters. The Americans were unwittingly launching their attack waves against non-carrier ships, believing they had found the Japanese fleet carriers.

Far to the south, events in the Japanese task force roughly mirrored the Americans' erroneous actions. A Japanese floatplane spotted the fast oiler *Neosho* and the escorting destroyer *Sims* at 7:22 AM, radioing excitedly that an American aircraft carrier and a cruiser lay 163 miles south of 5th Carrier Division's position. Takagi hesitated to act on a single report, but at 7:45 AM, another floatplane crew made the same mistake.

Now convinced that the *Neosho* was the *USS Saratoga,* Takagi and Hara unleashed a massive 78-plane attack against the American vessels to the south. Beginning around 8:30 AM, the attack consisted of 36 Aichi D3A2 dive bombers (relatively slow aircraft at 267 mph, carrying a single 551-lb bomb), 24 Nakajima B5N2 "Kate" torpedo bombers (capable of being equipped with a single 1,760-lb Type 91 torpedo, one 1,760-lb bomb, two 551-lb bombs, or six 293-lb bombs as payload), and 18 agile, long-range Mitsubishi A6M "Zero" fighters.

A short time later, as the American strike flew north and the Japanese strike flew south, both against incorrectly identified targets, each commander abruptly received new information apprising him of his error. However, each commander, for his own reasons, proved reluctant to recall his strike force, which led to very different outcomes for the two sides.

Nielsen, returning from his scouting mission, dropped a message on the deck "confirming" the sighting of four light cruisers and two destroyers. He then brought his F4F in to land. Queried about his earlier statements regarding two enemy carriers, the pilot maintained he had said nothing of carriers. An examination of his coding device revealed that the poorly designed mechanism substituted one type of ship for another. According to Lieutenant Forrest E. Biard, a *Hypo* code-breaker aboard Fletcher's flagship, the Admiral responded with anger and despair, screaming at Nielsen, "Young man, do you know what you have done? [...] You have just cost the United States two carriers!" (Toll, 2012, 340).

Conversely, the rest of the bridge crew, several of whom left their own accounts, failed to notice this outburst. Throughout Biard's account, Fletcher constantly looks "foolish," "stupider" than any other officer Biard has seen, or admits in ludicrous distress to being pathetically inadequate to his job. Given the fact that Fletcher and Biard engaged in an acrimonious dispute over codes immediately after the latter boarded the *Yorktown*, Biard's later account of Fletcher's reactions appears more as a venomous attempt at character assassination for personal reasons than a sober description of the admiral's actual behavior.

Either way, Fletcher thought about the situation briefly and then decided to allow the sortie to continue. After all, the faulty intelligence at his disposal placed the Japanese carriers somewhere to the north, and the American craft might also find some excellent targets of opportunity among the Port Moresby Invasion Force. General Douglas MacArthur, meanwhile, did his best to assist Task Force 17 by sending out B-17 bombers on scouting and search missions over the Coral Sea.

At 10:22 AM, almost simultaneous with the first attack on the *Neosho* far away in the south, one of the B-17 crews radioed a sighting of *Shoho* and a handful of escorts to MacArthur's HQ. The *Lexington* and *Yorktown* strike groups would have a target after all.

In the meantime, confusion grew among the Japanese admirals. Reports soon indicated that the American ships in the south consisted of an oiler and a destroyer, and Takagi decided to recall his attack force. However, it proved too late do so rapidly, as the strike leader already dispersed his aircraft to search the sea for a carrier. Japanese flying boats located and shadowed Task Force 17, but they botched their reports, making the American force seem further away than in reality. Other scouts reported Crace's detached Task Force 17.3 variously as a group of battleships or carriers, creating even more difficulties for the Japanese decision-makers.

The only Japanese officer who looked at the data and correctly analyzed the situation, Vice Admiral Goto Aritomo, commanded the Moresby Escort Force, including cruisers and the light aircraft carrier *Shoho*. He ordered the actual invasion force to turn back north until the battle ended. He then moved his cruisers to support the *Shoho*, but the gap between had grown too large for them to close up and provide anti-aircraft shelter to the small flattop.

Just three aircraft formed a combat air patrol over *Shoho* – the "Auspicious Phoenix" – when the American squadrons sighted the carrier and moved in for the kill. The first visual contact with the Japanese vessel consisted of slender threads of white against the deep blue of the ocean, the unmistakable wakes of large ships on the move. With the clear air in the northern Coral Sea, the USN pilots spotted the wakes at a range of 40 miles.

The American squadrons banked east and closed. Lieutenant Commander Weldon Hamilton soon made out the pale rectangle of a flight deck gleaming in the sun. Thumbing on his radio, he announced, "I see one flattop bastard." But despite being caught completely by surprise, Captain Izawa Ishinosuke immediately issued an order for an evasive turn, to which the crew responded crisply. The carrier drew a semicircle of foam on the sea as it came around to port, just as the first American aircraft streaked down from the sky.

Commander William Ault and Lieutenant Commander Robert Dixon led their respective sections of aircraft in bombing runs, but missed the carrier. Some of the bombs landed close enough to throw Japanese airplanes off the deck with their concussive force, and the SBDs' machine gunners raked the deck and the Japanese manning sponson-mounted anti-aircraft guns. Though the Japanese sent up a barrage of anti-aircraft fire, none of it hit. American doctrine emphasized marksmanship and often brought down many Japanese attackers, while the Japanese, training their men to use "spray and pray" barrage fire, enjoyed much less success with their carriers' anti-aircraft batteries throughout the war.

After Ault's and Dixon's runs, Weldon Hamilton brought his SBD-3 in for a bombing run, along with 14 other SBDs of Bombing Two. Hamilton achieved the first hit on the carrier, a devastating direct hit: "The Jap was exactly downwind as I nosed down, simplifying my problem tremendously. My bomb, which was the first 1,000 pounder to hit, struck in the middle of the flight deck's width, just abaft amidships. As I looked back the entire after-portion of the flight deck was ablaze and pouring forth heavy black smoke." (Toll, 2012, 342).

The explosion on the *Shoho*

Aboard the *Shoho,* the first hit reduced the deck to shambles. Akira Tendo, a reporter on the aircraft carrier, recounted that after the "breath" of the explosion rushed over the ship, an officer near him began shouting insults at the Americans while holding a hand to his cheek where a fragment had slashed it open. Another nearby sailor bled out and died from a severed arm, while a third tried to keep his station with enough of the flesh blown off his thigh to show the bone. Looking down, Akira saw blood soaking into his pants from a leg wound, but he felt too much shame at the worse injuries of the other men to seek medical aid.

The *Shoho* managed to launch three more fighters to reinforce its CAP, but this action represented too little, too late. The skilled *Yorktown* squadrons roared down, pummeling the burning ship with 1,000-lb bombs and torpedoes. Squadron leader William O. Burch landed another direct hit, and 11 more bombs punched into the shattered vessel after that. Seven torpedoes also ripped into the hull, bursting it open like wet cardboard.

The Americans circled back around the ruined carrier, this time snapping photographs with their K-35 cameras. As the men watched, most elated, a few sickened, the *Shoho's* bow sank until the flight deck sliced into the water. The ship's propellers, still turning at full speed, helped drive the *Shoho* under the surface; the ship "ploughed herself under" according to Harold Buell, and the reporter Akira's account agrees. Out of the 834 men on board the *Shoho,* only 203, including Captain Izawa, survived to be rescued by *Sazanami,* an IJN destroyer. For their part, the Americans lost just three SBD Dauntless dive bombers in the attack. Built extremely tough like many American aircraft of World War II, the SBD-3s could often sustain multiple machine gun hits without crashing.

As the American airplanes streamed away from the spreading patch of reddish fuel oil on the clean blue Coral Sea's water, Lieutenant Commander Robert Dixon of the *Lexington* radioed an ecstatic message to Task Force 17: "Scratch one flattop! Dixon to Carrier, Scratch one flattop!" (Toll, 2012, 343).

When squadron commander Joseph Taylor landed on the *Yorktown,* he reported to the bridge with the other strike leaders, while his rear seat man hurried off to the ship's photo darkroom. When Taylor reached the bridge, Admiral Fletcher asked him what he had seen on the mission. Taylor responded that in a minute, he would show Fletcher. Fletcher at first believed Taylor sought to make him the butt of a joke, but in a short time, the rear seat man arrived with fully developed photographs of the *Shoho* burning and then sinking. The Admiral and the *Yorktown's* captain forgot their dignity when they studied the still-dripping but conclusively detailed photos: "'When they looked at those pictures and heard the story,' said Joe, 'they jumped up and down like a couple of old grads in the grandstand when a last minute touchdown saves the day. Captain Buckmaster and Admiral Fletcher just threw their arms around Bill Burch and me and hugged us... they were so excited and happy.'" (Ludlum, 2006, 122).

The morning's error had paid off with the destruction of a light IJN carrier and all 21 attack aircraft on its deck. Better yet, the strike aircraft returned before any major Japanese raiding force arrived, despite the presence of skulking floatplanes for much of the day and the increasing crackle of Japanese radio traffic.

While the Americans celebrated their success, Crace's detached trio of cruisers and three destroyers came under air attack by Japanese land-based aircraft. The Australian and American ships maneuvered frantically, managing to avoid all the bombs dropped on them by the poorly trained land-based pilots. The latter returned to their bases with bombastic tales of victory, multiple "battleships" sunk, and the near-destruction of a major Allied surface fleet.

After the Japanese had flown off, a trio of American B-26 bombers spotted the Australian naval officer's command and, mistaking them for part of the Port Moresby Invasion Force, attacked. Crace later remarked, "Fortunately, their bombing, in comparison with that of the Japanese a few minutes earlier, was disgraceful." (Layton, 1985, 400).

To the south, the men aboard the fast oiler *Neosho,* skippered by Commander John Spinning Phillips, remained unaware of their peril until the wide formation of Japanese strike aircraft roared over the northern horizon at 10:28 AM. With skies rapidly clearing, the officers and sailors on *Neosho* and *Sims* clearly discerned the overwhelming force bearing down on them and scrambled to action stations despite the odds.

The first squadrons of Japanese aircraft dropped low and moved past the two American ships on a parallel course without immediately attacking. Though the USN personnel did not know it, these Japanese pilots radioed to their strike leader that a close visual inspection confirmed the *Neosho* was not an aircraft carrier. Accordingly, the strike leader sent most of the aircraft off in all directions in a search pattern, leaving 24 dive bombers and a handful of other aircraft to deal with the *Neosho*. These decisions made clear that the Japanese still assumed the scouting report had been correct and that an aircraft carrier had been present earlier, refueling from the fast oiler. Therefore, rather than returning to Vice Admiral Takagi's task force, the detached portion of the strike unit spent two hours combing the expanse of waters around the *Neosho*'s location, using up considerable fuel for no practical gains.

Grimly standing at their guns, the American crews raked the sky with a steady hail of anti-aircraft fire. The destroyer *Sims* fired flak shells from its 5 inch guns, while the *Neosho's* crew kept up a rapid barrage with their 20mm cannons and 40mm guns, as well as their 5-inch/38-caliber DP (dual-purpose) guns. The well-armed *Cimarron*-class fast oilers featured guns similar to those on American destroyers, though fewer in number (and the oilers also lacked the torpedoes found on all destroyers).

Three Nakajima B5N2 "Kate" torpedo bombers opened the attack, dropping a payload of bombs rather than Type 1 torpedoes. Under Phillips' coolheaded directions, the *Neosho* swerved hard to starboard, narrowly evading the bombs, which struck the sea surface in thunderous fountains of spray.

At this point Phillips ordered the *Neosho's* communications officer, Lieutenant William Driscoll, to radio the main task force with news of the situation. Driscoll, too terrified to function, merely radioed that three aircraft had bombed the *Neosho* and missed. Fletcher thus thought a small band of floatplanes had attacked the oiler and sent no fighters to its aid. Phillips later censured Driscoll sharply in his after-action report: "When contact with the enemy was made, the Commanding Officer directed this officer […] to send out contact reports […] The contact reports, and subsequent reports of this vessel's position when sinking, were not despatched correctly […] His conduct under fire is questionable. […] he should at least make an attempt to appear courageous even though inwardly frightened." (Phillips, 1942, 16).

The Japanese dive bombers took some time to set up their run. Finally, at one minute after noon, the Aichi D3A2 dive bombers stooped like falcons on their quarry. Dropping down the air in a long file, the Japanese pilots suddenly dispersed, their formation disintegrating as each man lined up to attack from a different direction.

The multidirectional attacks made both evasion and anti-aircraft fire more difficult. The *Sims* fired its five-inch guns as fast as the gunners could aim them. One shell struck a dive bomber full on, blasting the aircraft and its pilot into fragments that skimmed into the sea like buckshot, spattering the surface with small, foaming splashes.

However, at 12:15, the *Sims'* luck ran out. A Japanese bomb struck the aft deck, punching through into the engine room and exploding. Three more bombs hit the ship as it slid to a halt, no longer able to move or maneuver. Knowing an explosion would soon follow, the assistant chief engineer ordered the men nearby to put the whaleboats and life rafts in the water. The first whaleboat, damaged by bomb shrapnel, filled and sank immediately. A current pushed the second away from the ship,

Chief Signalman Robert Dicken and Fireman 2nd Class Vito J. Vessia, known to his shipmates as "Bill," swam to the drifting whaleboat, started its engine, and turned it back towards the *Sims*. The bomb hits had already thrown some men into the water, and Dicken witnessed the final moments of the sinking destroyer: "One outstanding act was done by an enlisted man named E.F. MUNCH, MM2c, just before he jumped over the side to be picked up by my boat, he secured a depth charge to the deck so it would not go over the side or accidentally explode on deck. The last I saw of the Commanding Officer he was standing on the bridge when the ship was blown up by the explosion. He showed an example of courage throughout the entire engagement." (Dicken, 1942, 3).

The *Sims*

When seawater flooded into the after engine room, the boilers exploded, followed almost immediately by a secondary explosion deep inside the hull. The central section of the *Sims* blew apart violently, splitting the destroyer in half. As the two halves abruptly sank, the forward five-inch gun crew fired a last defiant shot at the Japanese dive bombers, seconds before they vanished under the water.

Out of the crew of 192, only 15 survived to clamber aboard the whaleboat captained by Dicken and Vessia. Two of these men later died. The rest of the destroyer's crew, including skipper Lieutenant Commander Wilford Hyman, died in the explosions or drowned immediately afterward.

As the *Sims* met its demise, *Neosho* kept up a desperate fight against its tormenters. Bomb fragments sliced the head off one of the 20mm gunners and killed another, but the rest of the men stayed at their stations and continued firing. Two Japanese planes burst into flame and crashed into the ocean, while a third pilot, fatally hit, swerved his Aichi D3A2 into one of the 5-inch/38-caliber guns, inflicting tremendous damage on the fireroom just above the after engine room. The *Neosho* also took five direct hits from bombs, three near the bridge and two in the after section.

At 12:18 PM, the Japanese dive bombers ceased their attacks and flew away northward, believing the American oiler doomed. Phillips and his crew fought on doggedly to keep the ship afloat. With the ship afire and listing, steam blasting out of ruptured boilers, and wounded men screaming, some of the officers passed along the order to stand by to abandon ship. Many men only heard "abandon ship" in the confusion, however. They threw the inflatable life rafts over the side and leaped into the sea after them.

A picture of the burning ship

Nonetheless, Phillips managed to keep his ship afloat. He ordered the starboard wing tanks flooded to counteract a dangerous list to port which might have resulted in the oiler capsizing. The boilers lost steam without exploding, and the men brought the fires under control.

At this point, Phillips realized nearly two-thirds of the *Neosho's* 304-man crew had abandoned the ship prematurely. He sent out the whaleboats to tow them back, but the men in the boats found only a few of the rafts, whose gray color blended with the waves. 154 men and 4 officers disappeared into the vastness of the Coral Sea on tiny rafts.

The Japanese aircraft finally reached the relative safety of the *Zuikaku* and *Shokaku* after a 7-hour mission against one oiler and one destroyer. The men had no sooner climbed down from their cockpits, however, exhausted and ravenously hungry, than officers informed them that they would fly out on another strike as soon as a hasty refueling and rearming occurred. "King Kong"

Hara wanted to attack the actual American carriers without waiting for the morrow.

Obediently, Commander Takahashi Kakuishi, the strike leader, and his bone-weary aviators climbed back into their cockpits and took off into the failing evening light under heavy clouds. Part of the southern strike force still could not find the Japanese carriers, though radio traffic indicated their relatively close proximity. Takahashi accordingly led a reduced force against the two American carriers to the west.

The Japanese flew west, expecting a long flight to Task Force 17. In fact, the two armadas sailed quite close. The Americans' radar picked up the incoming attack formations and Fletcher ordered additional F4Fs scrambled, bulking up his combined carrier combat air patrol (CAP) to 30 Wildcats. As a result, Takahashi's attack group ran directly into an ambush set by F4Fs under two "hotshot" pilots, Lieutenant Commanders Paul Ramsey and James Flatley. The American pilots attacked the unsuspecting Japanese suddenly, accompanied by a radioed "Tally ho!" from Flatley. In short order, the Americans shot down eight Japanese aircraft, four of them accounted for by Ramsey alone.

Takahashi realized that if he lingered, the Wildcats would tear his whole force to ribbons. Accordingly, he ordered his surviving air crews to jettison their ordnance into the sea to lighten their loads, making them faster. Then he ordered his men to turn for the Japanese carriers and reach them as quickly as possible. As his strike force trailed away eastward, the *Lexington* and *Yorktown* began recovering their F4F fighters, working quickly due to the approach of dusk.

While the carriers recovered most of their aircraft by nightfall, they continued to cruise close to the same location in case any more stragglers arrived. Suddenly, at 7:09 PM, the men aboard the aircraft carriers observed large numbers of aircraft lights appear over the horizon. Most of the USN officers assumed that these numerous airplanes must belong to their other carrier's complement, since they had access to a count of only those aircraft that had returned to their own deck.

However, as the dark silhouettes of the aircraft flew closer, Lieutenant Commander Stroop on the *Lexington* spotted something amiss: "These planes were in very good formation. I remember noticing the port running lights of the formation all in a beautiful echelon, and one of the things that struck me as odd was that the red color of the port running light was different from the shade of running lights that we had on our own planes. They had a sort of a bluish tint, red-blue tint. About the time that we sighted these lights, one of our screen destroyers began firing at the planes." (Wooldridge, 1993, 39).

The sharp-eyed destroyer captain discerned that the silhouettes of the aircraft were those of Japanese, not American dive bombers. He therefore ordered his entire ship's anti-aircraft armament to open fire on the massed formations of Japanese craft. The flagship sent a desperate radio call to him to cease fire, to which the captain replied tartly that he knew Japanese airplanes when he saw them.

Incredibly, the Japanese aircraft were sending out identification queries and beginning to drop lower and slow as they prepared to land on the two American carriers, which they mistook for the *Zuikaku* and *Shokaku*. They suddenly found themselves in a sky blossoming with glaring bursts of flak and the brilliant stitched streamers of tracers. Abruptly, the Japanese pilots broke formation, swooping in all directions to baffle their opponents' aim as they streamed away across the sky.

The remaining F4F pilots eased back nervously to the *Lexington* and *Yorktown*, hoping that a nervous anti-aircraft gunner did not blow them out of the air. The Americans used radar to watch the Japanese aircraft retreat for approximately 40 miles before they faded from the display. This put the already battle-ready American crews even more on edge. While the relatively weak radar of the early World War II period could drop contacts at a range of several dozen miles or even less in sufficiently bad weather, the disappearing radar signatures could also mean the IJN carriers had moved extremely close.

The Japanese carriers, in fact, lay closer to their American counterparts than at any other moment in the battle, partially explaining the error of the Japanese pilots. A later estimate placed the two forces just 60 miles apart. The Americans listened in surprise to crystal-clear uncoded radio chatter between the carriers and the returning aircraft. Stroop once again furnished a vivid description: "One of the Japanese pilots couldn't get his wheels down, and the carrier told him [...] he'd have to land in the water. They wouldn't take him aboard, didn't want to clutter up their flight deck with a crash [...] So after he got this order from his air group commander or the captain of the Japanese carrier, he then requested that the carrier shine a light on the water so he'd have a spot to land on." (Wooldridge, 1993, 40).

As the interpreters provided rapid translations of the radio signals, the Americans heard the Japanese pilot repeat himself, this time angrily demanding that the ship switch on the spotlight. The chatter soon died down as the aircraft landed.

On the American side, the mistaken landing attempt by the Japanese cost two pilots their lives. 26-year-old Ensign John Drayton Baker, piloting an F4F Wildcat, attempted to land at the same time as the Japanese aircraft. Met by a spouting wall of anti-aircraft fire, Baker took his F4F away to the northeast to avoid the "friendly" batteries, and he soon lost his way amid the squalls. Unfortunately, a second Baker, Paul Baker, also flew his F4F through the darkness, but on the opposite side of the Task Force and in the opposite direction.

Admiral Fletcher took a personal interest in retrieving the unfortunate pilots. The fighter directors, Frank "Red" Gill of the *Lexington* and Oscar Pederson on the *Yorktown*, worked hard at their radios to bring the two desperate aviators in. Unfortunately, both pilots grew confused as to which directions they should be following; John Baker flew off northeast and Paul Baker flew off to the south to vanish forever.

John Baker, at around the same time Pederson attempted to give him directions to the nearest land, sent an ominous transmission hinting at his fate. He stated that he finally saw the *Yorktown* and began to circle it, yet the men on the *Yorktown* saw that his radar signature appeared dozens of miles away to the northeast, suggesting Baker had probably found a Japanese carrier and, like the Japanese earlier, mistook it for a "friendly." His final transmission at 8:28 PM stated, "Why don't you take me aboard? I'm almost out of fuel and am coming in to land." (Ludlum, 2006, 126).

While Paul Baker simply flew onward until his Wildcat likely nosed down into the remote expanse of the southern Coral Sea and he drowned, John Baker probably suffered a more violent end. Whether he crashed into the ocean, was thrown overboard after questioning by the Japanese, shot down, was killed later at a POW camp, or was slain accidentally when the Americans savaged the Japanese fleet carriers the following day, John Baker vanished without a trace.

Stuart D. Ludlum, a naval reservist, preserved the firsthand accounts of the two Bakers' deaths after conducting extensive interviews with the *Yorktown*'s aviators immediately after Midway. Later in the war, a "heroic myth" version of the story sprang up in which Paul Baker deliberately lured the Japanese aircraft wave away from the carrier group at the cost of his own splashdown and drowning.

Whatever the actual case, both Bakers received a posthumous Naval Cross. The USN named a *Cannon*-class destroyer escort, USS *Baker*, DE-190, after John Baker, while Paul Baker, who shot down three Japanese aircraft that day and damaged a fourth, had a *Buckley*-class destroyer escort, USS *Paul G. Baker*, DE-642, named after him.

To the east of Task Force 17, Admiral Takagi ordered his cruisers and destroyers to create a box of searchlight beams around his twin carriers. He knew the Americans' approximate location and thus felt safe in framing the two crucial vessels with light as a navigational aid to returning pilots. Presumably, the angry pilot asking for a spotlight on the sea surface also got his wish, enabling the retrieval of one more trained, experienced Japanese pilot from the water. By 9:30 PM, all surviving Japanese aircraft gathered back on the *Zuikaku* and *Shokaku*. Adnurak Takagi sailed east, while the Americans sailed southeast. This had the effect of slowly but steadily widening the gap between the hostile armadas. Morale on the Japanese ships suffered a severe blow upon learning of the *Shoho*'s destruction. Even the naval command experienced a wave of pessimism.

Around midnight, Fletcher and Fitch determined the American plan for the following day. Task Force 17 turned south, then due west, sailing further from the nearest Japanese land-based bomber bases. Fletcher intended to turn southeast at first light, whereupon Fitch would launch a full-circle search with *Lexington's* scouts. The admiral set the search radius at 200 miles northward and 125 miles southward.

May 8

Planes taking off from the *Shokaku* on May 8

Brilliant tropical sunlight greeted Task Force 17 on the second day of the main Battle of the Coral Sea. The cold front had moved away to the north overnight, depriving the Americans of weather cover. The Japanese, however, still benefited from heavy squalls and cumulus towers, making the *Shokaku* and *Zuikaku* considerably less vulnerable.

Many of the men on board the two American aircraft carriers understood exactly how vulnerable the treacherously fair weather might prove, as noted by Signalman Floyd Beaver: "The next morning found us out in bright sunlight under clear skies with no place to hide. We got off our dawn searches and settled down to our usual waiting. But this time the wait was not so long as usual. Two of our search planes found the Japanese fast carriers, and we swung into the wind to launch our own attack [...] Unfortunately, the Japanese had found us as well and sent their airplanes winging against us." (Beaver, 2009, 166).

Many of the men, Fletcher included, got only three hours of sleep in the early morning of May 8th. Task Force 17 steamed west during the night, then turned southeast and used the trade winds to launch scouting aircraft and a strong CAP. At 8:20 AM, Lieutenant Joseph Smith spotted the Japanese carriers 175 miles away to the north of Task Force 17's position. Fletcher ordered the launch of two strike groups, then turned over tactical command of both carriers' complements to Fitch. The *Yorktown* put 15 SBD-3 dive bombers, 12 TBD-1 Devastator torpedo planes, and 9 F4F Wildcats into the air, while the *Lexington* launched 24 SBDs, 9 TBDs, and 6 F4Fs.

At around 9 AM, Dixon, who had announced "scratch one flattop" the day before, found the Japanese fleet and gave a more accurate location and distance, 191 miles from Task Force 17. The intrepid pilot shadowed the Japanese for an hour, slipping between storms to escape the Zero fighters that soon began hunting him, all the while transmitting valuable data to Fitch.

The Japanese immediately changed course and launched 69 aircraft against Fletcher's armada – 18 torpedo bombers, 33 carrier bombers, and 18 fighters. Once again, Commander Takahashi served as the strike leader. Once all the aircraft left the carriers' decks, Hara ordered the two vessels and their escorts up to a speed of 30 knots, making directly for the American battlegroup. This eased his retrieval of his own aircraft but also brought the *Zuikaku* and *Shokaku* deeper into the USN aerial strike force's attack zone.

One of the Japanese scouts, Kanno Kenzo, located Task Force 17 at 8:22 AM and gave "King Kong" Hara surprisingly accurate location, heading, and distance information. The USN CAP pilots never spotted the wily Kanno, who switched on his homing signal as he flitted ghostlike around the task force's periphery, guiding the Japanese strike planes directly to his location. The F4F Wildcats flushed out a land-based flying boat, however, and destroyed it.

Fletcher deployed Task Force 17 in an anti-aircraft circle, with the carriers in the center about two miles apart, a ring of destroyers around them, and the cruisers in an outer ring. While the Japanese expressed scorn for this formation, apparently relying purely on anti-aircraft firepower, Fletcher actually expected maneuvering by the carriers to form an important part of the defense.

The American strikes reached the Japanese carriers slightly before the Japanese attack reached their targets, at 10:32 AM. However, William Burch, the strike leader for the *Yorktown's* aircraft, opened the action with a serious mistake. Both *Zuikaku* and *Shokaku* sailed in the open when he and his dive bombers arrived on the scene, but Burch delayed, waiting for the slower TBD-1 torpedo bombers to catch up. During this time, *Zuikaku* slid neatly into a heavy squall and vanished from sight.

When the torpedo bombers finally arrived at around 10:52 AM, both sets of aircraft launched attacks against the *Shokaku,* the only remaining target. The Japanese aircraft carrier swerved and turned to avoid the bombs and torpedoes, while Zero fighters darted out to harass the American aircraft, shooting some down, damaging others, and spoiling the attack runs of yet others.

The first squadron, that of Burch, scored no hits at all on the *Shokaku.* As the Americans dove from the cold air aloft to the warm, humid air closer to sea level, their canopies and telescopic sights fogged over in precisely the same manner as at Tulagi. In the meantime, the TBD-1s, unable to approach the Japanese carriers due to their fighter cover, launched their torpedoes vainly from extreme range.

The second attack, led by Lieutenant Walter Short, involved 17 SBD-3s. Once again, the pale obscurity of fogging blinded the pilots as their dive bombers streaked downward across the sky. Nevertheless, Lieutenant John Powers dove lower than the rest, determined to score a hit no matter what the cost. Having told others pilots in the attack force that he would "get a direct hit if I have to lay it on the flight deck," Powers plunged to 900 feet altitude and released his bomb. The stout, capsule-shaped piece of ordnance hurtled across the gap and plunged into the *Shokaku's* deck, followed by a shattering explosion just aft of the Japanese carrier's bridge. Touching off aviation fuel, the blast started a ferocious blaze, whose glare the other pilots compared to an acetylene torch.

Powers paid heavily for his courage. Possibly damaged by the blast of his own bomb, his SBD-3 flashed downwards towards the sea to the starboard of the *Shokaku*. Powers tried to pull up at 200 feet, but the Dauntless dive bomber smashed into the sea surface, killing both Powers (who received a posthumous Medal of Honor) and his copilot. A second SBD-3 scored a hit during this attack.

Powers

The Japanese made excellent use of the weather cover provided by the "quasi-stationary" cold front, which now covered them rather than the American carriers. Lieutenant Noel Gayler described the conditions prevailing during the action: "You couldn't see much [...] Big towering columns of rain clouds, sort of like pillars. You'd go around them and all of a sudden you'd see the carrier. Here he is, and there he's gone [...] It was just such an incredibly confusing, mixed-up, screwed up situation. Poor visibility and people yelling on the radio." (Toll, 2012, 354).

The American aircraft lost track of *Shokaku* after Powers' attack, despite the extensive fires burning on the deck and the huge cloud of black smoke trailing from the wounded carrier. Slightly later, William Ault of the *Lexington* and three other SBD pilots found the *Shokaku* once more, using a "box" search pattern.

A picture of the *Shokaku* under attack

A picture of the *Shokaku*'s crew fighting fires on deck

A picture of damage to the bow

The quartet of aircraft immediately attacked, scoring another hit on the carrier – the third and last of the day. Though the TBDs launched many torpedoes against the *Shokaku,* all either missed or struck the hull and failed to detonate, both characteristic flaws of the inferior quality of the torpedoes used by the U.S. Navy in the early war years.

Meanwhile, two American ensigns flying TBD-1 Devastator torpedo bombers located the *Zuikaku* and tried to attack. Thomas Bash and Norman Sterrie released their torpedoes regardless of the Zeros trying to shoot them down, but only at extreme range. Neither torpedo came close to hitting its target, and the Americans lost two SBD-3s and three F4F Wildcats to the Zero CAP during the action, while many others suffered damage.

As this took place, the Japanese strike located the American carriers, utterly exposed on the sunlit ocean. Kanno Kenzo, the scout who successfully shadowed Task Force 17 for over an hour without being seen, matched courses with strike leader Takahashi. With consummate professionalism and samurai fatalism, Kanno guided the Japanese squadrons over the last few miles to their objective, ensuring the attack reached its target in the fastest time possible. This represented a death sentence for Kanno and his two crew, who exhausted their fuel during the shadowing and guiding.

As his radar screen suddenly lit up with 69 incoming "bogeys," the *Lexington*'s fighter controller, "Red" Gill, shouted into the radio the decades-old rallying call of carnival personnel at the start of an all-out fight: "Hey, Rube!" The Americans had 17 F4F Wildcats airborne, along with a supplemental force of SBD-3 Dauntlesses Fitch wanted to use in an air-to-air role.

Unfortunately, the order went out to fly low to guard against torpedo bombers, enabling the Japanese to pass over some of the American CAP. The Japanese aircraft brushed past the outer CAP and went into the attack runs. A furious melee between the combat air patrol and the escorting Zeros broke out, while the dive bombers and torpedo bombers sought their targets. Most of the aircraft to be used against *Yorktown* had been shot down in the dusk ambush the night before, so the preponderance of the attacking force made their runs at the *Lexington*.

The leader of the Type 97 torpedo bombers, Lieutenant Commander Shimazaki Shigekazu, left a vivid account of the scene as he brought his aircraft in for an attack on the *Lexington*, which he nearly accidentally rammed as he pulled out of his attack run: "Never in all my years in combat have I even imagined a battle like that! When we attacked the enemy carriers, we ran into a virtual wall of antiaircraft fire; the carriers and their supporting ships blackened the sky with exploding shells and tracers. It seemed impossible that we could survive our bombing and torpedo runs through such incredible defenses. [...] Burning and shattered planes of both sides plunged from the skies. Amidst this fantastic 'rainfall' of antiaircraft and spinning planes, I dove almost to the water's surface and sent my torpedo into the *Saratoga*-type carrier." (Okumiya, 1956, 103).

The Type 99 dive bombers also screamed in to drop bombs on the *Lexington* as smaller numbers of each type attacked the *Yorktown*. The *Lexington*, huge and unwieldy, tried to turn out of the way of the attacks, but too slowly to avoid some of them. The *Yorktown*, on the other hand, showed itself much more nimble, moving rapidly out of the way of torpedoes and even dodging bombing runs with abrupt zigzags. Only a single bomb struck the *Yorktown*, inflicting relatively minor damage and a quickly extinguished fire, and at some point during the melee, the strike leader, Lieutenant Commander Takahashi Kakuichi, suffered a hit from either the innumerable flak bursts or an F4F Wildcat. His plane plunged burning into the sea, killing him.

While the *Yorktown* avoided serious damage, the *Lexington* lacked the good fortune of its lighter cousin. Captain Sherman, calm despite the "majestic" slowness of his vessel, tried to turn his ship out of the way of the Japanese torpedoes streaking the water in every direction. The torpedoes porpoised, leaping out of the water and then plunging back in as their powerful motors drove them forward. This gave Stanley Johnston, aboard the *Lexington*, the eerie feeling of the ordnance as living creatures hunting his ship: "Their wicked noses look to me like death incarnate. I have the illusion they are alive, and breaking water to peek at us, only to dive again after having made sure of their courses." (Johnston, 1942, 184).

The huge aircraft carrier, skillfully handled, managed to avoid damage for several minutes. At one point, Sherman kept the vessels on a straight course to allow a pair of torpedoes to pass it by, one running parallel to the hull on either side. But eventually, the large number of attackers and the ship's own ponderousness caused its luck to run out. Two bombs exploded on board the *Lexington*, and two torpedoes struck home in its hull, ripping away armored plate. The explosions killed dozens of men with shrapnel or flame that instantly baked them into carbonized lumps, and they started raging fires.

After a desperate fight with firefighting foam, the Americans managed to put out the flames and began taking the F4Fs aboard. Unfortunately, the ship's doom gathered below decks even as the men began to relax. Thick gasoline fumes from leaking tanks filled the air, growing ever more concentrated until the sparks from a damaged power cable near the telephone switchboard touched them off. The colossal blast wrenched the vessel from the keel up and sent a flaming blast through the ship, instantly killing 25 men and injuring dozens more.

Lieutenant H.E. Williamson later recalled in an interview: "Immediately following the explosion, a gale of wind with the force of a hurricane blew through the door from Central and pinned me to the board. The wind seemed to be made up of streams of flame and myriads of sparks [...] and left nothing but heavy choking fumes. [...] There were cries from the surrounding rooms, so I shouted at the top of my voice, 'Take it easy and hold your breath, and we'll all get out.'" (Johnston, 1942, 244).

The first blast occurred at 12:47 PM, and at first, the captain and crew did not realize the fatal situation of the carrier. However, the explosion ripped open doors and bulkheads, enabling the volatile fumes to spread throughout the ship's interior. Firefighters continued struggling with the flames for hours, but dozens of small explosions occurred, each adding to the inferno and spreading it to new areas.

Pictures of the *Lexington* on fire

At 2:42 PM, a huge explosion destroyed the forward elevator. Another shattering blast rocked the ship at 3:25 PM, after which both Sherman and Fitch realized the necessity of abandoning the *Lexington*. At 4 PM, the captain ordered the engines shut down and the remaining steam vented to prevent a boiler explosion. The men then began a massive rescue operation, combing the burning decks below for wounded or trapped men. The heroic efforts of the crew, who showed great courage and steadiness in the face of the perilous situation, saved hundreds of men who would otherwise have perished in the depths of the vessel.

At 5:07 PM, Admiral Fitch issued the order to abandon ship, seemingly tired of waiting for Sherman to issue the command. The crew did so without panic or haste in a remarkably orderly fashion. Harold Littlefield noted the calm atmosphere aboard the "Lady Lex" during its final moments, despite the possibility of a massive explosion: "Those who were back aft had a treat that we on the bow missed out on. The ice cream locker was aft on the main deck so they broke her open and all the fellows there had all the ice cream they could eat. [...] The morale of the men was excellent; I don't remember seeing any signs of panic. In fact, shortly before leaving ship I saw one fellow lying on the flight deck reading a magazine!" (Hoehling, 1971, 171).

Last to leave the ship at around 6 PM were the executive officer, Mort Seligman, and Captain Sherman himself. Sherman lingered for a moment until a huge explosion erupted through the deck, filling the air with broken airplanes. Seligman shouted for him to follow, and as the two men slid down the rope into the water, Sherman remarked, "I was just thinking, wouldn't I look silly if I left this ship and the fires went out?" (Toll, 2012, 366). In fact, Sherman left just in time.

30 minutes later, a vast explosion went up into the night sky as the *Lexington* blew apart from the inside. Debris and aircraft rained down on the sea for hundreds of yards around as the *Lexington* turned into a pyre of dark red flames. The destroyers and cruisers moved in to rescue the crew, with the USS *Minneapolis* saving Sherman from the water. With the survivors safely aboard, Fletcher sent the USS *Phelps* in to sink the hulk with torpedoes. Shortly after the colossal wreck slid under the waters, a huge explosion occurred, its shock felt and heard by ships 10 miles distant. Out of 2,951 men on board the *Lexington*, 216 died, and 36 aircraft on the carrier's deck sank into the sea.

The Results

Fletcher, knowing the loss of the *Yorktown* could turn the situation into a complete disaster, ordered a retreat. Task Force 17 sailed south, then east, slipping out of the Coral Sea to refuel at Tonga. Task Force 17.3 under Crace, nearly out of fuel, sailed for the Australian ports, while the fast oiler *Neosho*'s crew, working tirelessly, managed to keep the ship afloat for four days despite its gaping wounds and shattered boilers. The whaleboat captained by Dicken and Vessia came alongside, taking on containers of food and water from the larger ship. The oiler and the whaleboat remained together during the four-day wait for rescue. Finally, the destroyer USS *Henley* arrived on May 11th and took the survivors of both the *Neosho* and *Sims* aboard. The *Henley* then used its torpedoes to sink the tattered oiler and the whaleboat lashed to its side.

The USS *Helm*, another destroyer, found one of the *Neosho's* life rafts drifting five days later, on May 16th, 1942. The *Helm* picked up four survivors from the raft, of whom one died soon after rescue. The three survivors reported that they originally numbered 68, crowded onto four life rafts lashed together. However, 64 of the men died from thirst while awaiting rescue. The *Helm* took the three to Brisbane for medical treatment, where another man died. Thus, only two of the 158 officers and men who abandoned the *Neosho* survived.

In light of these facts, Phillips made a list of four recommendations as part of his report. The first addressed the problem of finding life rafts: "That all life rafts be painted yellow, and provided with a tarpaulin which can be quickly slipped off; tarpaulin to be painted the color of the surrounding structure. The Neosho life rafts were painted grey and were extremely difficult for the men in the water, and personnel on board ship, or for searching ships or aircraft, to locate in the water." (Phillips, 1942, 16). While no direct link exists, the USN soon adopted chrome yellow life rafts, which remained in use until replaced by even more visible red life rafts in 1952. The *Neosho's* experience in the Coral Sea may well have helped prompt the change to colorful rafts.

The Japanese also retreated. Inoue requested permission to retreat from Admiral Yamamoto, the architect of the attack on Pearl Harbor, who initially angrily refused. With no forces left opposing them, the Japanese could have readily taken Port Moresby, but they declined to do so. Though *Shokaku* required repairs and could not support air operations from its mangled deck, *Zuikaku* remained and the invasion force also remained intact. Okumiya Masatake later blasted his commanders in a postwar book for abandoning the opportunity of a notable strategic success and a continued Japanese advance: "The truth of the matter was that our senior naval commanders in the Coral Sea area lacked the fighting spirit necessary to engage the enemy. This failure to pursue a temporary advantage later proved to be of tremendous advantage to the Americans (Okumiya, 1956, 110). As at the Battle of Leyte Gulf, Japanese commanders proved remarkably fragile once the enemy pierced their feelings of invincibility, "giving up" too soon and squandering the opportunities won for them by the courage and blood of their subordinates.

The fame of engagements such as the Battle of Midway overshadows the Battle of the Coral Sea in historic memory, but Coral Sea proved quite significant to the course of World War II in the Pacific. Though the Japanese claimed a victory after sinking the USS *Lexington,* the battle actually gave the Imperial Japanese Navy its first bloody nose in a conflict which, until then, had been going entirely their way. This dented Japanese morale and raised that of the Americans, Australians, and British, beginning a tidal shift in the balance of confidence which previously favored the warriors of Japan over the Allies. Rather than being in "high spirits for an adventure" as had been the case just a few days before, Inoue's official diary revealed a new, anxious, almost pessimistic outlook: "The dream of a great victory is gone. The battle belongs to the enemy. It was impossible, as feared. When the expected enemy raid came, we could not even mobilise the slightest united strength. In the end, we cannot even blame inadequate reconnaissance seaplanes. I am all the more concerned." (Bullard, 2007, 63).

While the outcome of the tactical engagement represented something of a draw, or a result slightly in the favor of the Japanese, the Americans clearly won on the strategic level. The Japanese carriers withdrew, and in doing so they aborted the seaborne invasion of Port Moresby. A land attack on the key port also failed thanks to the hard-fighting Australians. The base never fell to the Japanese and became an important center in the counteroffensive that eventually crushed the Empire of Japan in the coming years.

More immediately, the Battle of the Coral Sea helped the Americans achieve their notable victory at the Battle of Midway in several ways. The sinking of *Shoho* prevented the light carrier's possible deployment at the June naval encounter, and *Shokaku* suffered too much damage to participate in the later fight. *Zuikaku*, though still in fighting condition, lost most of its aircraft complement in the battle off Australia, and therefore the Japanese did not deploy it at Midway either. As a result, the outcome of the May 7th to 8th naval encounter reduced the number of Japanese carriers at Midway by at least two vessels, and possibly three.

The Battle of the Coral Sea likewise firmly established the reputation of Joseph Rochefort as a master codebreaker, known to the highest levels of the USN hierarchy, including Admirals Chester Nimitz and Ernest King. These men therefore gave considerable weight to his pronouncements about Midway as the next Japanese objective, based on his unique analysis of signals intelligence, when planning their countermeasures against Yamamoto Isoroku's next move. As Rochefort later stated, "We were a little surprised that [King] would ask us what our views were. I personally felt that he was not even aware of our existence." (Carson, 2011, 282).

The Coral Sea operation provided a superb "proof of concept" for Joe Rochefort's skills and the methods of the whole *Hypo* code-breaking team. Therefore, when he later made one of his penetrating leaps of intuition that a mysterious objective labeled "AF" corresponded to Midway Island, and he telephoned Lieutenant Commander Edwin Layton, Nimitz's intelligence chief, to announce, "I've got something so hot here it's burning the top of my desk," Layton worked to convince Nimitz of the code-breaker's accuracy. The Admiral, knowing Rochefort's earlier work, soon agreed.

Thus it transpired that Yamamoto arrived at Midway with four rather than seven carriers in his armada, and, rather than a weakly defended island, he found a powerful American carrier force awaiting him. The reduced carrier force at his disposal and the presence of the American fleet had a decisive impact on the ensuing results at Midway, and they sprang from events that unfolded exactly one month before during the somewhat forgotten but pivotal Battle of the Coral Sea, the first naval battle in history to be fought entirely by carrier sorties rather than gunfire.

The era of the aircraft carrier had fully arrived.

Midway

GMT 2006 Sep 27 16:16:27 ONC - Martin Weinelt

km
0 1000 2000

Midway is marked by the white dot in the middle of the Pacific

Japanese Planning

By the time of the Coral Sea engagement, Admiral Yamamoto, Commander of the Japanese Combined Fleet, had won his own political battle; his view that the priority in the Pacific should be the American fleet had finally prevailed. The fact that American carrier-borne bombers had hit Tokyo in April during the famous Doolittle Raid had helped him. Though militarily insignificant, the raid had nonetheless badly shaken Japanese national pride. By the time Japan's military leaders were on board with Yamamoto's intentions of striking the American fleet, Yamamoto had conceived a bold plan for drawing these units out into a pitched battle. He knew that the Americans, now fighting a naval war in two oceans, were nervous about exposing their precious carriers. Another lunge towards Pearl Harbor would surely force them to fight, but the strong garrison and numerous aircraft now based on Hawaii made this too risky. Instead, Yamamoto would threaten Midway, the tiny island base which represented America's most western toehold. Midway lies about 1,200 miles directly west of the Hawaiian islands, and about 2,300 miles east of Japan. Thus, "Operation MI" was born.

Midway in November 1941

The plan was to use a carrier strike force to bomb the island, with a separate invasion fleet putting troops ashore in the aftermath. Both would be supported by the main Japanese battle fleet, again operating separately. Meanwhile, another force including two light carriers would strike north towards the American held Aleutian islands ("Operation AL"). Given the damage done at Coral Sea and the decision to send two carriers north, Yamamoto only had four fleet carriers and two light carriers for the Midway operation, but he also knew that the *Lexington* had been sunk and suspected that the *Yorktown* would be in dry dock for months. Assuming that the Americans would keep at least two carriers in the Atlantic, Yamamoto thought his fleet was big enough, and in terms of the raw numbers, this was a reasonable judgment to make at the time.

Unbeknownst to the Japanese, the main disadvantage Japan would have at Midway was the fact the U.S. could read their radio traffic. With the success of their codebreakers, Americans were able to understand Japan's communications in the Pacific in the days leading up to the battle, and even when the routine issue of new Japanese code books meant that the Americans were once again in the dark, analysts working for the Navy in Hawaii were reasonably confident that as the Japanese units left port, Midway was their target and June 4 would be the date of their arrival. This intelligence was enough to allow Admiral Chester Nimitz, the commander of the Pacific Fleet, to prepare an ambush.

Although Nimitz had strong intelligence, he also had to be very mindful of the limitations of his own forces. The two key indices of naval power in 1942 were the battleship and the aircraft carrier, and even though modern writers are apt to point out that the days of the former were numbered (since the aircraft carrier could deliver its punch before a battleship could get anywhere near close enough to engage it), this was still a period of transition. Carrier operations at night remained a highly risky proposition, leaving open the possibility that battleships might be able to close the range under cover of darkness. At the same time, carriers were highly vulnerable to submarine attacks.

In the summer of 1942, Nimitz had plenty of issues to deal with. Most of the American battleships were either sunk at their moorings in Pearl Harbor, supporting the British in the Atlantic, or back in San Francisco, so Nimitz had an unbalanced fleet in Hawaii. He had to ensure that the American carriers did not get caught by the powerful Japanese battleships, and he also had to make sure the American carriers could win the action against Japan's own carriers.

Nimitz had two carriers in Task Force (TF) 16: the *Enterprise* and the *Hornet*. He also had a third, the *Yorktown*, in TF 17. *Yorktown* had been rushed to Pearl Harbor for emergency repairs after the battle of the Coral Sea, but in an astonishing feat of teamwork and repairs, she was patched up in time to sortie just 72 hours later. These two Task Forces were escorted by heavy cruisers and destroyers, and operating separately were several flotillas of submarines, as well as land-based aircraft flying out of Midway. The Midway air base had been reinforced from Hawaii on the basis of the new intelligence.

The USS *Enterprise*

The USS *Hornet*

Nimitz based himself at Pearl Harbor, while the two carrier task forces were under operational command of Rear Admiral Spruance (TF 16) and Rear Admiral Fletcher (TF 17). Fletcher was the senior commander at sea because Admiral Halsey, who would normally have been at sea in command of all carriers, was hospitalized in Hawaii. Spruance and Fletcher lacked Halsey's experience with carrier operations, setting up one of the great controversies of the campaign. TF 16 and TF 17 linked up about 350 miles northeast of Midway on June 2 and were positioned with the aim of pouncing on the Japanese force, which was expected to arrive from the west. The two squadrons remained within supporting distance, about 20 miles apart, and TF 17 was to move more to the northwest on June 4 in order to launch search aircraft in that sector. At the same time, Submarine pickets were spread out to the west of Midway in an effort to pick up the Japanese as early as possible. Although the Americans had radar on board their ships, at this stage in the war its range was limited to about 50 miles, not much considering the speed of an attacking aircraft. Indeed, the emphasis was on search, with planes from Midway pushing out as far as they could on the 3rd.

Spruance

Fletcher

While the Americans were moving into position, the Japanese were surging westwards towards Midway. In the lead was Admiral Nagumo with his carrier group, the 1st Kido Butai (Mobile Force). It consisted of four carriers - the *Kaga, Akagi, Hiryu* and *Soryu* - with plenty of escorts, including two battleships and two heavy cruisers. Nagumo reported to Admiral Yamamoto, architect of the attack on Pearl Harbor and Commander in Chief of the Nihon Kigun (Imperial Japanese Navy).

Nagumo

Yamamoto was a long way behind Nagumo, aboard the *Yamato*[2], and his was the main battle fleet, including three battleships and the light carrier *Hosho*. There was also the Midway invasion force, which consisted of two battleships, another light carrier, and the troop transports. Each force was supplemented by destroyers, light cruisers, tankers and other logistical vessels. Therefore, they were all powerful mixed surface groups, with the overwhelming bulk of the aircraft in Nagumo's command. This was necessary because the Japanese task forces were not close enough to each other to offer realistic support in the event of a fight, meaning they were all essentially operating as independent units.

In addition to the three large formations described, there was a simultaneous mission to the Aleutian Islands in the far north, and a submarine group supposedly operating ahead of the surface ships. This last command was scattered across the Pacific, tasked with refuelling float planes, reconnaissance, picking up downed pilots, and attacking the U.S. fleet when it sortied. As a result, its targets ranged from the Aleutians through the Californian coast, and even to Hawaii

---

[2] At 72,800 tonnes, the largest battleship ever launched.

itself. Since the submarine command was kept out of the loop in terms of Yamamoto's overall plan and issued its complicated orders far too late, it is not surprising that the Japanese submarine arm was not in position on time. Its contribution to the battle at Midway would prove minimal.

A layout of the opposing forces in the Pacific at the start of June 1942

As dusk fell on June 2, the Americans knew the Japanese planned a major offensive towards Midway that would undoubtedly include carriers and battleships, but they had little inkling of the makeup or deployment of the force beyond that. Early histories have often overstated the degree of intelligence detail available to the Americans at this stage. Fletcher rightly expected the Japanese carriers to be split into two strike forces, and that they would approach from the west or north, but he would later need to respond to a single carrier group approaching from the southwest. For their part, the Japanese knew that the American heavy units were not at Pearl Harbor, but it seems likely that Nagumo was not given specific confirmation of this. Yamamoto knew about it back with the main force, but his concerns about communicating via radio kept him from tipping off his deputy. As such, the plan for an initial strike against Midway by the carriers went ahead.

The First Blows

The first positive contact with the approaching Japanese was made by an American PBY flying boat at 8:45 on the morning of June 3. At the absolute limit of its patrol range, some 700 miles out from Midway, it reported sighting the "Main Body", but it had actually encountered the invasion force. The far deadlier Kido Butai, with its four heavy carriers, was further to the north. After the patrollers had located the Japanese force, 9 B-17 Flying Fortresses were dispatched from Midway, locating the convoy four hours later. The first blows of the battle were delivered in the form of 500 and 1,000 pound bombs from medium altitude heavy bombers, but despite wild claims from the air force, the raid was totally ineffectual. Indeed, this type of bombing was rarely successful against ships underway. That said, even though the Japanese were unscathed, their invasion force had been compromised, and they could be certain there would be more attention from the Americans shortly.

An American PBY during World War II

A B-17 Flying Fortress

Later that day, it was the turn of the Flying Boats, also operating from Midway but using torpedoes and flying by night. The four aircraft that flew out to attack the Japanese pressed home their attacks bravely, but again their success was limited. One Japanese tanker was damaged in the bow, and one of the troop ships was sprayed with machine gun fire, but that was the only damage inflicted.

The American aircraft returned safely despite lively anti-aircraft fire from the Japanese, but as they got back to Midway, they quickly discovered they would have to divert elsewhere because the base was under attack; Nagumo had launched 108 aircraft in an all-out assault on the U.S. facilities at Midway. The attackers swept in at 6:30 on the morning of the 4th, in an ugly echo of Pearl Harbor and Darwin, but this time the hangars and runways were empty, with no planes on the ground for the Japanese to strafe and bomb. There were two reasons for this. First, the Americans had finally received intelligence regarding the Japanese carrier fleet. Earlier that morning (at about 5:00 a.m.), reports from several patrolling flying boats came in, so by the time the Japanese carrier planes hit Midway, the base's own bombers were airborne on their way to hit those same carriers. Second, the fully alerted base had picked up the incoming air attack on radar, and the Japanese planes had also been spotted by one of the PBY's, enabling all of the defending fighters to be scrambled for defense.

Picture of the Japanese attack on Eastern Island, one of the Midway islands

In terms of knocking down intruding Japanese aircraft, the defending fighters achieved some limited success, but at a terrible cost to themselves. 10 Japanese bombers and one escorting fighter were shot down, while another 40 Japanese planes suffered damage, but out of the defending 25 American fighters, 15 were destroyed by Japanese fighters and a further 8 were badly damaged. That left only two serviceable American fighters to defend the base in the case of more attacks. The reason for the attrition was straightforward; the Japanese Zero fighter completely outclassed the American F4 and F2 defenders. 18 Zeros had accompanied the attacking force as escorts, and the F2 Brewster Buffalo in particular had no chance against the nimble Zero. Furthermore, Japanese naval pilots were better trained and more experienced than their American counterparts.

A Japanese zero

An F2 Brewster Buffalo

What saved the Midway raid from turning into a disaster was the fact that the American bombers were now away on their own mission. As at Clarke field in the Philippines in December, they would have been sitting ducks had they been on the ground. And while the relatively light payload of Japan's naval bombers would have been more than enough to destroy parked aircraft, it was not very effective against buildings and emplaced troops, ensuring that damage was minimal.

Burning oil tanks on Midway during the battle

Early Attacks on the Kido Butai

At 7:00 a.m. on June 4, Nagumo could draw some satisfaction over the manner in which events were progressing. As he waited for news from his strike force, he could take assurance from the fact that he had half of his bombers still aboard ship and configured for anti-shipping attacks, with many of the Val D6 dive bombers equipped with armor-piercing bombs and the Kate bombers loaded with torpedoes. On the direct instructions of Yamamoto, this reserve was held back in case the Japanese encountered the American fleet before the other planes returned and re-armed.

It was not long after 7:00 that the first American planes from Midway appeared over Nagumo's fleet, where they ran into heavy anti-aircraft fire and combat air patrols mounted by the deadly Zero fighters. Four brand new B-26 Marauder medium bombers had set off from Midway at dawn, equipped with a torpedo apiece, but despite being fast and well-armed, they were no match for the swirling Zeros above the Japanese carriers. Two were shot down before releasing their torpedoes, and one of these, flown by Lieutenant "Herbie" Myers, came close to nose-diving straight into the bridge of the Akagi, which would have wiped out Nagumo and his command team. The two survivors dropped their torpedoes, but the novice crews missed their targets. Both planes were badly shot up but managed to make it back to Midway. The only damage inflicted was the downing of one of the Zeros.

A B-26 bomber

As the Marauders swept in at low level, six TBF Avengers attacked the fleet from the opposite direction at the same time. These were also torpedo bombers and also a brand new design, one which the Navy had high hopes for. The planes were normally based aboard the *Hornet*, but they had missed her departure a few days earlier and had thus relocated to Midway. Simultaneous attacks such as these had a chance of swamping the defenses, but the Japanese had too many Zeros. Only one of the Avengers made it back to Midway, with one of its crew dead and the other two injured. The others were cut down by the Zeros, and even though two of them did manage to drop torpedoes at the *Hiryu* and one at a light cruiser, every torpedo missed.

A TBF Avenger

Nagumo's carrier force was cutting the Americans to pieces, and the key was the superlative Zero, organized into a permanent Combat Air Patrol which put at least 30 of the fighters over the fleet at any given time. The next Americans to launch their death rides were the Dauntless dive bombers of the Marines. Their attack might have been more successful had they actually employed dive bombing tactics, by far the most accurate method of bombing moving ships during this period, but the pilots were inexperienced and their commander instead ordered a shallower glide bombing attack. Such a trajectory was much easier for anti-aircraft gunners and the lethal fighter pilots to follow. Of the 16 planes that went into the attack, only 8 came out. Nevertheless, as they returned to Midway, the Marine pilots were jubilant despite their 50% casualty rate because they mistakenly believed they had set three carriers ablaze. In fact, the Marines had hit nothing.

A Dauntless dropping a bomb

The Japanese had little difficulty in brushing off these early attacks, and this successful defense, along perhaps with radio reports from his pilots over Midway, may have influenced the decision Nagumo was about to take. Around 7:15, Nagumo decided that he needed to launch a second attack against Midway, and to do this, he ordered his reserve aircraft to be rearmed with conventional high explosive bombs.

However, half an hour later, as the Japanese aircraft were still being rearmed, Nagumo's order was rescinded. He had received a new report from one of his spotter aircraft that there was a large American surface fleet (Spruance's TF 16) about 100 miles away to the northeast, but even though that task force had been located, poor reporting left Nagumo uncertain whether the enemy formation included aircraft carriers. Both Task Force 16 and Task Force 17 had yet to receive definitive news of the attacks on Midway, but that was about to change, and now there was some degree of disorder on board the Japanese carriers, as ground crews sought to change the bomb load of their aircraft for the second time that morning. Although historians continue to debate exactly what state Nagumo's aircraft were in during the deadly American assault about to follow, it is clear that they were not ready to launch a concerted strike against the American carriers.

The organization of high-tempo air operations from carriers remains an extremely challenging proposition even today, but in June 1942, the Japanese were world leaders in this field. Their fleet carriers would typically hold about 90 aircraft, confined into a very tight space. There were two hangar decks, with lifts connecting them to the flight deck above. Japanese ground crews were very well trained, with the result that they could turn around aircraft much faster than their British or American counterparts. Nonetheless, these were crowded ships, and they were already coming under attack from the Midway-based American aircraft. Furthermore, in addition to switching armament for Nagumo's reserve bomber force, the crews were maintaining a rotating force of covering fighters. There were always Zeros on deck waiting to take off, being refuelled, or just having landed. Hoisting heavy torpedoes into the bomb bays of the Kates was also a very skilled operation that only specialist torpedo armorers were able to undertake. In short, this was a recipe for delay and confusion, even given the superb quality of the Japanese ground crew, and as Nagumo changed his mind twice in the span of less than an hour, the issues the Japanese faced on the carriers were exacerbated.

By 8:00, Nagumo's Kido Butai force had been under continuous attack for an hour, and even though they were successfully fighting off American attacks, there was plenty of chaos aboard the ships. As the reserve bombers were switching their bomb loads below decks, the anti-aircraft guns were blazing above them. Now came more planes from Midway; high up in the sky, the air force's huge B17s were making a second appearance. Originally routed out to find and engage the invasion fleet they had attacked the day before, the heavy bombers had their target switched in mid-flight to Nagumo's newly discovered carrier force. The Flying Fortresses were lucky in that the Zeros had no time to climb to their altitude and engage, and the flak from the ships' anti-aircraft guns was relatively ineffective at such heights. Notwithstanding this, and despite being equipped with the much vaunted Norden bombsight, the bombers again failed to score a single hit.

Navy picture of the Japanese carrier *Hiryu* maneuvering to avoid bombs dropped by the B-17 Flying Fortresses on the morning of June 4

The fifth and final attack by aircraft based at Midway took place shortly after the B17's had departed the scene. Another Marine squadron, this time flying elderly Vindicator dive bombers, arrived over the Japanese fleet despite having been harried by swirling Zeros for the final 30 miles of their run. Astonishingly, the plodding Vindicators had thus far not suffered any casualties, and all 11 of them commenced a shallow glide attack on the battleship *Haruna* as the Zeros followed them down. It was at this point that their luck ran out, as 3 were splashed down by the defending Zeros and intense flak barrage. Nevertheless, the others pressed home their attack, with the survivors zooming out the other side of the fleet and heading up into the clouds to escape. Like those before them who had managed to get back to base that day, there were plenty of reports of hits on the Japanese vessels. All were subsequently proven to be ill-founded.

A Vindicator taking off from Eastern Island on June 4 to attack the *Haruna*

The *Haruna*

In five separate bombing attacks on the Japanese, the Americans had managed to achieve almost nothing, other than to clock up the kill rate of the elite Zero pilots. Many brave young aircrew had gone to their deaths, with obsolete aircraft, poorly trained men, and a lack of any coordination all playing a part in the failures. It is tempting to speculate what might have happened had the American command control been sophisticated enough to put all of these aircraft over Nagumo's ships at the same time, but the planes had been hastily thrown into the air as soon as the fleet was detected in an effort to strike quickly and avoid being caught on the ground by Nagumo's own attacking planes. Would their colleagues from the three American carriers be able to do any better? The tired crews aboard the Japanese carriers were about to find out.

The Tide Turns

At just after 6:00 on the morning of June 4, Fletcher's carriers got word of the Japanese carrier group, and as more details came in, general quarters were sounded and aircrews donned their flight gear, rushing to the briefing rooms to learn about the missions ahead. By the time the Americans launched their strikes, Spruance's TF 16, including the *Hornet* and *Enterprise*, was about 30 miles south of Fletcher's TF 17, which included the *Yorktown*. At 6:07, Spruance had been ordered south and authorized to attack the Japanese carriers as soon as they were firmly located. Fletcher lingered to the north with the *Yorktown* in order to recover his patrol aircraft, which were searching in that direction for what he believed was a second Japanese carrier group.

The launch arrangements for the American carriers, the conduct of their air groups, and the associated navigational and command issues continue to cause controversy, and even today, over 70 years after the battle, a number of important matters remain open to question. What seems to have been lacking was a firm command grip on the overall American effort. Nimitz had rightly called for caution in the use of his carriers and identified a broad plan to capitalize on the American intelligence advantage by deploying to the north of Midway, waiting until the Japanese had committed their planes to an attack on the island, and then launching an all-out assault on the carriers. But coordinating such a plan from Hawaii was impractical, so he had left it to Fletcher and Spruance to firm up on the details, depending on the tactical situation.

Fletcher was the senior Rear Admiral at sea with the fleet, but he was some way to the north, coordinating a peripheral and ultimately fruitless search for a phantom second Japanese carrier group. Thus, the main offensive effort against the already identified Kido Butai was initially left to Spruance and the two carriers of TF 16. They were to rely heavily on the aviation experts sailing with them on the carriers, but even within TF 16 itself, although both *Enterprise* and *Hornet* were ordered to launch strikes, they were permitted to do so independently of each other. To their north, the *Yorktown* was eventually to change course and launch a strike of her own. In essence, the Americans would end up launching three entirely separate air attacks on Nagumo's fleet, and any notion of coordination over the target among the three carriers would therefore be a sheer matter of luck. If the five brave but disorganized attacks from Midway, which had already been comprehensively defeated by the Japanese, were any indication, this was a recipe for disaster.

The men launching their attack from the *Hornet* had perhaps the most miserable story to recount. With a total of 76 aircraft available for the attack, on paper the *Hornet* had the most firepower of the three carriers, and the aircraft were led by Commander Stanhope Ring, a highly experienced naval aviator, albeit one with little actual combat experience (like most of those at Midway).

Ring

Unfortunately for Ring and his crew, their actual combat experience was greatly lacking in comparison to their Japanese counterparts. Ring's aircraft began to lift off from *Hornet* at about 7:00 on June 4, but they were not actually ready to depart for another hour; it took that long just for each aircraft to take off, circle and take position within Ring's formation. By contrast, the Japanese were able to achieve this in less than 10 minutes with over 100 aircraft. Compounding the problem, the estimated range to the target was in excess of 100 miles, already a stretch for the shorter-ranged American aircraft. They could hardly afford to waste fuel circling the carrier for an hour.

As if that wasn't enough, the precise heading taken by Ring's force when it did depart is still the subject of debate, but whatever the case, Lt. Commander John C. Waldron, the leader of Ring's torpedo squadron, was unhappy. In fact, he was so unhappy with the plan that after just 50 miles out from the *Hornet*, Waldron ordered his aircraft to peel off to the right and take a completely different course, not only openly disobeying his commander's instructions but even breaking radio silence in order to do so. His loyal squadron followed him.

Despite now missing half of his bombers in formation, Ring kept his course, but by 9:30 he had yet to sight a single Japanese ship. He then decided to turn south towards Midway, where he hoped to spot Nagumo's Kido Butai, but at that point, Ring's fighter escort, low on fuel, abandoned him and turned back towards the *Hornet*. Ultimately, Ring and the remaining dive bombers eventually landed at Midway itself, but nearly all of the fighters failed to make it back to the *Hornet*, forcing most to ditch into the sea in hopes of being rescued. Very few would.

While Ring was in the middle of a debacle, Waldron's torpedo bombers, which had peeled away from the rest of the group early on, did find the Japanese fleet. He had been right in his navigational judgment (if completely insubordinate in his behaviour), and his aircraft would be the only ones from Hornet to attack the Japanese fleet that morning. Of course, without the rest of Ring's aircrew, they proved to be sitting ducks. At about 9:00, Waldron's 15 Devastators skimmed in towards the Japanese carriers at a sedate 120 mph, in a macabre naval version of the Charge of the Light Brigade. The waiting Zeros pounced, and Waldron's squadron was wiped out by them and the concentrated flak. Of the 30 crew involved, only Ensign George Gay would survive, clinging to a piece of wreckage from his plane. It was brave, it was costly and it was completely ineffective; of the several torpedoes launched, apparently no hits at all were scored[3]. By 9:30, the sky above the Japanese aircraft carriers was clear of enemy planes, while the Japanese planes returning from the Midway attack had safely landed. On board, the crews frantically worked to stow the returning planes, maintain the rotating fighter patrol, and prepare an anti-shipping raid to hit the American carriers.

---

[3] There are those that contest this, claiming some damage was inflicted.

Ensign Gay (right) posing with one of his plane's rear gunners before the attack on June 4.

The lull in the fighting would not last long, because after just past 10:00, Nagumo's carriers began enduring sustained attacks from the *Yorktown* and the *Enterprise* air groups. The following 30 minutes would turn the tide in the Pacific. The *Enterprise*'s air group had finally pulled away from the ship at about 7:45, but even before they did so, their own escorting fighter squadron had disappeared, mistakenly chasing after planes from the distant *Yorktown*. In addition, the slower torpedo bombers got away a full 11 minutes after the Dauntless dive bombers, so this was hardly a compact and well balanced air wing as it made its way toward the Japanese fleet. These were not good omens, but the bombers from the *Enterprise* pressed on unescorted nonetheless.

TBD-1 Devastators on the deck of the *Enterprise* getting ready to take off on June 4

By 9:30, they had still not spotted the Japanese carriers, and matters were now critical in terms of fuel. Unbeknownst to the American planners, Nagumo had changed direction. He had landed all of his returning planes, and now aware of the American carriers, had turned his force to a northeasterly heading. Thus, the Japanese carriers were not where they should have been.

Ultimately, luck and a shrewd command decision worked in the Americans' favor. Lt. Commander Eade McClusky, leading the air group, spotted a lone Japanese destroyer travelling northeast at high speed and guessed (correctly) that it might be returning to the main force after having been detached for some earlier duty. Sure enough, that destroyer had been chasing an American submarine, the *Nautilus*, which had managed to penetrate and discomfort the Japanese destroyer picket earlier in the morning. One of the fleet's older subs, *Nautilus* had picked up a message from a patrolling flying boat at about 4:30 a.m. identifying the approximate location of Nagumo's fleet. Making as good a speed as possible, *Nautilus* managed to slip into the middle of the Japanese formation and fired a salvo of torpedoes at one of the battleships around 8:00, shortly after the first unsuccessful American air attacks from Midway. *Nautilus* then stalked a carrier (probably the *Soryu*) before firing again, this time at a light cruiser. Throughout this adventure, the *Nautilus* was chased and attacked by aircraft and destroyers, so much so that it had to withdraw. All of the submarine's torpedoes misfired or missed, as was usually the case with the U.S. Mark XIV, but the destroyer which was tasked to hang back from the fleet and hunt down the *Nautilus* was the *Arashi*. *Arashi* was ultimately unsuccessful in that mission, and it was this same destroyer which was spotted by McClusky. By following the destroyer, McClusky's air group was effectively vectored straight to Nagumo's fleet, which they sighted some half an hour later. Nimitz would later state that McClusky's decision "decided the fate of our carrier task force and our forces at Midway..."

McClusky

Meanwhile, the *Yorktown*, dashing south to rejoin Spruance's carriers, launched her own raid at about 9:00, but after a last minute change of plan, one squadron of Dauntless dive bombers and most of the fighters remained aboard the carrier. Still suspecting a second Japanese carrier force (his intelligence had so far only confirmed two cruisers with Nagumo), Fletcher was being cautious, leaving his attacking air group with only six escort fighters. Furthermore, like the planes from the *Enterprise*, the attacking squadrons were strung out rather than concentrated. But as fate would have it, the planes from the *Yorktown* did not experience the navigational difficulties which bedevilled those from TF 16's carriers, because updated intelligence enabled them to fly straight to the target, which they sighted at 10:10.

Thus, just after 10:00 that morning, by luck rather than good judgment, the Americans had managed to assemble three squadrons of dive bombers and two squadrons of torpedo bombers over the Japanese carrier fleet at roughly the same time. The slow torpedo bombers, as they had been all day, were the target of most of the Japanese fighter opposition, due mostly to their potential for damaging ships, as a successful torpedo hit was far more lethal to a carrier or battleship than a bomb strike was likely to be. Thus, it may have been a tactical choice. On the other hand, the Japanese had sufficient fighters to do both jobs, with at least 30 and probably 40 in the air at any given moment[4]. Most of these stayed at low level and attacked the torpedo bombers, and some took on the dive bombers as they came down to release their bombs, but in most cases this was after they had done so and were on their way back up. In other words, there were no fighters allocated to engage the dive bombers as they approached the fleet at higher altitude. This points to another problem the Japanese had: coordination of their immediate fleet defense was difficult. Unlike the Americans, they had no radar and therefore relied on visual contact for the identification of intruders. Second, their radio equipment was poor and often ignored by the pilots[5]. Third, the fighter pilots, while highly skilled, were imbued with bushido, the Japanese martial tradition that emphasised individual aggression rather than teamwork.

None of this was good news for the torpedo bombers that attacked the *Kaga* and *Soryu*. Of the two attacks, the attack by the planes of the *Enterprise* against the *Kaga* was the more sophisticated. The 14 aircraft came at the *Kaga* from two directions in a textbook pincer attack, but of the eight torpedoes dropped; all of them missed. The price was again high, with 9 of the aircraft being shot down. Of the 12 torpedo planes from *Yorktown* that attacked the *Soryu*, only four were to survive. Hits were claimed, but the carrier emerged unscathed yet again. The American torpedo attacks at Midway were therefore an expensive failure. No damage was done to the Japanese fleet, and dozens of Americans were killed. It now seems possible that some of the torpedoes may have hit their targets but failed to detonate, since the American Mark XIV torpedo used at the time was hopelessly unreliable.

In one sense though, the attacks did serve a useful purpose by keeping the Japanese fighters off the dive bombers. The Dauntless dive bombers, consisting of two squadrons from *Enterprise* and one from *Yorktown*[6], were a new type optimized for this specialist role, and on this occasion they employed it, eschewing the easier glide bombing technique used earlier in the day by the Marines from Midway. The steeper angle of a true dive bombing run (about 70 degrees) was far less vulnerable to flak and far more accurate. Japanese carriers had thin unarmored flight decks,

---

[4] Bicheno, P93.
[5] Smith, P. p154-5.
[6] Yorktown's second Dauntless squadron remained on board in reserve.

and on board the ships there were hundreds of aircraft, many of them being refuelled and re-armed. All the factors were now aligned for a devastating attack.

Yorktown's VB3 dive bombing squadron hit the *Soryu* just as *Yorktown's* torpedo bombers had made their unsuccessful run in at wave-skimming altitude. The VB3s dropped out of the sky right on top of the ship, like sinister birds of prey, and at least five hits punched through the *Soryu's* flight deck, immediately causing devastating fires and mass casualties. Additional near misses sent huge shockwaves ringing through the hull. Soryu was doomed.

Aerial photo of *Soryu* earlier on June 4

The fate of *Kaga* and *Akagi* would be similar. In the confusion of combat, most of the attack by the crews of the *Enterprise* went in against the *Kaga*, which suffered at least five direct hits and was soon ablaze from bow to stern. *Nautilus*, the only submarine to make any significant contribution to the battle, returned to the scene during the mid-afternoon and fired three torpedoes at the crippled Kaga, but once again, the submarine was let down by faulty ordnance.

One torpedo hit the carrier and failed to explode. Meanwhile, the *Akagi*, despite only being attacked by one section of VB-6s, took two direct hits that started fires on board, and a near miss off the stern jammed the rudder over, making all attempts to steer the ship impossible.

The men of *Enterprise's* **VB-6s**

Within 10 minutes, the entire complexion of the battle had changed. Three of Nagumo's carriers had been crippled, leaving only the *Hiryu* undamaged. Carrier doctrine had long emphasised the importance of getting in the first blow, and even though it took so many attempts to land such a blow, Nimitz's three carriers nonetheless remained completely unscathed, while three of Nagumo's were on fire.

A Navy diorama depicting the damage they believed they had inflicted on the Japanese on June 4. The diorama depicts the *Soryu* (center foreground), *Kaga* and *Akagi* (both in the center background) all burning.

On board the stricken ships, the carnage and chaos was appalling. Fires quickly became uncontrollable, and the *Soryu* was abandoned at 10:45, sinking three hours later. *Kaga* was left to her fate at 4:40 p.m., and it finally exploded at 7:25. Admiral Nagumo left his flagship, the *Akagi*, at 10:46, to resume command from the light cruiser *Nagara*. The engines onboard the *Akagi* were successfully restarted at noon, but the rudder damage meant that the ship could only circle hopelessly. The carrier was finally abandoned later that afternoon, and after remaining afloat into the night, the Japanese finally sunk the *Akagi* themselves at 2:00 a.m. on the 5th.

Though badly damaged, Nagumo's fleet continued to sail north towards Fletcher's carriers, now only 90 miles away. The Japanese group still included dangerous battleships and heavy cruisers, which would cause mayhem if they got in amongst the lighter American ships. They also still had one unscathed aircraft carrier, the *Hiryu*. The Japanese were not done yet.

The *Hiryu* Strikes Back

On board the *Hiryu*, the Japanese crews had been far from idle. In addition to accommodating orphaned Zero fighters needing somewhere to land, the *Hiryu* had been preparing a strike of her own. At 10:45, 18 Val dive bombers and an escort of six Zeros left her deck, and the closest enemy group was now Fletcher's TF 17, with the *Yorktown* at its center. Aware of the capabilities of American radar, the Japanese approached at low level, so the *Yorktown* did not spot them until they were only 30 miles out. At that point, around noon, 14 F4 Wildcat fighters were in the air above the carrier, and these were immediately ordered to intercept what the Americans thought were Kate torpedo bombers.

An F4 Wildcat

Once again, Japanese fighter tactics let them down. On the short flight across to the *Yorktown*, the Zeros spotted a group of American bombers returning to their own carriers after the earlier strikes against Nagumo's fleet. The undisciplined Japanese fighter pilots left the bombers they were supposed to be escorting in order to take on those American planes, resulting in the loss of two Zeros. More importantly, the remaining four Zeros were unable to catch up with the Vals until after they had attacked the *Yorktown*, meaning the bombing attack went in without the advantage of a fighter escort.

The Wildcats tore into the Vals as they climbed prior to making their dives, and 11 of the 18 attacking dive bombers were shot down before they could even begin their bomb run. Others were knocked down by flak as they bore in on the *Yorktown*. It would not be enough to save the ship from damage, however. By 12:30, the *Yorktown* had taken three bomb hits, damaging the flight deck, starting a series of fires, and stopping her engines. At 12:38, Admiral Fletcher moved his command to the heavy cruiser *Astoria*. The returning Japanese pilots reported that they had left an American carrier ablaze and at least crippled. This would end up causing an important misunderstanding in the Japanese command.

Less than two hours later, 10 Kate torpedo bombers and 6 escorting zeros approached TF 17 as part of *Hiryu's* second strike of the day (or third if the attack on Midway itself is counted). However, what the Japanese pilots saw upon approaching TF 17 was a carrier making good speed with an even keel and no apparent fires. Unsurprisingly, the Japanese concluded that they were about to pounce on a second American carrier, not the *Yorktown* again. In a remarkable feat of damage control, the men on the *Yorktown* had put out the fires and restarted the engines. The carrier was thus able to launch fighters to intercept the new attackers.

The *Yorktown's* fighters would join other F4's from TF 16, which appeared just over the northern horizon, but this battle would be much more even handed because the Japanese had six Zeros with their bombers. These went a long way towards neutralizing the F4's, but as many as three Kates were splashed down before being able to launch torpedoes.

Nevertheless, the defense would not be enough to save the *Yorktown*. At about 2:45, the carrier took two torpedo hits adjacent to each other in the middle of its port flank, and the blasts ripped a single giant hole in the hull. The ship began to flood and list badly, and Captain Elliot Buckmaster ordered the surviving crew to abandon ship and go aboard the escorting destroyers. Unaware that they had launched another attack on the *Yorktown*, which they thought had already been badly damaged, the Japanese returned to the *Hiryu* thinking they had critically damaged or sunk a second U.S. carrier. Operating under this incorrect assumption, Nagumo believed the fight was still very much on.

Japanese plane and anti-aircraft fire as the *Yorktown* attempted to defend itself.

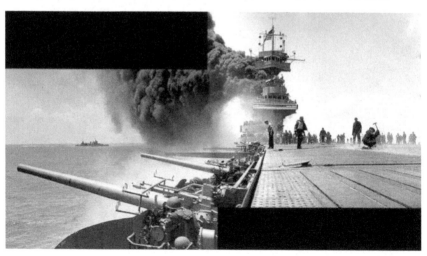

The End of *Hiryu*

While *Yorktown* fought for her life, Spruance was weighing his next move. Though technically second in command, evidence suggests that Fletcher was essentially now allowing Spruance to run the offensive battle while he concentrated on the defense of TF 17. But like Fletcher, Spruance was cautious and unsure of the number of intact Japanese carriers there might be left in the area. The dogfight over the *Yorktown* proved there was at least one, but his aviators had led him to believe that they had mortally wounded all of the carriers in the Kido Butai. That implied a second Japanese task force.

Eventually, Spruance received a detailed report firmly declaring that one of the carriers in the Kido Butai was unscathed and heading north. With it were two battleships, two heavy cruisers and four destroyers. Spruance's mind was made up; he now prepared another attack.

This time, the American attack was launched in two waves, though again this was due just as much to command confusion as anything else. *Enterprise* launched a force of 25 dive bombers around 2:30, and they were on their way towards the target at 3:30. Once again, the Americans' ability to coordinate and form up an attacking carrier air wing was not getting any better. There were no fighters with this group because all that could be spared were either assisting TF 17 or held back for any attacks that might develop against TF 16. Meanwhile, the *Hornet* had at least as many Dauntless dive bombers aboard, having returned from Midway after their unsuccessful attempt to locate the Kido Butai earlier that morning. These were rearmed and ready to go, but the order to do so did not come for another hour, well after the *Enterprise* force had swept south across the horizon. Even when *Hornet's* planes did begin to launch, they were stopped from doing so after the departure of the first squadron: Spruance had decided he would hold some of his bombers back after all. Just like the *Enterprise's* bombers, those from *Hornet* would be unescorted.

Once again, it seemed the American command had done all in its power to ensure a piecemeal, uncoordinated attack, and the ingredients were now in place for the kind of catastrophe which had blighted the Americans at the start of the battle. Nagumo's Combat Air Patrol, although now down to only about 10 Zeros, was still very much in action, and they were even more determined to defend their one remaining carrier because they could not land without it. Had they enjoyed the American advantage of radar, they might have picked up the *Enterprise's* attackers earlier, but regardless, with no low level torpedo bombers to distract the Zeros, the Dauntless dive bombers from the *Enterprise* immediately received the full attention of the defending fighters. From the moment they began their dives, they were set upon, and the Japanese pilots knew that it would only take one Dauntless to get through in order to potentially cripple the *Hiryu*. Three were shot down before completing their dives, and others were badly shot up. The anti-aircraft flak being shot from the ships was heavy as well.

By the time the remains of the shattered first wave arrived back on board the *Enterprise*, only four aircraft were deemed fit for further operations; but they had done their job. At least four (and possibly as many as six) bombs had smashed into the deck of the Hiryu, and even as the battered Dauntless bombers struggled to escape while being harried by the defending Zeros, their crews could see that the carrier was ablaze throughout its length. The Hiryu was a stricken ship.

The damaged *Hiryu*

This was also apparent to the second wave of Dauntless bombers, which were now approaching the fleet as the first pulled away. There seemed little point in attacking the Hiryu yet again, since it appeared to be clearly neutralized at least for the remainder of the battle. The commander, Lt. Stebbins, thus ordered his squadron to go for the heavy cruisers. This decision has since been criticized, with some arguing that Stebbins should have made sure the *Hiryu* was sunk. After all, earlier that day the *Yorktown* had seemingly come back from the grave after being set afire by dive bombers, and the light bombs of the Dauntless planes would be unlikely to penetrate a heavily armoured ship. Of course, all of this is easy to point out in hindsight, and even though the attacks on the cruisers achieved nothing, Stebbins' snap assessment of the *Hiryu's* state proved accurate. The *Hiryu* was already fatally wounded.

Meanwhile, in another example of the ineffectiveness of high altitude level bombing at sea, *Hornet's* planes had to fly through a curtain of bombs dropped by the American Army Air Force itself. B-17's had attempted to intervene yet again from their base on Hawaii, but like before, the B-17's hit neither friend nor foe.

Regardless of the ineffective final attacks, the events of June 4 had been decisive. The last of Nagumo's once proud carrier strike force was engulfed in flame. Before the night was out, the *Hiryu* would be deliberately sunk by torpedoes from one of Japan's escorting destroyers.

The Aftermath

Although they did not yet know it for certain, the Americans had wiped out the Japanese offensive air arm with the loss of only one carrier, but that did not mean the battle was over. Later on the evening of June 4, aircraft from the two surviving American carriers again set out to attack the Kido Butai, in the belief that there might be a fifth Japanese carrier. As dusk fell, they failed to find anything but wreckage, and the subsequent night landings only caused confusion and additional casualties. That same night, the American submarine *Tambor* encountered a force of four Japanese cruisers. These had been detached by Nagumo to bombard Midway in preparation for the intended amphibious assault, but after being called back to the rest of the fleet, they saw the *Tambor*'s periscope and took evasive action. During these maneuvers, two of the cruisers collided, suffering substantial damage. As the submarine withdrew, the two damaged cruisers were left behind by their compatriots to make as best a speed as they could.

The dawn of June 5 found TF 16 heading south, then northwest, in a hunt for a phantom fifth Japanese carrier. Meanwhile, Yamamoto and Nagumo were still hoping to concentrate their forces and entice the American carriers westwards. If they could achieve that, they might be able to bring on a close range night action or move the battle within range of their land-based aircraft on the island of Wake.

However, the main forces of both sides did not establish contact with each other throughout the day. Instead, the action would focus on the two damaged Japanese cruisers, which were now joined by an anti-submarine escort of two destroyers. This latter precaution would actually prove unnecessary, because in one of the more peculiar decisions of the battle, the American submarine commander had already ordered all of his subs to pull back.

However, the damaged cruisers had left a highly visible fuel slick on the surface of the ocean, making it easy for an aircraft to follow, and they were also less than 100 miles from Midway itself. Thus, it was not long before they came under attack by American land-based bombers. There were three such assaults, starting at about 7:00. The first two were pressed home by the Marines, who were flying their elderly Vindicator dive bombers yet again, but this time there were no Japanese Zeros to counter them. Nevertheless, the anti-aircraft flak screen was intense. Although some damage and casualties were inflicted on the cruisers, these attacks were unlikely to sink such well-protected vessels. The much circulated story of one of the Vindicators intentionally nose-diving into a cruiser in a kamikaze-like "suicide" appears to be a myth; the plane had been shot down and crashed close by the ship. Once again, brave Marine aviators had taken significant losses for little in return. They were followed by the even less successful air force heavies, flying in at 20,000 feet and predictably dropping their bombs harmlessly into the ocean. After the attacks, the two cruisers and their escorts continued limping back toward the rest of the Japanese fleet.

Further north, Spruance's two carriers launched their own strike later that afternoon after a suspected contact with the Japanese about 250 miles northwest. There were heated arguments on board the *Enterprise* about the tactics to be employed, because this would be a long reach for the Dauntless bombers even if the carriers sailed after them in the same direction at full speed. Bomb loads were eventually reduced, and the launch was delayed, all in an effort to ensure the attackers could return safely to the carriers. Ultimately, 58 aircraft took off and set off in a fruitless search for another Japanese aircraft carrier. Unable to find the nonexistent carrier, they settled on attacking the *Tanikaze*, but they did not heavily damage that maneuverable Japanese destroyer.

June 6 was the last day of active combat in the three day mini-campaign that became known as the Battle of Midway. Early that morning, the *Hornet* launched a dive bomber mission, with fighter escort, against the two damaged Japanese cruisers. About two hours behind the *Hornet's* aircraft came those from the *Enterprise*, again escorted by fighters. Ironically, these two waves enjoyed more fighter support than had been available to the bombers that had taken on the full might of the Kido Butai only two days earlier. Of course, the escort fighters had no Zeros to worry about this time, and despite a heroic defense, the two cruisers and one of the escorting destroyers were badly hit by the dive bombers. Eventually, the fire on board one of the cruisers reached the torpedoes stored on deck, causing a large explosion and sinking the cruiser a few hours later. In an episode characteristic of the U.S. tactical intelligence effort during Midway, the attacks on this modest force had repeatedly been reported as being against one or two "battleships". It was only later in the evening that aerial photography confirmed the sunken vessel had been the heavy cruiser *Mikuma*, with her damaged sister ship *Mogami* getting away. The brave defense of this little force over two days, and the fact that three out of the four ships eventually made it back to port, stands testimony to the professionalism and abilities of the Imperial Japanese Navy.

The damaged *Mikuma*

The final chapter of the Battle of Midway exemplified the difficulties of even finding and identifying the enemy. Despite the fact there had been heavy engagements the previous two days, a force of B-17 Flying Fortresses managed to bomb an American submarine during the afternoon of June 6, mistaking it for a Japanese heavy cruiser.

Ironically, the last aircraft carrier to sink as a result of the Battle of Midway was an American one. By the early afternoon on June 6, there was some optimism about the prospect of saving the *Yorktown*, as salvage crews had put out the fires and stabilised the vessel using pumps. The *Yorktown* was also surrounded by 6 protective destroyers as an escort. However, these destroyers failed to detect the Japanese submarine I-168, which crept to within easy torpedo range. In the middle of the afternoon on June 6, the submarine fired four torpedoes, two of which punched through the *Yorktown's* hull, causing more extensive flooding. The third hit the destroyer *Hammann*, sinking the destroyer within three minutes and causing mass casualties. The fourth torpedo missed, and the I168 was chased off by the remaining American destroyers. Abandoned yet again, the heavily listing *Yorktown* eventually slipped beneath the waves at 5:00 the following morning.

Picture of the Hammann sinking

By June 7, it was evident to Yamamoto that the Americans were not going to be drawn far enough west to be subjected to attacks from Wake island, nor were they foolish enough to risk a surface action against Yamamoto's heavy units. Yamamoto had already called off the invasion of Midway, and there seemed to be little more to be gained by remaining in the area. Fuel was also becoming scarce, so a general withdrawal to Saipan and the home islands of Japan was ordered.

For the Americans, triumphant in what was arguably the most important carrier battle of all time, there was little real hope of exploitation. The U.S. aircraft carrier *Saratoga* had now arrived at Pearl Harbor from California, but even adding her aircraft would not make up for the huge losses suffered over three days of fighting. With only a weakened carrier force and still no battleships, Nimitz concluded that this was not a good time to go chasing the enemy back towards their home bases. Midway was safe, and the enemy was in retreat. Nimitz decided it would be wiser to pause and take stock of the situation.

Meanwhile, 2,000 miles to the north, the simultaneous Japanese offensive against the Aleutian Islands had provided a measure of success for Yamamoto. Despite a spirited defense from locally based fighters, aircraft from the two Japanese carriers raided Dutch Harbor, and amphibious assaults were successful at the islands of Attu and Kiska. The Japanese had a toehold in the Aleutians, and it would be a year before American and Canadian troops eventually ejected them. Nevertheless, debate continues as to whether this was a diversionary raid or a strategic move in its own right. Despite their proximity to mainland Alaska and an important maritime route, the Japanese invasion of the Aleutians would not have the impact Japan hoped for. At best, it served as a deterrent against a U.S. thrust from that direction.

While the Japanese had more success in the north, the Battle of Midway ensured the center of the action in the Pacific would subsequently move south. Within three months of Midway, the Americans would launch their first real counter-offensive: the amphibious invasion of Guadalcanal in the Solomon Islands. The tide had truly turned.

The Americans had won a stunning victory at Midway, and it allowed for the U.S. not only to even up the crucial carrier numbers game but also buy time. American shipbuilding would prove more than able to do the rest, and henceforth, it would be difficult for Japan to challenge America's might in the field of carrier warfare. The U.S. still lagged behind in terms of battleships and tactical competence in "old fashioned" surface actions, but the Guadalcanal campaign would give the Americans plenty of experience as well.

Perhaps the most ironic aspect of the Battle of Midway is that the battle, which would prove so decisive in terms of the outcome in the Pacific, was neither a positional nor territorial battle. Midway was merely a convenient target chosen by Yamamoto to draw the Americans out, and both sides' objectives were attritional attempts to degrade their opponents' carrier units. Nevertheless, the result created space for the Americans to begin their cautious advance back across the Pacific. This started with Guadalcanal and proceeded along two axes. Nimitz would command the larger and predominantly naval effort across the central Pacific, and island fortresses such as Saipan and Iwo Jima would soon go down in military legend. To the south, General Douglas MacArthur led a campaign across New Guinea and the Philippines, with a more land-based focus. Notwithstanding that, it was off Leyte Gulf in the Philippines in October 1944 that the Imperial Japanese Navy suffered a fatal blow in the largest naval battle in history, during which four carriers and three battleships were lost. Japan's Southern Resource Zone was thus collapsed from two different directions, and by early 1945, with the fall of Manila and Okinawa, the end was clearly in sight.

Guadalcanal

In the middle of 1942, both sides would end up focusing on the Solomons, a long chain of mostly volcanic islands stretching nearly a thousand miles from the southeast to the northwest. The western edge of the Solomons is about 600 miles due east from the coast of New Guinea, and as much as a thousand miles northeast from the coast of Australia. The indigenous population consisted of about 100,000 people, largely Christian and overwhelmingly Melanesian, and they had been subjects of a British protectorate since the 1890s.

A map of the Solomons

A map of Japanese bases on the Solomons, including one (E) on Guadalcanal

Guadalcanal itself is a mid-sized island just over 2,000 square miles near the southeastern end of the chain. Honiara, on the island's north coast, is today the capital and largest city of the independent Solomon Islands, but the interior of Guadalcanal is highly mountainous, and the terrain that greeted the combatants was largely dense tropical rainforest, buzzing with insects and crawling with lizards and rodents. The climate is punishingly hot and extremely humid year-round, with some of the world's heaviest rain falls and daytime temperatures ranging from 77-90 degrees Fahrenheit. August, when combat began, is somewhat cooler and drier than average, but as the campaign wore on, soldiers and sailors on both sides were subjected to the tropical wet season, with warmer temperatures, more frequent rains, and occasional cyclones in the Coral Sea.

A map of Guadalcanal Island and nearby naval battles fought during the campaign

Prior to the Guadalcanal Campaign, few in either Japan or the United States had envisioned a major confrontation in the Solomons. Within the Imperial Japanese Navy, strategic doctrine had held that upon the outset of hostilities with America, the Navy would seize the Philippines and the Western Pacific. The American fleet would then be forced to steam west to confront Japan's combined fleet in a decisive battle. Interestingly enough, the US Navy's Plan Orange for war with Japan outlined essentially the same sequence of events. Neither side had imagined a conflict to the south in Melanesia; in fact, at the outset of the war, the US Navy did not even have detailed nautical charts of the region.

As it happened, however, while Japanese forces did indeed overrun Southeast Asia and the Western Pacific, no decisive fleet engagement came, in part because the Americans, focused on Atlantic convoys and the European theater, were in no position to dispatch a major offensive battle fleet across the Pacific. The Japanese, having won a Pacific empire on the cheap, were not disposed to risk their precious aircraft carriers in any but the most advantageous circumstances.

The results at Midway created space for the Americans to begin their cautious advance back across the Pacific, and this directed new attention to the South Pacific, where the situation was more ambiguous. In January and February of 1942, Japanese forces under Vice Admiral Inoue Shigeyoshi and Major General Horii Tomitaro had overtaken Rabaul on the island of New Britain, part of Australian New Guinea. At Rabaul, Inoue took advantage of the caldera-formed deepwater harbor to establish a major naval and air base as his headquarters, and from there, the Japanese proceeded to invade the north and west of mainland New Guinea and bombard Australian forces in Darwin.

Inoue

The Battle of the Coral Sea had forced Inoue to abandon his plans for a seaborne invasion of Port Moresby on New Guinea's southeast coast. It did not, however, prevent him from occupying the capital of the British Solomon Islands Protectorate: Tulagi, a small island no more than 3 miles wide and just off the southern coast of the larger Florida Island (now called Nggela Sule). Tulagi is about 25 miles north across the Savo Sound from the much larger island of Guadalcanal. On June 8, a Japanese construction battalion from Tulagi landed on the north shore of Guadalcanal, established a small outpost, and began construction of an airstrip.

Picture of the construction of the airstrip on Guadalcanal

When it reached American war planners through radio intercepts and Australian coastwatchers, news of the Guadalcanal airstrip was greeted with alarm. With control of the skies over and around the Solomons, the Japanese could strike shipping to and from Australia, potentially dividing the United States from its most significant Pacific ally and setting the stage for a further advance southeast. Thus, denying the Japanese use of the Guadalcanal airstrip became a top priority for American military planners in the Pacific.

Leadership

As a target, Guadalcanal had other attractions as well. Control of the island might represent a valuable first step in an offensive operation aimed at taking Rabaul and driving the Japanese out of the southwest Pacific. Such a prospect, however, inspired conflict and rivalry among American commanders nearly as heated as that between the contending militaries.

Command of the American war effort in the southwest Pacific was a cumbersome hybrid that was split by service and geography and beset by rivalry and miscommunication. On one side was the Navy, commanded in Washington by Admiral Ernest J. King, Commander-in-Chief of the US Fleet. King was a loner, an only child raised by his Ohio father after his mother had been institutionalized. A top graduate of the United States Naval Academy at Annapolis in 1901, King had experience in both surface ships and submarines, and he was qualified as a naval aviator in 1927. President Roosevelt, who appreciated King's drive and initiative, appointed him overall commander of the US fleet in December 1941, as well as one of the four members of the newly-established Joint Chiefs of Staff. King was abrasive, hot-tempered, and stubborn, but he had a penetrating grasp of naval strategy. He is reputed (perhaps anachronistically) to have said of himself, "When they get in trouble they send for the sonsabitches."

Admiral King

According to one of his assistants, the belligerent King frequently locked horns with General H. H. Arnold, another member of the Joint Chiefs. The two managed to avoid blow-ups only because of the urgency of the military situation: "King knew he had to get along. That was the compelling influence on all of them. They knew they had to get along." (Conolly, 375-76)

Arnold

On the other side, simultaneously cooperating and competing with the Navy, was the Army, still led by General Douglas MacArthur. This arrangement meant that any American offensive against the Japanese in the Solomons, New Britain and New Guinea would fall awkwardly between the army and navy, and thus the commands of MacArthur and King. Both officers yearned to go on the offensive and resented Allied war planners' "Europe-first strategy," which prioritized men and materiel for commanders preparing for the North Africa Campaign. For MacArthur, the motivations were personal; his retreat from the Philippines, after loudly proclaiming that he would turn the Japanese back from the beaches, was a humiliation that only victory could erase. For King, the notion of a defensive naval war was an absurdity. Strategic doctrine in the US Naval Academy, inspired by the theorist Alfred Thayer Mahan, stressed the need for offense to establish dominance of the seas. According to Mahan, "the nation that would rule upon the sea must attack" (Mahan, 68).

Thus, both King and MacArthur pushed hard for a southwest Pacific advance, albeit advances very different in character. King, in March 1942, argued for a naval advance along the Solomons chain and up to Rabaul and northern New Guinea. MacArthur, on the other hand, advocated a quick strike against Rabaul itself, claiming that he could capture the Japanese headquarters in three weeks if provided with a division of amphibious assault troops and a navy task force with two aircraft carriers. The argument, which was more about who would command the offensive than over how it would proceed, roiled the Joint Chiefs of Staff. In fact, King went so far as to threaten General George Marshall that the navy would proceed with its advance on the Solomons "even if no support of army forces in the southwest Pacific is made available." MacArthur, for his part, claimed that King's obstinacy was part of a navy conspiracy aimed at "the complete absorption of the national defense function by the Navy, the Army being relegated to merely base, training, garrisoning, and supply purposes" (Hayes, 208-9). At its heart, this was merely a bureaucratic dispute over America's limited war supplies, and for all their mutual recriminations, both King and MacArthur agreed that it was essential the forces in the Pacific get their fair share. As an assistant with the Joint Chiefs of Staff described the controversies of the time, "They were fighting for men and supplies. The money was insignificant. You could get all the money you wanted but there were just so much supplies in the US." (Silverthorne, 265).

George Marshall

After considerable acrimony, the Joint Chiefs managed to hammer out a compromise. The advance would be divided into three phases: an occupation of Tulagi, including the airstrip on nearby Guadalcanal, followed by a simultaneous advance up the Solomon chain and along the northern coast of New Guinea, and finally an all-out attack on the Japanese regional headquarters in Rabaul. The final two phases would be under MacArthur's command, but the first, even where it extended into the army's "Southwest Pacific Area," would be controlled by the navy. King, who managed the naval war from the yacht *Dauntless*, which rode at anchor in the Washington Navy Yard, delegated command of the Pacific theater to Admiral Chester Nimitz, a quiet and capable West Texan of German ancestry. Nimitz, in turn, delegated the southwest Pacific area to the command of Rear Admiral Robert L. Ghormley.

Portrait of Nimitz

Ghormley

Ghormley would probably have been an ideal commander to oversee the defensive operations American war planners had initially assigned to the navy in the southwest Pacific. He was a skilled diplomat who could be expected to manage tensions among his Australian, New Zealand, and New Caledonian Free French allies, all while organizing, training, and equipping his troops for the large-scale advance to come. Ghormley was not, however, well-suited to the aggressive, improvisatory, shoestring operation which he suddenly found himself leading. Doubtful about the strategy in general, Ghormley besieged his superiors with requests to postpone the mission until his troops were reinforced and better-supplied. Expected by King and Nimitz to command the operation on site, Ghormley chose instead to remain at his area headquarters at Noumea, in New Caledonia. As the violence on Guadalcanal escalated through August and September, Ghormley became vacillating and despondent, hardly an ideal commander.

As for the Japanese, tensions between the Imperial Japanese Army and the Imperial Japanese Navy were even more bitter and longstanding than on the American side. Naval operations in the Pacific were overseen by Admiral Isoroku Yamamoto, Commander of the Combined Fleet. Yamamoto was, perhaps, a curious choice to manage Japan's war against America. He had advocated against going to war with the United States against the Axis alliance, opposed the

Japanese Army's invasion of China, and was in favor of naval arms limitation treaties. Yamamoto was by no means a pacifist, but he had a more realistic grasp than most of his colleagues of Japan's relative position in the world. Having spent time in Britain and America, Yamamoto understood that Japan had no hope of prevailing in a long war of attrition with the United States. Having lost the political battle over whether or not to go to war, however, Yamamoto acquiesced and threw himself into preparations for the war he had sought to avoid. The brilliant tactical success at Pearl Harbor had largely been his doing.

Yamamoto

Japanese army operations in the southwest Pacific were under the command of General Hyakutake Harukichi, who operated out of Rabaul on the island of New Britain. Hyakutake had been a part of the radical Kwantung Army during the "Manchurian Incident" of September 1931, in which radical junior officers deliberately precipitated a Japanese invasion of Manchuria, supposedly to defend Japan's South Manchurian Railway against "Chinese bandits." As commander of the Seventeenth Army, Hyakutake was primarily concerned with Japanese operations on New Guinea. He was slow to credit Yamamoto's increasing alarm about the American garrison on Guadalcanal, and he frequently discounted estimates of American strength as exaggerations.

Harukichi at his headquarters in Rabaul

The Invasion and Battle of Savo Island

A picture of equipment being prepared in New Zealand ahead of the invasion

Howitzers on the deck of transport ships

Picture of Marines entering transport ships in a landing rehearsal ahead of the invasion

Phase one of the new American offensive began in the predawn hours of August 7 when troops from the First Marine Division, under Major General Archer Vandegrift, landed on Tulagi and the north shore of Guadalcanal. The Marines were undertrained, consisting mostly of young post-Pearl Harbor recruits, and they were also poorly equipped. They had arrived in New Zealand in June as a small, forward-positioned contingent not expected see actual combat until sometime in 1943, and their transports had not even been "combat loaded," meaning they could not be unloaded rapidly in support of an amphibious landing. Upon learning of their new mission, the Marines rushed to reload the transports, dramatically cutting stocks of food, supplies, and even ammunition to save time.

Photo # 80-CF-112-4-63   RAdm. Turner & MGen Vandegrift aboard USS McCawley, July-Aug. 1942

Picture of amphibious crafts headed towards Guadalcanal

While this rush to battle left the Americans dangerously under-supplied, it also helped them to seize an advantage that had done so much for the Japanese in their six-month advance: surprise. The Japanese construction troops on Guadalcanal, unaware of the American landing until the moment that covering fire from naval guns began raining down upon them, initially offered little resistance. Most simply retreated into the jungle. On Tulagi and the nearby islands of Gavutu and Tanambogo, however, the main Japanese force pushed back tenaciously against the Marines. Outnumbered and taken by surprise, the Japanese defenders fought virtually to the last man, extracting the maximum possible price for control of the islands. Altogether, only three of the 350 Japanese soldiers on Tulagi survived, and only 20 of the roughly 500 on Gavutu and Tanambogo survived, a grim taste of the brutal combat that would come to characterize the Guadalcanal Campaign and the war in the Pacific as a whole.

A map of Guadalcanal and direction of the landings

A picture of Marines coming to shore on Guadalcanal on August 7

Aerial photo of Tanambogo and Gavutu Islands during the invasion

Aerial photo of Tulagi during the invasion

By August 8, the Marines had secured Guadalcanal, but even by then, ominous strains and fractures had begun to show within the American coalition before the first Marine waded ashore. The Guadalcanal invasion fleet initially consisted of 76 ships assembled piecemeal from Australia, New Zealand, Pearl Harbor, and San Diego, and at the heart of the force were three of the navy's four remaining aircraft carriers - *Enterprise, Wasp,* and *Saratoga* - under the command of Vice Admiral Frank Jack Fletcher. As operational commander of the US fleet at the battles of Midway and the Coral Sea, Fletcher had proven himself a daring and capable officer, but he was skeptical of the Guadalcanal operation and believed that so modest a prize was not worth the risk of bringing three precious carriers within range of Japanese air power. Even before the operation began, the dispute between Fletcher and Rear Admiral Richmond Kelly Turner, who commanded the transports and cargo ships, grew heated and personal, to the extent that Turner's chief of staff reported he "was amazed and disturbed by the way these two admirals talked to each other. I had never heard anything like it." (Dyer, 301). In the end, Fletcher insisted that his carriers would stay to cover the landings for no more than three days, enraging General Vandegrift, who argued that his Marines would require five days at the least to unload their supplies and equipment.

Fletcher

That would not be the end of the matter either. On the afternoon of August 8, not quite two full days into the operation, Fletcher received word of Japanese torpedo planes in the area. Convinced that large numbers of Japanese aircraft could be preparing to strike, and that the risk of losing his carriers outweighed all other factors, Fletcher sent a terse message to Admiral Ghormley in Noumea: "Fighter strength reduced from 99 to 78. In view of large numbers of enemy torpedo planes and bombers in this area, I recommend the immediate withdrawal of my carriers. Request tankers be sent forward immediately as fuel running low." (Dyer, 383). Fletcher didn't bother waiting for a reply; he readied his ships and departed at 6:30 that evening, leaving Vandegrift with his Marines only partly deployed and Turner with only a few surface ships for protection.

As a result of those decisions, the American forces found themselves in an incredibly vulnerable position when they encountered the first devastating Japanese counter-strike. Informed of the American incursion by the Japanese garrison at Tulagi, Admiral Yamamoto ordered Vice Admiral Mikawa Gun'ichi, commander of the Eighth Fleet (based in Rabaul), to assemble a group of five heavy and two light cruisers and steam southeast to destroy the American transport ships. Given that Mikawa's small force had no air support, the move was daring, if not reckless, but Fletcher's untimely departure considerably evened the odds, and the Japanese sailors were also well-trained in night-time operations.

The route of the Japanese airstrike

As it happened, Mikawa's small attack group arrived just as Turner was convening a conference of his officers to discuss whether or not they could continue to unload Vandegrift's Marines without air support. This meant that the perimeter of Savo Sound, where Turner's transports and cargo ships rode at anchor, was even more lightly defended than usual. Mikawa took advantage of his adversaries' lack of readiness, as well as the cloudy and moonless conditions, to launch what naval historian Samuel Eliot Morison labeled "the worst defeat ever suffered on the high seas by the US Navy." (Morison, 167). Mikawa's squadron slipped completely undetected through the south entrance to Savo Sound about 1:30 a.m., and by communicating via a system of hooded blinkers arranged so that they would only be visible to his own ships, Mikawa launched a furious assault on the ships patrolling the southern entrance. The Japanese sank the Australian cruiser *Canberra* and damaged *Chicago*, the flagship of the officer in command, Captain Howard D. Bode. In the confusion, Bode failed to alert his ships in the north entrance to the Savo Sound about the Japanese assault. As a result, 15 minutes later, when Mikawa swung around Savo Island and came up behind the heavy cruisers *Quincy*, *Astoria*, and *Vincennes* at the north entrance, he caught them completely by surprise. Under punishingly accurate fire from Mikawa's squadron, *Quincy* sank almost immediately, as did *Astoria* a few minutes later. *Vincennes* lasted through the night, heavily damaged, but slipped beneath the waters the next morning. Having sustained only minor damage to his ships, Mikawa steamed out of Savo Sound and back to Rabaul, leaving behind him four destroyed cruisers and almost 2,000 dead and wounded.

A picture of the *Quincy* on fire and sinking

The *Canberra* before being sunk

The Battle of Savo Island, as it was called, was a defeat for the Americans, and the damage was immediately recognized as such by Admiral Turner, who blamed overconfidence on the part of the Navy: "The Navy was still obsessed with a strong feeling of technical and mental superiority over the enemy. In spite of ample evidence as to enemy capabilities, most of our officers and men despised the enemy and felt themselves sure victors in all encounters under any circumstances. The net result of all this was a fatal lethargy of mind which induced a confidence without readiness, and a routine acceptance of outworn peacetime standards of conduct. I believe that this psychological factor, as a cause of our defeat, was even more important than the element of surprise."

Historian Richard B. Frank would later cite that battle as the point after which "the United States picked itself up off the deck and prepared for the most savage combat in its history," but the next morning, August 9, was a dark one for the Americans. While rescue ships plucked bodies and desperate survivors out of the sea and medics tended to the hundreds of wounded,

Turner and Vandegrift reconsidered their position. The only bright spot from the previous night was that in his hurry to leave the Sound before the Americans could mount any sort of adequate response to his incursion, Mikawa had failed to strike his main target: the transports and supply ships. Since those were still manned and intact, they could continue loading Marines and supplies onto Guadalcanal. Indeed, when Mikawa returned to Rabaul and sent his report to Yamamoto, the admiral was furious. The whole point of the operation had been to destroy the transports and prevent the Americans from landing any further troops on Guadalcanal, so Yamamoto questioned the value of a victory over the cruisers if the treasure they guarded remained unclaimed.

On the American side, however, the catastrophe of the previous night had driven home to Turner his fleet's alarming vulnerability. He decided that without air cover, he could not afford another night in Savo Sound. His crews worked feverishly throughout the day to unload everything they could onto Guadalcanal, but as the sun went down, they weighed anchor, turned south, and set off for Ghormley's headquarters in Noumea. Nearly 2,000 Marines who had not been able to unload in time sailed off with Turner.

The Marines who remained, about 11,000 on Guadalcanal and another 6,000 on Tulagi, could have been forgiven for feeling abandoned. In the rush to reload at Wellington, their supplies had been drastically scaled back, and in his own rush to leave Savo Sound with most of his fleet intact, Turner had only managed to unload about half of the little he had brought. Young, poorly-trained, isolated and alone, the remaining Marines were an obvious target for Japanese counter-strikes, and to top it off, they had no radio equipment, no radar, no construction equipment, and no barbed wire. They had no more than four days' worth of ammunition and ate only two simple meals per day. In the words of one officer, "We had no idea what was going to happen. We were all wondering where our planes were. The Navy had left, their carriers had left. We didn't have a thing there." (Pollock, 130-32)

From those inauspicious beginnings, conflict over control of the island and its airstrip would drag on for half a year.

Early Operations

The Marines' defensive perimeter in early August

Japan's greatest strategic failure in the early stages of the Guadalcanal Campaign was to misjudge the Americans' intentions and capabilities. The Battle of Midway had been a major setback, but even so, a great many Japanese officers believed that the dynamic of the conflict was still one of Japanese advance and American response. Even canny strategists like Yamamoto, who understood and respected the war-making potential of the "sleeping giant," believed that the Americans could not possibly initiate a major offensive until 1943.

To be fair, these were hardly unreasonable expectations, because most American strategists held more or less the same opinion. Without the stubborn, reckless determination of King and MacArthur to seize the initiative at any cost, the Americans would never have launched a Solomons campaign so early. Indeed, had Roosevelt and his other Joint Chiefs understood just how expensive the Guadalcanal Campaign would end up being, they probably would never have even agreed to it in the first place.

Moreover, Mikawa's easy success in the Battle of Savo Island suggested that the Americans were not fully committed to holding Guadalcanal, and Fletcher and Turner's hasty retreats to Noumea implied the same. On that basis, even astute Japanese strategists like Admiral Yamamoto concluded that there could be no more than 10,000 Marines on Guadalcanal and perhaps as few as 2,000. Yamamoto further assumed that these Marines were likely isolated, undersupplied, and demoralized. The American garrison was badly undersupplied and, for a time, cut off from headquarters in Noumea. Nonetheless, Vandegrift's Marines were closer to 20,000 strong and by no means ready to surrender.

Making matters worse, Army General Hyakutake, at Rabaul, was at this time still more focused on the New Guinea operation, and he considered Guadalcanal the navy's problem. Even when he began receiving reports that thousands of Americans were on the island and that the Japanese contingent was threatened with total defeat, he did not believe them.

In addition to being underestimated, the Marines held one key asset: the airstrip. The Japanese construction troops had nearly completed it before the August 7 invasion, and Vandegrift's men used captured equipment to rush the airstrip to completion. The airstrip was renamed Henderson Field in honor of Lofton Henderson, a Marine major who had died at the Battle of Midway. On August 15, a small contingent of destroyer-transports managed to deliver equipment, including aviation fuel and bombs, as well as a team of badly-needed aircraft technicians. Within the week, 19 fighters and 12 dive-bombers managed to fly into Henderson Field from the escort carrier *Long Island*. These were the beginnings of the so-called "Cactus Air Force," a name based off the Allied codeword for Guadalcanal ("cactus"). The Cactus Air Force maintained American control of the air around Guadalcanal, an essential advantage in the months ahead.

Aircraft at Henderson Field

Since all these warning signs went unread, it was unsurprising that the Japanese response was initially piecemeal and somewhat half-hearted. Admiral Yamamoto did detach a number of destroyers from Rear Admiral Tanaka Raizo's Destroyer Squadron Two to form the Guadalcanal Reinforcement Force, and this force, which American Marines would soon be referring to as the "Tokyo Express," was tasked with transporting men and supplies to the beleaguered Japanese troops on Guadalcanal. Admiral Tanaka reportedly considered the assignment beneath his dignity, but he would eventually learn to his dismay that the mission was also beyond his abilities. In addition, Yamamoto persuaded General Hyakutake to begin assembling a 6,000 man force to retake the island.

Tanaka

Before this full force was prepared, however, Yamamoto and Hyakutake dispatched Colonel Ichiki Kiyonao, with just over 900 men, to strike the Americans. On the night of August 18,

Ichiki and his men landed at Taivu on the north coast of Guadalcanal, just east of the American garrison, and began marching through the jungle. Expecting to encounter a small contingent of malnourished soldiers, Ichiki was surprised on August 21 when his men clashed with a large, heavily-armed Marine force. The Battle of the Tenaru, fought at the mouth of Alligator Creek, was a bloodbath, and when Ichiki mounted a foolish frontal assault, the Americans, armed with machine guns and light tanks, virtually annihilated his invasion force. Nearly 800 of the Japanese soldiers were killed, with most of the rest of the survivors fleeing back into the jungle. Only one surrendered, and Ichiki himself committed suicide when he saw that the battle was lost. It was a moment full of added significance because Ichiki had commanded the Japanese troops in the 1937 Battle of Lugou Bridge, also known as the "Marco Polo Bridge Incident," the opening of Japan's invasion of coastal China and widely considered an event that truly marked the beginning of World War II.

Ichiki

Dead Japanese soldiers after the battle

Buildup

Following the disaster of the Ichiki mission, the Japanese navy turned its attentions more seriously toward dislodging the Americans from Guadalcanal. For Admiral Yamamoto in particular, conflict over the Solomons appeared to be not just a threat but an opportunity to finally lure the American fleet into the long-awaited "decisive battle" advocated by naval doctrine. On August 24, the Battle of the Eastern Solomons was an evenly-matched carrier confrontation between Fletcher and Admiral Nagumo Chuichi, who had been the operational commander of the Pearl Harbor attack. Nagumo's fleet, including the heavy carriers *Shokaku* and *Zuikaku* and the light carrier *Ryujo*, was providing air support for a convoy landing reinforcements for General Hyakutake's troops on Guadalcanal. Reports of the large-scale Japanese action had brought Fletcher's fleet, including the carriers *Enterprise*, *Wasp*, and *Saratoga*, up from Noumea. On Fletcher's approach, Nagumo immediately broke off from supporting the convoy to strike at the American carriers, a far larger prize, in his eyes, than recapturing Guadalcanal.

The *Enterprise* during the battle

The outcome, yet again, was less than decisive. American pilots managed to sink the light carrier *Ryujo*, but bombers and torpedo-planes from *Shokaku* and *Zuikaku* returned the favor, damaging *Enterprise* so badly that she had to be sent back to Pearl Harbor for repairs. As historian Richard B. Frank put it, "The Battle of the Eastern Solomons was unquestionably an American victory, but it had little long-term result, apart from a further reduction in the corps of trained Japanese carrier aviators. The (Japanese) reinforcements that could not come by slow transport would soon reach Guadalcanal by other means."

Following the exchange, both carrier groups retreated, anxious to avoid any further losses, but in one bright spot for the Americans, the convoy of Japanese troop transports and destroyers was now bereft of air support. The next day, Marine dive-bombers from Henderson Field and B-17 bombers from Espiritu Santo managed to locate and destroy the convoy before it could land reinforcements on Guadalcanal.

Still, while the flow of Japanese reinforcements had been delayed, it was not stopped. Yamamoto's Reinforcement Force under Admiral Tanaka began running regular convoys from Rabaul through the Solomon chain ("up the slot") and onto Guadalcanal. The "Tokyo Express" operated largely by night and frequently attempted to dampen American air power by bombarding Henderson Field. By the end of August, having taken advantage of dark, moonless nights, Tanaka managed to convoy nearly 6,000 well-armed reinforcements under General Kawaguchi Kiyotake onto Guadalcanal.

Japanese troops climb aboard a destroyer on the Tokyo Express

The Cactus Air Force over Henderson Field

After the fiasco that was the Battle of the Tenaru, Kawaguchi's orders, from General Hyakutake, were cautious and ambiguous. He was to reconnoiter Henderson Field, try to determine the enemy's strength, and estimate whether he would need further reinforcements before mounting an assault. Kawaguchi, however, threw caution to the wind and decided to attack immediately without sending out scouts or reconnoitering the area. On the night of September 13, after marching through dense jungle, his troops crawled up a low ridge about a thousand yards south of Henderson Field. Attempting to overrun and outflank the Marine perimeter, Kawaguchi's troops, supported by heavy mortar fire, launched at least a dozen charges up the face of the ridge. The Marine defenders, led by Lieutenant Colonel Merritt Edson, slowly pulled back but managed to hold the final knoll of the ridge. By morning, the ridge was littered with dead bodies, lending the battle its name, "Bloody Ridge." 20% of Edson's Marines were dead or wounded, but Kawaguchi had fared even worse, losing more than half of his men. He retreated back into the jungle, with the Marines too weak to pursue.

Edson

Dead Japanese soldiers after the battle

In both Washington and Tokyo, news of Kawaguchi's defeat at Bloody Ridge merely bolstered each side's determination to make a stand at Guadalcanal and thus accelerated the steady buildup of forces on both sides.

On September 18, a convoy under Admiral Fletcher managed to land the entire Seventh Regiment, 4,000 thousand Marines with all their weapons and equipment, in the face of Japanese air and submarine attacks. Meanwhile, the "Tokyo Express" ensured a steady flow of Japanese reinforcements, including General Hyakutake, who arrived on October 9 to personally direct the Japanese offensive. Meanwhile, Admirals Ghormely and Turner resisted calls from their subordinates on Guadalcanal to direct all their resources to the campaign, but they did eventually agree to reinforce the Marines with the 3,000 former Dakota National Guardsmen of the 164th Regiment, who arrived on October 13. Their escort of surface ships, under Rear Admiral Norman Scott, had managed a few days earlier to beat back Tanaka's "Tokyo Express" in the Battle of Cape Esperance.

As the conflict expanded, the popular press in the United States had begun to invest Guadalcanal with an outsized psychological importance, portraying it as a chance to redeem the many humiliating losses of before. A *New York Herald Tribune* editorial of October 16 stated, "The shadows of a great conflict lie over the Solomons." On October 24, President Roosevelt, a keen judge of popular opinion, directed the Joint Chiefs of Staff to "make sure that every possible weapon gets into that area to hold Guadalcanal." (Frank, 405) Despite the reinforcements, these raised expectations proved too much for Admiral Ghormely in Noumea, who complained to Nimitz, "My forces [are] totally inadequate to meet [the] situation." Concluding at last that it was Ghormley who was inadequate to the situation, Nimitz replaced him with the aggressive and determined Vice Admiral William "Bull" Halsey, already something of a legend in the navy. Meeting with Vandegrift in Noumea for the first time, Halsey was blunt: "Go on back. I'll give you everything I've got." With that, the Guadalcanal Campaign had entered a new phase.

Halsey

Interlude

After the first few weeks, the action at Guadalcanal fell into a regular pattern that held for several months. Each side struggled to supply and reinforce its own forces on the island, while simultaneously attempting to interdict the supply convoys of its enemy. While control of Henderson Field gave the Americans a built-in advantage in the air, Japanese mastery of night operations meant that Tanaka's "Tokyo Express" could maintain a steady flow of Japanese troops and supplies onto the island. Air and naval battles frequently revolved around attempts at resupply on one side or the other.

For troops on Guadalcanal itself, the environment could be just as threatening as the enemy. Aside from the narrow beaches, the island was covered with a profusion of giant hardwood trees, creeping vines, twisting roots, and undergrowth. Visibility was often as low as a yard or two, and soldiers would be lucky to march a mile or two in a day. Furthermore, both Japanese and

Americans were largely unused to the tropical climate, which bred fungus, skin infections, jaundice, and acute attacks of dysentery. Of course, the jungles were crawling with spiders, leeches, giant ants and wasps. Worst of all was the malarial mosquito; as dedicated as each side may have been to eliminating the other, malaria was often a greater threat than enemy action.

As bad as the environment was, the supply situation wasn't much better. Soldiers on both sides lived in tents if they were lucky and muddy dugouts if they were not. The Marines, for the most part, subsisted on canned C-rations, dehydrated meats and vegetables, and, when they could get it, captured Japanese rice. The Japanese, particularly as the conflict dragged on, often found their rations sharply reduced or even eliminated, surviving where they could on roots, coconuts, and moss.

Naturally, the stress and anxiety of the conflict weighed heavily on Japanese and American soldiers alike. Marines often spoke of "going Asiatic," which would now be called battle psychosis. As one Marine described the Japanese to John Hersey, a war correspondent: "They hide up in the trees like wildcats. Sometimes when they attack, they scream like a bunch of terrified cattle in a slaughter house. Other times they come so quiet they wouldn't scare a snake. One of their favorite tricks is to fire their machine guns off to one side. That starts you shooting. Then they start their main fire under the noise of your own shooting. Sometimes they use firecrackers as a diversion. Other times they jabber to cover the noise of their men cutting through the underbrush with machetes. You've probably heard about their using white surrender flags to suck us into traps. We're onto that one now." (Hersey, 20).

American soldiers, particularly those stationed at or around Henderson Field, frequently suffered through nightly bombardments by the "Tokyo Express." One Marine, recalling a particularly extensive episode in mid-October, wrote, "It was the most tremendous thing I've ever been through in all my life. Anyone who says a naval bombardment isn't worse than any artillery shelling is absolutely crazy....There was one big bunker near our galley in the First Marines...a shell dropped right in the middle of it and practically everybody in the hole was killed. We tried to dig the men out but it wasn't any use." (Pollock, 117).

Japanese bombardment of Henderson Field in October 1942

For the American pilots at Henderson Field, the stresses of the Guadalcanal Campaign could be extreme. They faced many of the same challenges as other soldiers, including heat, humidity, disease, insects, poor diet, and uncertainty, but in addition to those problems, the "Cactus Air Force" struggled with shortages of fuel, spare parts, and ammunition, not to mention the poor condition of the airfield and almost nightly Japanese bombardments of it. The average flier could only last 30 days on Guadalcanal before being judged physically or psychologically unfit to fly. For example, Marine Air Group Twenty-Three was the first contingent of dive-bombers to operate from Guadalcanal, but of that group's pilots, "only one would eventually be able to walk to the plane that carried him away from Henderson Field." (Merrillat, 103).

One particular stress for American pilots was the fact that during the Guadalcanal Campaign, Japanese fliers still enjoyed a technological edge. The Mitsubishi Zero fighter was substantially faster, more maneuverable, and more reliable than both the Marine Wildcat fighter and the Army Air Force P-40 fighter. Indeed, the Wildcats had immense difficulty just making their way up to combat altitude, often requiring 35-40 minutes of advance warning in order to engage incoming Japanese bombers. In addition, the B-17 bombers, which military planners had hoped to use against enemy ships, proved nearly worthless. Nonetheless, American control of Henderson Field proved invaluable because the Japanese Zeroes, forced to fly in from Rabaul, could only afford to spend a few minutes at a time over Guadalcanal before returning to base to refuel.

A True Offensive

General Hyakutake had arrived on Guadalcanal to personally oversee a massive Japanese offensive aimed at capturing Henderson Field, and he believed his men were ready by mid-October. The plan was for a three-pronged land offensive, with elements from the Combined

Fleet prepared to intercede to prevent American warships from reaching and supporting the Marines. On October 16, some 20,000 Japanese troops began struggling through the dense jungle to position themselves for the assault, and with a 30 mile trek ahead of them, the soldiers each carried a full ammunition pack, 12 days of rations, and an artillery shell.

Perhaps not surprisingly, while contending with heat, insects, rough terrain, and anxiety, the three "prongs" lost track of each other and the detailed timetable they had worked out in advance. According to the plan, Lieutenant General Maruyama Masai's Second Division was meant to strike from the south, but it was repeatedly delayed, and when a communications failure prevented Major General Sumiyoshi Tadashi (to the west) from learning of the postponement, he launched his assault as originally scheduled on October 23. Without support from the other two "prongs" of the attack, Sumiyoshi's forces faced the full brunt of the Marines arrayed against them. His troops, already tired and weak from their march through the jungle, fell into line behind their nine light tanks, but the Marine artillery were already sighted and prepared for the assault. They quickly knocked the tanks out of commission, after which Sumiyoshi's force was virtually annihilated.

Dead Japanese soldiers and disabled tanks

A Marine howitzer defending on the western side of the perimeter

At the very least, Sumiyoshi's ordeal did keep the Americans focused on the west while the main body of the assault formed up unobserved to the south, along Bloody Ridge. In fact, with one Marine battalion reassigned west to support the action against Sumiyoshi, defenses on the south side of Henderson Field were relatively light. Just one unit, the First Battalion, Seventh Marines, under Lieutenant Colonel Lewis "Chesty" Puller, manned the 4,000 yard perimeter to the south of the airfield.

Map of the three prongs

General Hyakutake launched his major assault late on the night of October 23 in the midst of a major rainstorm. Hitting all along the southern side of the perimeter at once, the Japanese threatened to overwhelm and outflank Puller's Marines, and they did manage to break through the defensive line in a few places, but these holes were rapidly filled. As Puller's Marines fell back, from the force of the Japanese assault, they were reinforced by elements of the 164th Regiment. The Dakota National Guardsmen, though considerably older than the Marines, managed to hold their own.

While Hyakutake's march through the jungle had secured him the element of surprise, he made poor use of such a hard-won prize. Wave upon wave of poorly-trained rural recruits were ordered to make pointless and suicidal *"banzai"* charges, running up the ridge directly only to be mown down by disciplined automatic fire. By morning, the assault had broken off, leaving more than a thousand Japanese dead.

Hyakutake struck the next night as well, again attempting to charge up Bloody Ridge to break the Marine perimeter and take Henderson Field, but with no better results. Altogether, as many as 3,500 Japanese may have died in this, the Second Battle of Bloody Ridge.

Dead Japanese soldiers after the attacks on October 25-26

On October 26, Hyakutake's support fleet, which was stationed to the northeast off the Santa Cruz Islands, clashed with an American carrier task force under Admiral Thomas Kinkaid. The Japanese fleet, under Vice Admiral Kondo Nobutake, managed to sink one American carrier, *Hornet*, and badly damage another, *Enterprise*. On the flip side, Kinkaid's men damaged two carriers, *Zuiho* and *Shokaku*, but were not able to knock them out of the fight. The Americans ultimately had to withdraw, but while Kondo had shown that Japanese naval aviators could still hold their own against the Americans in an equally-matched contest, the Japanese were perpetually harassed by ground-based aircraft out of the invaluable Henderson Field. Unable to strike Henderson, running short on aircraft and experienced pilots, and worried about his carriers' vulnerability after learning that Hyakutake's ground assault had been a failure, Kondo figured he had no operational justification for continuing to risk the safety of his ships. As a result, Kondo withdrew his forces.

Combined, the Second Battle of Bloody Ridge on land and the Battle of the Santa Cruz Islands at sea marked an important watershed. Though few suspected it at the time, the operations turned out to be Japan's last major attempt to claim Henderson Field from the Marines. Furthermore, Kondo's dilemma off the Santa Cruz Islands demonstrated just what a valuable prize the Americans had claimed. With more than 100 aircraft operating out of Henderson Field, the Americans held unquestioned mastery of the air in the eastern Solomons, which ensured that Guadalcanal would remain a secure beachhead and jumping-off point for further incursions into Japanese-held territory. Finally, the steep losses the Japanese suffered at Bloody Ridge and the Santa Cruz Islands demonstrated to Japanese military planners that they could no longer afford to mount offensive operations. The loss of so many aircraft and experienced pilots was particularly alarming. The Americans, with their massive industrial and population base, might have made up for such losses, but the Japanese could not.

The End of the Campaign

The final major phase of the Guadalcanal Campaign after the Second Battle of Bloody Ridge was a grim war of attrition. This was precisely the sort of war that Japanese military planners, especially Admiral Yamamoto Isoroku, had desperately sought to avoid, a contest of brute numbers in which America's massive industrial economy, now fully mobilized for war production, would slowly grind down Japan's much more limited material base. In a sense, the final phase of the Guadalcanal campaign was a preview of the Pacific War battles yet to come: brutal contests of strength in which American numbers would ultimately overwhelm Japan's desperate, determined resistance.

In retrospect, the outcome was probably never in doubt after October, but for the Japanese military command, however, the Guadalcanal Campaign did not yet seem a lost cause. As one officer at the Imperial General Headquarters put it, "We must be aware of the possibility that the struggle for Guadalcanal in the southeast area may develop into the decisive struggle between America and Japan." (Hattori, 21). Indeed, even Admiral Yamamoto, who had warned against descending into just such a conflict with the Americans and ought to have known better, sometimes fantasized that the struggle at Guadalcanal might still be used to draw the Americans into the long-awaited "decisive battle."

Early in November, the new Eighth Area Army, under General Imamura Hitoshi, took command in Rabaul and began overseeing Army operations in both New Guinea and the Solomons. In a good omen for the Japanese effort in Guadalcanal, Imamura and Admiral Yamamoto enjoyed a far better relationship than those between most generals and admirals. In their youths, the two had served together in London, where they frequently played bridge together, but while meeting with Imamura, Yamamoto warned his old friend that American war mobilization, finally kicking into high gear, was badly hurting Japan's prospects in the southwest Pacific. In the air, the Americans already enjoyed a 3:1 advantage. In addition, American pilots and sailors were becoming better trained and better equipped as the war progressed. "Our emphasis on intensive training and discipline isn't wrong," Yamamoto argued, "but we should have made sure it was accompanied by scientific and technological improvements as well. I have a strong sense of responsibility for our failure in that regard." (Agawa, 342).

Imamura

Throughout November, the Japanese continued to pour men and material - resources they could scarce afford to lose - into the forlorn cause of retaking the island. Admiral Tanaka's "Tokyo Express" continued to dispatch men and supplies to Guadalcanal, but increasing American control of the air and sea gradually constricted the flow to an irregular trickle. Meanwhile, Admiral Yamamoto, who had moved his headquarters to the Micronesian island of Truk in order to be closer to the action in the Solomons, prepared for one last major offensive in mid-November. A large convoy of 11 high-speed transports carrying 3,000 naval landing troops and a full army division would land at Tassafaronga, to the east of the American garrison. Simultaneously, a task force of battleships and cruisers would bombard Henderson Field to prevent the Americans from using their "Cactus Air Force" to interdict the reinforcements.

Unfortunately for the Japanese, by this point the Americans had cracked Japan's naval code (the "Magic" decrypts), so Halsey had advance warning of the operation and enough time to put together a strong response force of his own, including the carrier *Enterprise*, which had just returned from the naval repair yards at Pearl Harbor. The conflict, now referred to as the Naval Battle of Guadalcanal, began on November 12 when the Japanese task force (two battleships, a light cruiser, and six destroyers) under Vice Admiral Abe Hiroaki steamed down the "slot" of the Solomons chain to bombard Henderson Field and cover the landing at Tassafaronga. Admiral Turner, alerted to the impending Japanese operation, spotted Abe early and dispatched Rear Admiral Daniel J. Callaghan with five cruisers and eight destroyers to confront him. The Americans also had the advantage of functioning radar systems, which detected the Japanese task force early, but the officials were so unused to the new technology that Callaghan held his fire for too long, giving Japanese lookouts a chance to spot him and thus conceding the element of surprise.

The arrows represent the routes taken by the fleets toward each other.

Nevertheless, while the engagement proved a costly victory for the Americans, it was a victory. Abe managed to sink the cruiser *Atlanta*, as well as three of Callaghan's destroyers. In addition, the cruisers *Portland* and *San Francisco* were heavily damaged, and Admiral Callaghan himself was killed. The exchange was relentless and at very close range, at times so close that Callaghan reportedly could not even lower his big guns to fire on the enemy. One Marine described the action, "The star shells rose, terrible and red. Giant tracers flashed across the night in orange arches ... the sea seemed a sheet of polished obsidian on which the warships seemed to have been dropped and were immobilized, centered amid concentric circles like shock waves that form around a stone dropped in mud."

In the end, Abe's force sustained so much damage that he was forced to call a retreat, and his flagship, the battleship *Hiei*, was so badly damaged that it could barely limp back up the slot. The next morning, aircraft from Henderson Field - the very aircraft that Abe's bombardment had been designed to keep out of the air at all costs - located the *Hiei* and finished the job Callaghan had started, sending it to the bottom of the sea.

Aerial photo of the bombing of the *Hiei*

Without any relief from American air power based out of Henderson Field, the resupply and reinforcement convoy under Tanaka was dangerously exposed. Even so, the convoy continued on toward Guadalcanal. On the night of August 14, a small group of Japanese cruisers did manage to bombard Henderson Field, but not badly enough to do any significant damage. The next morning the Cactus Air Force was back in the air, sinking six of Tanaka's precious transport ships, as well as one of his cruisers.

The night of November 15, Kondo dispatched his remaining forces, the battleship *Kirishima* along with four cruisers, in one final attempt to knock Henderson Field and its aircraft out of the fight. Unbeknownst to Kondo, however, the *Kirishima* would face a new and dangerous foe. Rear Admiral Willis A. Lee had just arrived at Guadalcanal with two battleships from Admiral Kinkaid's task force. The battleships, *Washington* and *South Dakota*, were new models, faster, more maneuverable, and more heavily armored. They were perfect examples of the technological superiority that America was beginning to enjoy as the conflict wore on. Moreover, unlike most of his peers, Admiral Lee understood and appreciated the value of radar, a tool he believed could make up for the long-standing Japanese advantage in naval night-fighting. As historian Eric Hammel noted, "On November 12, 1942, the (Japanese) Imperial Navy had the better ships and the better tactics. After November 15, 1942, its leaders lost heart and it lacked the strategic depth to face the burgeoning U.S. Navy and its vastly improving weapons and tactics. The Japanese never got better while, after November 1942, the U.S. Navy never stopped getting better."

With the help of radar, the confrontation between Lee and Kondo was a hard-fought but decisive American victory. As the clash began, the power system on *South Dakota* failed, leaving it separated from *Washington* and helplessly exposed to enemy fire. However, the new battleship's improved armor proved its worth. Suffering no fewer than 42 large-caliber hits, *South Dakota* simply continued steaming ahead, damaged but unbowed. Shortly after that, *Washington* used its radar to direct a highly accurate rain of shells onto the deck of *Kirishima*. Within minutes, Kondo's battleship was sinking, one of his destroyers was maimed, and the rest of his task force was in retreat. At the cost of three American destroyers (and the damaged *South Dakota*), Admiral Lee had saved Henderson Field from bombardment.

The *Washington* firing at the Japanese during the battle

With no protection from American air power, Tanaka's transports suffered through a rain of fire in their attempts to land at Guadalcanal. Four of the transports did manage to beach themselves on a point near Tassafaronga, but aircraft based on Henderson Field and *Enterprise* strafed and bombed their decks mercilessly as the hapless soldiers attempted to disembark. In all, no more than 2,000 Japanese reinforcements made it onto Guadalcanal, and they were already traumatized, isolated, and poorly supplied. In Washington the next day, Navy Secretary Knox told reporters, "We can lick them. I don't qualify that. We'll defeat them." (Griffith, 205).

Pictures of wrecked Japanese transport ships on the beach

In the weeks following the Naval Battle of Guadalcanal, the Americans finally wrested full control of the sea lanes in the southeastern Solomons from the Japanese and the garrison around Henderson Field expanded steadily. By the end of the year, there were more than 60,000 airmen, Marines, soldiers, sailors, and other personnel on the island. By contrast, after their last major successful convoy in October, the Japanese struggled to land reinforcements and supplies on Guadalcanal. By December, American control of the sea had advanced so far that an increasingly desperate Japanese Navy had begun running stealth groups of high-speed destroyers up to the coast at night to hurl drums of rice and other supplies overboard and speed off before the Americans could detect them. Responding to the new supply tactics, American pilots and PT-gunners took to searching out and sinking the drums before Japanese shore parties could recover them.

With all of this occurring, the remaining Japanese troops on Guadalcanal found their position rapidly deteriorating. Outnumbered nearly two to one, isolated from headquarters in Rabaul, and with little to no air or sea support, they found themselves reduced to increasingly depleted rations. By the end of the year, malnutrition and starvation had set in, accompanied as always by tropical diseases that wracked the bodies of the already weakened soldiers. In some, dysentery and malnourishment had proceeded so far that their hair and nails stopped growing. The commander of one division of 6,000 soldiers estimated that only about 250 of his men were actually fit enough for combat, and one officer observed the precarious mortality of his troops as follows:

"Those who can stand -- 30 days

Those who can sit up -- 3 weeks

Those who cannot sit up -- 1 week

Those who urinate lying down -- 3 days

Those who have stopped speaking -- 2 days

Those who have stopped blinking – tomorrow" (Frank, 527).

As the Japanese capacity to mount offensive operations collapsed, the initiative passed to Vandegrift and his Marines. In the wake of the Second Battle of Bloody Ridge, he had begun pushing his defensive perimeter slowly and patiently outward while sending out teams to locate and destroy any isolated Japanese detachments that still clung to survival in the jungle. Finally, after four months of the most punishing jungle combat of the war thus far, Vandegrift and his long-suffering First Marine Division were transferred out of Guadalcanal in early December, replaced by the Second Marine Division under Army Lieutenant General Alexander M. Patch.

Altogether, Vandegrift's Marines had lost 650 dead and 1,300 wounded. About half of his men had contracted some tropical disease, usually malaria. For this steep price, however, Vandegrift could claim to have purchased a stunning success. In the first weeks after his men had waded onto the shores of Guadalcanal, they had been severely undersupplied and undermanned, an isolated garrison with a barely-functioning airstrip that struggled to keep more than a dozen planes in the sky. By December, there were more than 35,000 Americans on Guadalcanal, and more than 200 planes on Henderson Field. They controlled the air and increasingly the sea lanes as well. The Japanese forces on the island, while by no means negligible, were outnumbered and barely supplied. The tide had turned.

By the time General Patch took over command of the Guadalcanal Campaign on December 9, the Japanese had been decisively defeated in the Solomons. As the closing years of the war would demonstrate with horrible clarity, however, defeat and surrender are two completely different things. While the Japanese had no realistic prospects of retaking Guadalcanal, the task of dislodging them completely from the island would be a long and costly one. Early in December, Japanese destroyers covertly running supplies and equipment to their beleaguered ground forces on Guadalcanal were challenged by a group of American cruisers. The Japanese sunk one and damaged three others, and while these victories were growing increasingly rare, they made clear that Guadalcanal was not yet safe for the Americans.

Undeterred, General Patch was determined to complete the job of driving the Japanese from the island. He planned to spend the remainder of December neutralizing dangerous Japanese positions on the high ground overlooking Henderson Field. With that work accomplished, in early January, he would begin an all-out advance across the island west from the Marine garrison. He hoped to clear Guadalcanal of all Japanese forces by April.

As it happened, however, the campaign ended sooner than even the most optimistic American military planners had expected. In the wake of their crushing defeat in the Naval Battle of Guadalcanal, Japan's military leaders made the highly uncharacteristic decision of choosing to pull back. The Emperor approved the decision on December 31, and in February 1943, the Japanese demonstrated that despite all the setbacks they had suffered in the Solomons, they were still capable of executing complex, demanding military operations in complete secrecy and in the dead of night. Over the course of about a week, they evacuated more than 10,000 men from Guadalcanal. American leaders were so unfamiliar with the concept of a Japanese retreat that when Admiral Halsey noted the increased activity, he assigned extra forces to guard Henderson Field because he feared yet another attack was coming. By February 8, an advance force of Patch's Marines marched west across the island, encountering nothing but a few abandoned boats and supplies on the far western coast. The next day, Patch radioed to Admiral Halsey, "Tokyo Express no longer has terminus on Guadalcanal." After a grueling campaign that took almost half a year, the Guadalcanal campaign had ended with an American victory.

The significance of the campaign, launched by both the Japanese and the Americans on a shoestring and escalated in an unsteady, piecemeal, tit-for-tat pattern, came as a surprise to military planners and observers on both sides. Barely aware of the Solomon Islands prior to the Pacific War, both nations found themselves committed to triumphing in a contest of wills whose import at times seemed just as much psychological as practical. In the end, Guadalcanal represented the inevitable point where the military balance in the Pacific tipped in favor of the Americans. As strategists like Admiral Yamamoto Isoroku well understood, given the time and determination necessary to mobilize its massive population and industrial economy for war, the United States was bound to crush Japan. The remainder of the Pacific War was merely the working out of that destiny.

When King and MacArthur had won the Joint Chiefs' approval for the Guadalcanal operation in mid-1942, it had been conceived as merely the first and smallest phase of a campaign to capture Japan's southwestern Pacific headquarters in Rabaul. As the Guadalcanal conflict metastasized into an essential win-at-all-costs campaign, however, concern with the prize of Rabaul gradually withered away. In the end, King and MacArthur elected to bypass Rabaul.

Effectively cut off from contact with the rest of the Japanese war effort, frequently bombarded, alone and impotent, Rabaul was never actually invaded. Instead, the Americans turned their attentions to the north and west, to the Philippines, the Central Pacific, and beyond. Having reached the practical outer limits of their Asian-Pacific empire, and having gambled away so much at Midway and Guadalcanal, the Japanese hunkered down behind an extensive defense perimeter, awaiting the inevitable American advance. Conversely, the Americans, having finally succeeded in mobilizing their massive population and industrial economy on behalf of the war effort, began to overwhelm their Japanese opponents with men and materiel. The next few years would be marked by incredibly deadly campaigns like Iwo Jima and Okinawa, with poorly-supplied Japanese island garrisons attempting to hold out against a much larger American invasion force. These confrontations often proved unprecedentedly brutal, with desperate suicide tactics on the Japanese side and indiscriminate area bombing on the American side.

The tide had turned, but there was still plenty of bloody war ahead.

The Battle of Leyte Gulf

The Background Before the Battle

By March 1944, the Joint Chiefs instructed MacArthur to prepare his men to move into the southern Philippines by the end of the year, and then into Luzon by early 1945. They also ordered Admiral Chester Nimitz to prepare for an assault on Formosa for early 1945.

Nimitz

Meanwhile, between March and June of 1944, American intelligence had learned that Japan was in the process of reinforcing areas under their control in the western Pacific, especially Formosa. This meant that the longer it took for the Americans to begin their attack on the island, the better-prepared Japanese forces would be to defend it. For the Joint Chiefs, this meant that in order to attack Formosa, they would have to move up their timetable to the fall of 1944 if they wanted to carry out an assault on the island.

Another complicating factor was the belief by American strategists that the Chinese resistance was in danger of collapsing against Japanese pressure. This would nullify one of the major reasons for privileging Formosa over the Philippines (aiding in the supply of Chinese forces on the mainland). By this time, both MacArthur and Nimitz were advocating the need to take the

Philippines to secure air bases from which the Allies could launch further operations across the Pacific. In July 1944, Roosevelt sailed to Pearl Harbor to discuss strategy. Although often cited as the key event in the lead up to the invasion of the Philippines, the truth is that the meeting was indecisive. It was not until September 1944 that President Roosevelt, the Joint Chiefs, MacArthur and Nimitz were all committed to the plan of invading the Philippines before engaging in further attacks on Japan. This made sense mostly in terms of aircraft ranges and the imperative to keep ground forces under the umbrella of short range fighters, but as MacArthur was soon to discover, the carriers were not up to the job on their own.

Once military leaders settled on the Philippines-first plan, they began to prepare for the upcoming campaign. The Allied strategy would comprise of four phases. First, naval and ground units would establish a foothold on southeastern Mindanao, where they could establish airfields that would support further operations. Next, Allied units would move into the central Philippines at Leyte, where MacArthur would set up air and supply bases for the attack on Luzon. The third phase involved taking Luzon, and then the fourth phase would involve dislodging Japanese troops from the minor Philippines islands that had been bypassed during the first three phases.

Ultimately, in September 1944, MacArthur revised the plan and eliminated the first phase at Mindanao, instead collapsing the plan into a three-phased assault that would begin at Leyte. Admiral William "Bull" Halsey, in command of the U.S. 7th Fleet and directly subordinate to MacArthur, was a keen advocate of an attack on Leyte, a large island to the southeast of the Philippine archipelago. General Walter Krueger, commander of MacArthur's 8th army, was less enthusiastic. Buttressed by upbeat intelligence reports, MacArthur opted for Halsey's plan.

Halsey

Krueger

A problem the Allied forces encountered as they prepared for the Philippines invasion was Japanese reinforcements. Since Japanese military leaders were constantly moving troops and planes around, it became difficult for the Americans to estimate Japanese ground and aerial strength. For example, American leaders estimated that the Japanese had 400-500 planes in the Philippines, but that an additional 300-400 planes might be moved from Formosa, along with carrier-based planes that could be sent to the region to contest the American attack.

A map of the Philippines

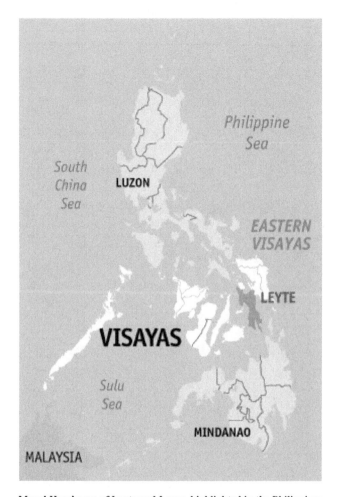

Magal Haes' map of Leyte and Luzon highlighted in the Philippines

Protecting the American landings at Leyte Gulf, two main forces of American vessels flanked the position to north and south. Vice Admiral Thomas Kinkaid watched the southern approach at Surigao Strait with a force of battleships, cruisers, destroyers, and torpedo boats (PT boats, or "patrol/torpedo"). This guarded the approaches from the Sulu Sea and the Mindinao Sea.

In the north, Halsey commanded the massive Task Force 38, containing a powerful grouping of

Essex-class aircraft carriers, plus fast modern battleships, heavy cruisers, and destroyers. Halsey undertook to guard the San Bernardino Strait to the north of Leyte Gulf, protecting the approaches from the Sibuyan Sea. On the Philippine Sea, three groups of 6 American *Casablanca*-class light carriers apiece, also known as escort carriers or jeep carriers (due to their small size rather than any onboard jeeps), provided air support to the American landings.

For their part, the Japanese planned a three-pronged attack against the American deployment. In the north, Vice Admiral Ozawa Jisaburo led the Northern Force, consisting of a single large aircraft carrier and three light carriers, plus supporting battleships, cruisers, and destroyers. The carriers lacked all but a handful of aircraft. The final remnant of Japan's once mighty carrier fleet, these craft would feint against the Americans' northern flank, hopefully drawing away the defenders of San Bernardino and Surigao Straits.

Ozawa

In the meantime, Center Force under Kurita Takeo, a massive flotilla centered around the two super-battleships *Yamato* and *Musashi*, would penetrate San Bernardino Strait via the Sibuyan Sea. A third task group, Force C, would cross the Sulu Sea and Mindinao Sea to force a passage through Surigao Strait. Coming from the north and south, these forces – if successful – would unite to sink the American *Essex*-class carriers if possible and wipe out the landing fleet in Leyte Gulf.

Kurita

The *Musashi*

A picture of Kurita's fleet anchored

Much of the plan depended on Northern Force's ability to lure the protective American warships away. The Japanese commanders later stated they believed they had a "50-50" chance of success, but with the Americans rolling ever closer to Japan, they believed the gamble worth the risk.

Palawan Passage and the Battle of the Sibuyan Sea

The first action of the battle occurred on October 23rd as Kurita's Center Force steamed across into the Palawan Passage, the western gateway to the Sibuyan Sea. However, danger lurked in the waters ahead, and the Japanese had no hint before it struck.

The American submarines *Dace* and *Darter*, commanded respectively by Bladen Claggett and David McLintock, patrolled the Passage on the early morning of the 23rd. At 1:16 AM, the two submarines, working in tandem, made contact with the Japanese force and reported its immense size and apparent heading to Task Force 38. Admiral Halsey heard the news approximately five hours later, after the message passed through the normal circuitous channels to his flagship.

Kurita's electronic warfare experts picked up the submarine radio signal, but Kurita – even more careless than Halsey – neglected to throw out a picket line of destroyers in advance of his force, moving through the Palawan Passage in three columns.

The two prowling submarines, unable to believe their good fortune, closed to attack at first light. Both fired a spread of torpedoes at Kurita's flagship, the heavy cruiser *Atago,* smashing its prow completely. Engulfed in black smoke shot through with bright orange flames, the cruiser sank rapidly by the bow almost immediately. Kurita leaped over the side along with the rest of his surviving crew, forced to tread water until the destroyer *Kishinama* came to his rescue and that of the other survivors.

The dawn attack continued with the torpedoing of the heavy cruiser *Takao,* which suffered so much damage its captain turned back to Brunei. The Americans completed their hit and run attack by firing a spread of six torpedoes into the cruiser *Maya,* one of which punched through its hull into the No. 7 boiler room. Almost instantly, internal explosions ripped the *Maya* apart, and the ship sank in 5 minutes. Ugaki reported that the cruiser simply "exploded, and after the spray and smoke had disappeared nothing remained of her to be seen" (Morison, 2002, 172).

The two *Gato*-class submarines, built at the same shipyard in Groton, Connecticut, shadowed the Japanese force for hours, trying to get in position for another attack. However, due to a navigational error, *Darter* ran aground on Bombay Shoal. After failed attempts to refloat the submarine and then failed attempts to sink it, the Americans finally transferred the crew to *Dace.* The overcrowded submarine set off for the Fremantle submarine base in Australia, enjoying what the crew described as a "pleasant voyage" despite running out of all food except mushroom soup and peanut butter sandwiches.

The two American submarines sank three of Kurita's heavy cruisers, but their most significant contribution perhaps consisted of the warning issued to Task Force 38. On the 24th, Center Force remained under American scrutiny as first the submarine USS *Guitarro,* then a reconnaissance aircraft, detected and reported its position.

The American carriers in the Philippine Sea launched strike after strike against Kurita's armada, with *Lexington, Essex, Intrepid, Franklin, Enterprise,* and *Cabot* contributing to the 259 sorties. The first squadrons arrived at 10:26 AM, formally beginning the Battle of the Sibuyan Sea. The Japanese ships put up heavy curtains of flak and, driven to desperation by their total lack of air cover, even fired their main guns at the flitting shapes of Hellcats, Avengers, and Helldivers as they swooped to deploy their ordnance, including both bombs and torpedoes, against the surface ships.

Pictures of Helldivers from Taskforce 38 during the battle

Picture of an Avenger during the battle

The Japanese only succeeded in destroying 18 aircraft in total, leading Vice Admiral Ugaki Matome, a profuse diarist who later flew a solo kamikaze mission rather than surrender, to remark, "The small number of enemy planes shot down is regrettable." (Morison, 2002, 184). Kurita requested air support time and again, but Vice Admiral Fukudome Shigeru deliberately ignored him, believing it better to deploy the aircraft directly against the American carriers once located.

The American aircraft damaged several battleships and cruisers, but the main feather in their cap consisted of the sinking of the super-battleship *Musashi*. This imposing *Yamato*-class vessel, armed with 18 inch guns, absorbed dozens of bomb hits and torpedo strikes over the course of several hours of air attacks.

Though doomed to never fire a shot in anger against another surface ship, the *Musashi* served some purpose at Sibuyan simply by being the main target. The Americans concentrated most of their wrath on the huge ship, which stubbornly refused to go down. The tremendous hull armor and resilient structure of the battleship came apart only very slowly under the impact of repeated strikes. No single hit sank the *Musashi* directly. Instead, it suffered a slow loss of power and hull integrity, which finally led to its sinking, with the loss of approximately half of its 2,400 man crew.

Pictures of the *Musashi* being attacked

In the face of the air attacks, the Japanese armada turned back and steamed the way it came. Kurita sent a report to Admiral Toyoda Teijiro, overall commander of the Japanese operation, explaining his situation and decisions: "As a result of five aerial attacks from 6:30 until 3:30 our damages are not light. The frequency and numerical strength of these enemy attacks is increasing. If we continue our present course our losses will increase incalculably, with little hope of success for our mission. Therefore, I have decided to withdraw outside the range of enemy air attack for the time being." (Hoyt, 1993, 147).

Halsey, who had assumed command from Vice Admiral Marc Mitscher – the actual commander of the American carrier force – ordered a halt to the airstrikes when his airmen reported the Japanese course reversal. Ironically, when Kurita took note of the cessation of air attacks, he was encouraged by this, so he reversed course again to make for San Bernardino Strait on the evening of the 24th.

In the meantime, Ozawa's Northern Force made its demonstration as noisily as possible, generating vast quantities of radio chatter to suggest a major carrier force moving to attack with full complements of strike aircraft. Halsey's scouts spotted the force at 3:40 PM, which led the impetuous "Bull" to charge off in search of a stunning naval victory. His own explanatory message to Chester Nimitz later stated, "Searches by my carrier planes revealed the presence of the Northern carrier force [...] which completed the picture of all enemy naval forces. As it seemed childish to me to guard statically San Bernardino Strait, I concentrated TF 38 during the night and steamed north [...] I believed that the Center Force had been so heavily damaged in the Sibuyan Sea that it could no longer be considered a serious menace." (Morison, 2002, 193).

In fact, Halsey took Ozawa's bait with a fervor even the Japanese could scarcely have hoped for. Gathering all his carriers, battleships, cruisers, and destroyers, he swept away northward in hot pursuit of what he believed represented a massive Japanese carrier fleet. In his wake, he left San Bernardino Strait unguarded by so much as a single PT boat, and he neglected to inform any of the other American commanders of his decision.

Not surprisingly, this would have a profound effect on the way the remainder of the fighting played out.

The Battle of Surigao Strait

A map of the two sides' positions at Surigao Strait

While the Japanese northern pincer sailed unopposed through San Bernardino Strait, rashly left unguarded by "Bull" Halsey as he pursued the adroitly flourished red cape of a Japanese decoy, Force C – the southern pincer – approached Surigao Strait. Beyond the narrows between Leyte's coast on the west and Hibuson Island and the north cape of Mindinao to the east lay a bounty of transport ships, anchored and apparently ripe for sinking in Leyte Gulf.

The feebleness of Nishimura Shoji's thrust through Surigao Strait during the early morning hours of October 25th all but guaranteed its defeat if it met determined resistance. Four destroyers led the way in a loose wedge formation. Behind these followed two battleships, *Yamashiro* and *Fuso*, with the heavy cruiser *Mogami* bringing up the rear. The second half of the southern pincer, consisting of two heavy cruisers and one light cruiser plus four destroyers under Vice Admiral Shima Kiyohide, had fallen 25 miles behind.

The Japanese sent reconnaissance aircraft up Surigao Strait during October 24th, but the pilots somehow missed any sign of the American surface forces gathering to meet Nishimura. The scouts returned with encouraging reports that no destroyers, cruisers, battleships, or aircraft carriers sailed in Surigao. Some even insisted on an absence of warships even in Leyte Gulf. Nishimura, heartened, decided on a fast passage into Leyte Gulf, where his ships could run amok among nearly defenseless transports.

On October 24th, American aircraft located and attacked a trailing group of vessels attempting to link up to Shima's force. They attacked, after which they claimed several sinkings, but in fact they had inflicted trivial damage. Other aircraft attacked Nishimura's ships, claiming hits on the *Fuso* which did not in fact occur. Though causing no damage, the air attacks gave the Americans invaluable intelligence of the position and heading of the southern pincer.

Japanese fleet doctrine called for using night attacks. At Guadalcanal a few years earlier, the IJN employed this tactic to devastating effect against American and Australian warships defending the landing areas, and avoidance of a repeat disaster ranked very high among the concerns of American commanders at Leyte Gulf. Vice Admiral Thomas Kinkaid commanded the southern flank of U.S. forces at the Battle of Leyte Gulf from his flagship on the USS *Wasatch*. Kinkaid received a message from Halsey at 8:45 PM on the 24th, informing him of the move to the north against Matsuda's carriers. Kincaid, however, assumed that Halsey left a strong force to guard San Bernardino Strait, and therefore had no idea that only chance prevented the Japanese northern pincer from falling on his unprotected rear.

Kinkaid

Kinkaid ordered Rear Admiral Jesse Oldendorf to deploy a powerful force of destroyers, battleships, and 39 patrol/torpedo boats (PT boats) in the 14 mile wide Surigao Strait to intercept Force C. Oldendorf, commanding the 7th Fleet Support Force, set about preparing what amounted to a massive naval ambush with skill and gusto.

Oldendorf

Starting at 2:45 PM on October 24th, Oldendorf began moving his ships into position. Though he believed he was facing a larger force than the one that actually approached, Oldendorf expected his plan to work, remarking grimly, "Never give a sucker a chance." (Woodward, 1947, 90). Nishimura, thanks to faulty intelligence that reported Surigao Strait void of large American surface ships, provided the perfect "sucker," as the diary of Ugaki corroborated: "The enemy fleet in Leyte Gulf had moved out and there were no large ships in the gulf [...] On the basis of the situation reports of the previous day, (Oct 24), that the enemy battleship force had sortied eastward and that no powerful force remained in Leyte Gulf, the Third Section carried out its penetration in a headlong rush." (Tully, 2009, 133).

The 39 PT boats, grouped into 13 tactical sections of three boats each, formed the forward picket line, dotted across the expanse of the southern Surigao Strait. The Japanese advance would trigger this line, providing ample warning to the rest of Oldendorf's force. Experienced, tough, confident, and aggressive, the PT boat crews also expressed readiness to launch the first attacks on the much larger Japanese ships. These 72-foot wooden hulled boats often sported colorful nicknames such as *Termite's Delight, Geisha-Gooser,* or *Ramblin' Wreck,* among many other humorous, ribald, or defiant appellations.

Darkness lay over the waters of Surigao Strait as the American crews waited tensely, eyes and radar probing southward for signs of the Japanese. Periodically, sprays of tracers erupted into the dark sky as jumpy anti-aircraft gunners fired at aerial phantoms.

Early in the night, stars glittered overhead and a brilliant moon rode in the sky, but as the early morning of October 25th arrived, a tropical thunderstorm approached from the south. Howard Sauer, an officer aboard the USS *Maryland*, reported the meteorological conditions at the northern extremity of Surigao Strait: "Squalls were reported in the area, but for us it was an increasingly overcast, black night, strangely still. The sea was smooth, the visibility good. Since we had no secondary battery radar, we practiced more than most on the development of night vision. You don't look directly at the object you wish to see. Using that technique, we could make out the looming darker shapes of the nearby vessels." (Sauer, 1999, 115-116).

A three-boat PT section near Bohol Island made first contact with the IJN task force before midnight and immediately went on the attack despite the lethal fragility of their completely unarmored craft. This group consisted of PT 131, *Tarfu* (i.e. Things Are Really F****d Up), under Ensign Peter R. Gadd; PT 130, *New Guinea Crud*, commanded by Lt. Ian Malcom; and PT 152, *Lack-a-Nookie*, skippered by Lt. Joseph Eddins.

Gadd's radarman picked out the approaching ships at 10:50 PM, and the three irreverently named craft immediately went into action, deploying towards the Japanese at full speed. However, the IJN lookouts, showing their usual professional acumen, spotted the distant bow waves and moving shapes of the PT boats almost immediately, even in the darkness under the storm-clouds.

That darkness did not last long. The destroyer *Shigure* fired two starshells, glaringly illuminating the trio of boats at a range of 3 miles, too far away for the short-range American torpedoes. With these targets available, the *Shigure* opened fire, soon joined by the guns of the battleship *Yamashiro*. Bracketed by well-aimed shells, the PT boats had no choice but to flee.

Shigure, however, turned to pursue, hounding the small vessels for a desperate 23 minutes. A shell struck Eddins' *Lack-a-Nookie*, destroying the bow 37mm gun, mortally wounding the gunner Charlie Midgett, and setting the PT boat afire. A near miss from a massive shell put the fire out with its splash, but the Japanese followed the tiny boat with a searchlight. Eddins' crew fired their 40mm gun at the searchlight, while PT 130, *New Guinea Crud*, laid smoke.

After a desperate, weaving chase, the searchlight finally blinked out, and the *Shigure* rejoined its formation. Despite coming very close to annihilation, the morale of the PT boat crews remained high, and they tried to catch up to the rapidly northbound Japanese force to exact revenge with their torpedoes, like chihuahuas harrying a herd of elephants: "Pullen and Eddins had no intention of calling it a day – or a night. *Lack-a-Nookie* roared off in pursuit of the withdrawing Nipponese DDs with the intention of launching a torpedo attack. The enemy warships were making at least twenty-two knots and had a big lead, so, after trying an hour to catch up, Pullen and Eddins had to call off the chase." (Breuer, 1995, 186).

In their excitement, the PT boat crews made a serious error in not radioing their contact to the fleet. During the chase, Japanese fire destroyed the radios on all three craft, rendering them unable to communicate once Force C resumed its northward course. Eventually, Malcolm's *New Guinea Crud* found PT boat Section 2 near Camiguin Island. Ensign Dudley Johnson of PT 127 finally informed Oldendorf's flagship of the Japanese presence at 12:26 AM on October 25th.

In the meantime, Shima's force began catching up to Nishimura's. This gave the admiral greater confidence and even the beginning of hope that he might successfully penetrate the Surigao Strait after all. Nevertheless, the Japanese remained on high alert, expecting the ambush that did in fact await them.

Over the next several hours, the PT boats continued their brave but futile attacks on the Japanese. Japanese jamming and the deteriorating weather both interfered with their radio signals, but enough transmissions leaked through to keep Oldendorf and his captains apprised of IJN progress northward. Despite launching many torpedoes, the PT boats inflicted no damage, in part due to the poor firing conditions caused by constant salvos of Japanese shells and other ordnance.

By now, a storm front had developed, and the Japanese used it skillfully to mask their progress. In fact, despite hours of PT boat attacks, Force C managed to take at least one section of torpedo craft completely by surprise. At around 2 AM on the 25th, the men in PTs 490, 491, and 493 saw the first squall line rolling towards them across the sea, blurred with rain underneath and shot through with lightning. As the violent storm rushed closer, the glowing blue barbs of St. Elmo's Fire formed eerily around the machine guns and radio equipment aboard many of the boats, a weather phenomenon well understood by 20th century seamen.

However, what was unbeknownst to the men waiting tensely on the wooden decks of the three boats was that Nishimura's force sailed just behind the rain front, screened from long-range visual contact and partially from radar by the torrential downpour. PT 491 (nicknamed *Devil's Daughter*) under Harley Thronson made contact with the Japanese force as the storm rushed over them, though different crew members recalled the scene differently, as Thronson's recollection and executive officer Terry Chambers' narrative both indicate: "Terry remembered the Japanese ships coming in right behind the squall line. 'I saw a lightning flash, and there they were in column.' Boat 491's skipper Harley Thronson's recollection had a different flavor. 'The weather was miserable – really poor visibility. Suddenly we were in the middle of the Japanese formation. They turned on searchlights and opened fire.'" (Sears, 2005, 115-116).

In addition to radio signals, the men aboard the lurking American warships now received visual confirmation of the Japanese approach. Gazing south, they suddenly perceived searchlights strobing wildly across the southern horizon, accompanied by the flashes of gunfire. The time to spring Oldendorf's trap had nearly arrived.

Moving behind the storm curtain, the Japanese force nosed into the narrowest point of Surigao Strait, the passage between Sumilon and Panaon Islands. *Devil's Daughter* and its two accompanying PT boats attacked the Japanese within moments, despite their crews' initial shock, and PT 134, *Eight Ball*, joined the attack alone. While the Japanese evaded all the torpedo wakes, which were clearly visible on the dark ocean surface, they lost headway in doing so.

Terry Chambers once again described the close-quarters action: "Somehow, we'd gotten inside their destroyer screen [...] We were facing big ships and all we could do was aim our guns at the lights and the ships' bridges – like sticking our fingers in their eyes. We'd knock one light out and another went on." (Sears, 2005, 125).

During the exchange of fire, a shell crashed into PT 490, *Little Butch,* Lt. John McElfresh commanding. The shell wounded a number of men and started a serious leak, only slowed when Engineer Albert Brunelle, formerly dismissed as a "sissy" but about to win the respect of his fellow crewmen, stuffed his lifejacket into the hole. The *Little Butch* limped away, eventually sinking near Panaon Island, but another boat rescued its crew.

The PT boat attacks ceased at around 2:25 AM, and darkness and deep silence fell as the Japanese ships sailed forward against the strong Surigao Strait current. In fact, the order had come through from Oldendorf's flagship ordering the torpedo craft to break off so they would not be sunk by friendly fire during the imminent destroyer ambush.

A PT boat after the battle

Nishimura, however, interpreted the American retreat as the end of the attempt to bar his ships from passing the Strait. Despite restrained protests from some of his captains, he ordered Force C forward at full speed without even waiting to resume battle formation. He wanted to make up for lost time and pounce on his Leyte Gulf quarry within a few hours, with Shima's armada joining in upon arrival.

At 3 AM, a Japanese searchlight swept over the sea surface and illuminated the five destroyers of Captain Jesse Coward's DesRon 54. Revealed suddenly to the presumably surprised Japanese, the American destroyers immediately sped forward, releasing their torpedoes, and then swerved away, generating smokescreens as they did so. The combination of rapid maneuvering and smoke kept them well clear of the retaliatory salvos launched by the Japanese.

Over the next 20 minutes, the destroyers used the same tactic, firing their torpedoes and then getting away to avoid Japanese gunfire. Japanese shells rushed overhead with a "freight train" sound, sometimes exploding beyond the destroyers and back-lighting them, providing a momentary target for the IJN gunners.

Many of the torpedoes missed, but one struck the massive battleship *Fuso* amidships. A tower of spray erupted from beside the mighty vessel's flank as the torpedo warhead detonated, punching through the armored hull. Two more strikes followed in quick succession. The force of the explosions sent a thunderous sound pulsating through the hull and threw the ship over almost on its side, before it rolled heavily upright again.

A picture of the wounded *Fuso*

The cruiser *Mogami,* following closely, swerved abruptly to avoid *Fuso,* already halted by the destruction of its boilers. The *Mogami* – named for a river in Japan frequently cited in *haiku* and other poems – passed the stricken vessel and fell into place astern of Nishimura's flagship, the *Yamashiro.* Nishimura glanced back, saw the *Mogami,* and assumed it to be the *Fuso,* failing to realize that one of his two battleships had suffered fatal damage in the first seconds of the engagement.

The *Yamashiro*

Like the caracoling pistol cavalry of an earlier age, the destroyers of DesRon 54 swooped away into the darkness, letting a second DesRon – DesRon 24 – move in. Consisting of 5 American destroyers and 1 Australian destroyer, the HMAS *Arunta,* the ships found a scene of devastation already unfolding. Just half an hour after the first shots of the ambush, Nishimura's force was almost finished.

The Japanese found themselves under attack by enemies they could barely discern in the stormy blackness. As a surviving Japanese lookout later explained, "It was very dark and the sky was heavily clouded, not to mention a fine haze [...] Suddenly, two or three torpedo wakes appeared at almost a direct angle from the direction of the island, racing toward the force. Their phosphorescent wakes became well visible, almost as if someone had suddenly turned the lights on. Nevertheless, neither the flashes from their launching nor the attacking DDs could be seen in the darkness." (Tully, 2009, 156-157).

Nishimura ordered his ships to turn to starboard to meet the threat, since most of the torpedoes raced out of the darkness from that direction. Shortly thereafter, however, he ordered a course change back to due north, putting the Japanese back in line astern. The Admiral's fatal choice hastened the inevitable, putting his ships broadside to the attacking swarms of American destroyers.

Nishimura's error in believing the *Fuso* was still present emboldened him to continue. The illusion strengthened due to radio chatter using the crippled battleship's name as Japanese vessels in Force C mistook one another for the missing vessel. *Fuso* itself had lost all radio communication permanently at the moment of the torpedo strikes.

The destroyer torpedoes took a massive toll from the understrength Japanese armada as it advanced. First to perish after the *Fuso*'s fatal wounding was the destroyer *Yamagumo,* captained by Shiro Ono, after it sustained a minimum of two torpedo strikes at 3:20 AM. These torpedoes, fired by the destroyer USS *McDermut,* tore through the large destroyer's hull and caused it to detonate immediately in a spectacular fireball which lit the sea, as one American observer described, like the "Fourth of July." All of the destroyer's torpedo tubes, loaded and ready to fire back at the Americans, exploded onboard instead, spreading the blast to the magazines and torpedo storage instantly.

The 230 men aboard died almost to a man at the moment of detonation. Pieces of debris, smashed human bodies, and severed limbs pattered down on the nearby Japanese ships, spaced at 600 yard intervals. Within a matter of minutes, the *Yamagumo* slipped under the waters, a gutted, fire-blackened husk smeared with the pulverized flesh and bone of most of the vessel's crew. Still heated by the blast, the sinking ship made a powerful hissing sound like a massive forging being quenched.

Almost simultaneously, an American torpedo hit the destroyer *Asagumo* in the bow, causing the forecastle to crumple in on itself due to a design flaw present in most classes of Japanese destroyers. Just one minute later, the destroyer *Michishio* took two hits, with one collapsing the forecastle and the second annihilating the port engine room, leaving the ship dead in the water with no power. Water rushed in through the hull breach as men struggled to escape in the pitch blackness inside the damaged vessel.

At this point, only the destroyer *Shigure,* the heavy cruiser *Mogami,* and the battleship *Yamashiro* remained in fighting trim. Nishimura, still improbably optimistic and believing his force intact – in part due to *Mogami*'s radio chatter with the nonexistent *Fuso* (which was actually mistakenly directed at his own ship) - continued the advance into the trap, towards the six battleships and flanking cruisers waiting in the darkness ahead.

The *Mogami*

In the meantime, *Fuso* suffered a lonely death in the wake of the other vessels. Its captain, Rear Admiral Ban Masami, turned the ship west, possibly trying to escape, or at least reach shallow coastal waters where his crew could more easily abandon ship. Hovering torpedo boats, headed by PT 495, *Miss Fury*, observed the battleship for some time, but decided not to attack due to earlier orders to stay out of the fight.

The *Fuso* turned southward after a time and continued underway for some time. While American after-action reports and numerous history books reported that a magazine fire blew the battleship in half, with the two halves floating separately for a time before sinking, this appears to have resulted from an error. The destroyers spotted two large fires on the sea surface following the torpedo strikes on *Fuso* and interpreted these as halves of the vessel. However, these likely represented no more than a pair of burning slicks created by oil leaking from the bunkers of the fleeing, damaged battleship.

Instead, the *Fuso* leaned more and more to starboard as it limped away under the storm-wrack, seawater welling up to overwhelm deck after deck. Soon, the ship's prow was running underwater, forcing the crew to crowd the after deck as they evacuated the deeper parts of the ship and the gun turrets.

The increasingly panicky men jostled and surged in a pitch-black night so dark that men standing next to them appeared as no more than anonymous shadows. They could see white water combing over the foredeck, however, creeping aft towards them as the sea began to swallow the *Fuso*. Only at this point did Ban order the "abandon ship." A strident bugle-call sliced through the near-silence, and men began pouring over the rails.

At that moment, the *Fuso* suddenly toppled over on its starboard side, throwing men into the sea. Then the ship writhed, its prow sinking while its stern rose into the air. One of the bare handful of survivors – 10 men out of a complement of 1,900 – named Ogawa Hideo, later reported the battleship's final moments: "In the darkness, the huge black hull of our ship stood high above the water, and the forward bridge was about to fall down sideways. [...] Soon the bridge disappeared into the water. The stern, about 60 meters long aft of No. 6 turret, was above water at an angle of about 50 degrees, stood still, which showed an awkward figure in the night sky. The screws [...] were running in the air hopelessly." (Tully, 2009, 177).

As Ogawa and other survivors swam, giant masses of stinking fuel oil suddenly bubbled up to the surface. Ogawa fought his way clear of the clinging petroleum slime, but behind him, the oil caught fire with a deafening sizzling sound. The agonized screams of hundreds of men burning alive in the liquid flame echoed over the water, prompting the survivors outside the inferno to swim faster. A pair of deep shocks through the water indicated the magazines might have exploded far below the surface.

The cruiser *Nachi* sped past the survivors, its crew hearing their desperate cries for help but ignoring them. Many surviving men swam to Leyte's shores, but the Filipinos, enraged by years of Japanese atrocities, slaughtered most of them as they lay exhausted on the beach or killed them with machetes or rifles in the coastal waters. PT boats picked up two or three Japanese they found swimming, while the rest of the *Fuso*'s remaining survivors were captured by the Filipinos, who brought them as prisoners to American intelligence officers. The Americans repatriated all 10 to Japan following the war.

These men found themselves in an internment camp with survivors from the other sunken ships. Speaking freely for the first time in years, they worked out a rough reconstruction of the battle for their own edification. Their account actually jibed remarkably well with the true development of the battle, though they believed the PT boats, rather than destroyers, inflicted the lethal defeat on Force C. With their habits of suicidal submission and obedience to authority broken by disaster and captivity, they also placed blame for the catastrophe squarely on Admiral Nishimura, Some expressed satisfaction at Nishimura's presumed death.

The final action at Surigao Strait unfolded to the north at the same time as *Fuso* endured its death throes. However, new players entered the scene at about this time also. Shima's force of ships, including the heavy cruisers *Nachi* (Shima's flagship) and *Ashigara*, the light cruiser *Abukuma*, plus the destroyers *Shiranuhi, Kasumi, Ushio,* and *Akebono*, steamed rapidly up the Strait towards the action.

The PT boats, obeying orders to stay clear of the main engagement by lurking in the darkness, quickly took note of this new selection of targets hastening past them. With predictable aggressiveness, some of the 72-foot boats shadowed the newcomers, waiting for the opportunity to launch attacks on Shima's much larger, but unprepared, vessels.

Furious rain squalls and swaths of sea-mist obscured the way, and Shima's force almost came to grief in a startling fashion due to the poor visibility. The navigators failed to account for the powerful southbound current rushing through the Surigao Strait, which distorted their course. With no visible landmarks, the error went unnoticed until *Abukuma* broke clear of a bank of sea-mist and observed the white tumult of breakers just ahead, with a mountain looming out of the clouds miles beyond; Shima's force was in danger of running aground en masse on the coast of Palaon Island. The ships turned desperately, only just managing to avoid a humiliating end on the rocks and beaches.

As *Abukuma* labored in the water, slowed to a crawl and highly vulnerable, the swift shapes of American PT boats materialized out of the night. PT 137, *The Dutchess*, led the attack. The Japanese cruiser, trapped with nowhere to maneuver, sustained several torpedo hits, one barely missing the magazine. 37 men died instantly and more suffered wounds. With gaping holes in the ship's side, the *Abukuma* fell out of formation. Though the crew immediately began work on emergency repairs, Captain Kimura Masatomi knew he would probably remain unable to join the battle in the north before it reached a decision, a fact which frustrated him immensely.

With course corrections now properly in place, Shima's force moved north to support Nishimura. The flashes of gunfire and torpedo explosions, augmented by the glare of burning ships, showed clearly that a fierce battle continued to the north. The reinforcements pushed their ships' engines as hard as they could, achieving a speed of 28 knots as they charged north to their comrades' aid at 3:38 AM.

As it turned out, Shima arrived too late to alter the doom of Nishimura's Force C. As the *Yamashiro* continued to steam directly ahead, it came within range of the massive guns of the line of six battleships blocking the strait ahead. The four remaining Japanese ships – *Yamashiro, Mogami, Shigure,* and the half-crippled but still bravely advancing *Asagumo* – now all had deck fires from the 5-inch shells of the destroyers' guns, making them visible for miles on the darkened sea.

Nishimura, with incredible optimism, seemed to believe victory lay within his grasp nevertheless. His ships' radar had informed him shortly before of the battleship line ahead, yet the incorrigibly positive Admiral believed he had "caught" the Americans totally unprepared and could sink the battleships before moving on to Leyte Gulf. Accordingly, he issued a radio order for the ships to slow and reassume an attack formation.

Nishimura issued this order at 3:50 AM. At 3:51 AM, Oldendorf gave the order to the battleship line to open fire. The IJN ships therefore slowed at precisely the moment the Americans chose to fire on them, making themselves immobile targets for the eager American gunners sitting in their sweltering turrets to the north.

The cruisers on the right flank opened fire first, pouring a total of 3,100 shells onto the burning ships, and soon the "bulldogs" – the battleships forming the main line – joined in. The whole line of ships erupted time and time again in blinding flashes of discharge, while the thunder of the cannons nearly deafened the men on board and shook ill-secured items loose throughout the vessels. The force of each salvo, indeed, caused the ships to "shunt" across the water tens of yards in the opposite direction.

A picture of the cruisers opening fire in the pitch black

American destroyer captain Roland Smoot, standing on the fragile bridge of his craft, admired the aesthetics of the lethal pyrotechnic display: "The devastating accuracy of this gunfire was the most beautiful sight I have ever witnessed. The arched line of tracers in the darkness looked like a continual stream of lighted railroad cars going over a hill. No target could be observed at first; then shortly there would be fires and explosions, and another ship would be accounted for." (Hornfischer, 2004, 98).

While Smoot admired the accuracy of the gunfire, friendly fire claimed at least one notable victim. The destroyers continued their runs against the Japanese despite the appalling risk, and USS *Grant* paid the price. Stricken by Japanese shells, but even more frequently by American shells from the cruisers and "bulldogs," the ship came to a sudden halt, racked by internal explosions. Bursting shells killed dozens of men and wounded many more, smashing boilers that boiled men to death or left them appallingly injured and shattering the ship's weaponry and decks. A frantic radio call brought a temporary halt in the American ships' firing, after which the destroyers *Newcomb* and *Richard P. Leary* hastened to the maimed vessel's aid.

Despite the pyrotechnics, the Japanese on the receiving end of the bombardment could not even see the distant muzzle flashes of the battleships pounding them to pieces. The tracers appeared out of the darkness with no apparent source, and the shells arrived with a whistling shriek that ended in great fountains of spray or the fiery thunder of a direct hit on the slowly-disintegrating vessels.

The Americans concentrated first on *Yamashiro*, pounding the battleship until pieces of dead men strewed its decks and fires burned across nearly every part of the ship. Some of the ships then switched fire to *Mogami*, inflicting heavy damage on the cruiser and starting several fires. Soon, the fires turned into a roaring tower rising from much of ship's superstructure, illuminating the sea around the wounded vessel. Aboard the *USS West Virginia,* men later reported a gunnery officer laughing triumphantly every time fresh explosions rocked the distant targets.

The *West Virginia*

Independently, the *Yamashiro* and the *Mogami* finally turned in an attempt to flee. The *Shigure* continued forward briefly, hoping to acquire torpedo targets. However, as dozens of shells landed in the water all around it, the immense shocks smashed every instrument on the bridge, including the radar. *Shigure's* captain decided that escaping would be preferable to firing blindly at targets miles away, hidden by darkness. "At 0413 or 0415, being unsuccessful in finding the enemy, and determining that the rest of our force had been annihilated, I decided to withdraw without receiving orders from anyone." (Woodward, 1947, 116).

For its part, the *Yamashiro* did not die without a fight. While turning, the huge battleship raked the American lines with gunfire, which, while it inflicted little damage (except on *USS Grant*) impressed the USN officers and men with its relative accuracy. When the American battleships ceased fire to enable the rescue of *Grant*, the Japanese flagship turned south and fled at long last.

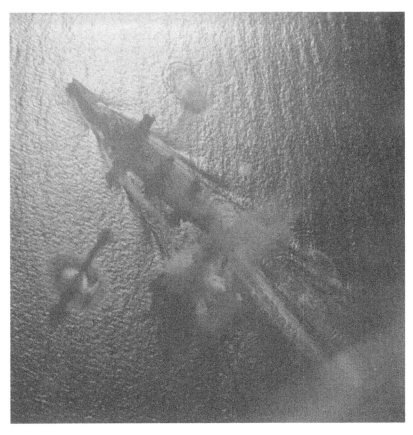

The *Yamashiro*

The *Yamashiro* did not get far, however. According to the few survivors later fished from the Surigao Strait, the battleship abruptly listed to port. Its towering "pagoda bridge" – an unmistakable feature of Japanese World War II warships – leaned towards the ocean, adding its weight to the rotational forces already in play. The captain issued an "abandon ship" order. However, just two minutes later, the battleship rolled over completely, pointing its keel towards the sky. Three minutes after that, it settled under the waves, sucking most of its officers and men down with it. Between 100 and 300 men managed to swim clear and reach Leyte. Here, again, they found vengeful Filipinos waiting, and only 10 men ultimately returned to Japan.

Shima's flotilla began reaching the scene of the action around 4:20 AM. The *Nachi* first passed the sinking *Fuso*, ignoring the men in the water who shouted for rescue. It then encountered the *Shigure*, partly on fire, listing, and laying down a smokescreen desperately as it steamed south. Seeking news from the fleeing ship, Shima received in answer only a terse message informing him that the *Shigure* was experiencing rudder trouble.

After these ominous sightings, the *Nachi* next encountered the burning *Mogami*. With remarkably bad luck, Shima decided *Mogami* must be dead in the water and ordered his ship to pass immediately in front of the cruiser's bow. Instead, *Mogami* was steaming south at the greatest speed it could muster. Unable to turn in time, the cruiser slammed into *Nachi*'s port flank, punching an enormous hole in the other cruiser. This accident rendered *Nachi* half-crippled and thus useless in a fight.

After sending his four destroyers north in a vain search for a parting shot, Shima ordered his ships to turn about and retreat southward also, trying to escape the deadly waters of Surigao Strait. The Americans, however, decided to pursue and finish off the Japanese remnants. When morning came, some destroyers crisscrossed the strait, attempting to rescue the numerous Japanese in the water. A few accepted help, but most ignored ropes thrown to them by the Americans. Many would not even look at the American ships trying to save their lives, instead floating silently in the waves waiting to die.

Even when a Japanese sailor allowed himself to be rescued, risks continued, as Tom Tenner aboard PT 127 reported, "I threw the guy a line and told him to climb up. He was small and soaking wet—if he weighed one hundred pounds that was a lot. He spoke a little English and told us the war was lost as far as he was concerned. We gave him a life jacket to wear [...] Then somebody said, 'We better search him.' We found he still had four hand grenades strapped to him. It showed what a bunch of bozos we were." (Sears, 2005. 169).

American destroyers, cruisers, and carrier aircraft hunted the surviving ships on the morning of the 25th, and they succeeded in sinking the *Asagumo*, the *Mogami*, and the *Abukumo*. Out of Nishimura's seven leading ships, only one, the *Shigure*, managed to escape, suffering 2 deaths on board. The rest sank, taking approximately 5,000 Japanese to their deaths.

Oldendorf, aboard the USS *Louisville*, toured the strait shortly after the sun came up, and the admiral appeared greatly pleased at the outcome, as well he should have been; his plan had worked, sinking a number of Japanese ships and forcing the rest to flee at minimal loss to his own forces. He received a congratulatory message from 7th Fleet at 7:28 AM.

Just 10 minutes later, however, his mood suffered a shattering blow. A desperate radio call came in at 7:38 sharp, informing Oldendorf that a second Japanese force was in his rear. Somehow, the Japanese had penetrated San Bernardino Strait, which Oldendorf and Kinkaid believed Halsey had left forces to guard. As a result, while Nishimura's last vessels fled south, the powerful ships of the northern pincer were about to surprise the fragile, nearly undefended

USN escort carriers in the ocean off Samar.

The Battle Off Samar

At the same time Nishimura was beginning his suicidal run into the teeth of Oldendorf's ambush far away in the south, Admiral Kurita Takao's Center Force moved cautiously into the San Bernardino Strait, north of Leyte Gulf, in the early morning of the 25th. Kurita had no way to know for certain if the decoy fleet to the north would lure Halsey away entirely or if the Americans would leave powerful ships to guard the key passage.

Kurita commanded an extremely powerful striking force, albeit one based on what was becoming a nearly obsolescent concept of naval combat. The Battle of Midway, a turning point in the Pacific, had been a battle between naval forces that never even sighted each other, and in many ways the Battle of Leyte Gulf would be the last major naval battle in which battleships fired at other surface ships rather than at targets onshore. Kurita had no choice, however, because he had no carriers, so he had to rely on land-based aircraft support, including the first dedicated kamikaze pilots to see action.

The centerpiece of his fleet, the super-battleship *Yamato*, represented one of the two mightiest cannon-armed ships to sail the seas, but the other, the *Musashi*, already resided on the floor of the Sibuyan Sea that morning. His force also included three regular battleships, the *Nagato*, *Kongo*, and *Haruna*; six heavy cruisers, the *Suzuya*, *Tone*, *Chikuma*, *Haguru*, *Kumano*, and *Chokai*; two light cruisers, the *Yahagi* and *Noshiro*; and 11 destroyers. In all, Kurita mustered 23 formidable fighting ships.

The Japanese ships moved eastward through the San Bernardino Strait in a stately column under clear moonlight at 3 AM on the 25th, debouching into the Philippine Sea. Despite keeping a tense watch, the IJN crews saw no signs of American surface ship activity. While the Americans sent carrier aircraft to patrol the Strait, and a trio of Catalina flying boats crisscrossed it, accidents of timing prevented them from spotting Kurita's powerful armada.

As a result, thanks to two strokes of luck – Halsey's impetuous decision to leave the Strait unguarded, and the failure of the American scouting aircraft and their Japanese targets to ever be at the same place simultaneously – Kurita achieved complete surprise. At 5 AM, shortly before sunrise, Kurita learned via radio chatter of the probable destruction of Force C in Surigao Strait, but undeterred, he formed up his ships and turned south around Samar, on course for Leyte Gulf and the American invasion fleet.

Ahead, three groups of tiny *Casablanca*-class US "jeep" carriers floated on the long, gentle swell of the tropical morning. These groups, designated Taffy I, Taffy II, and Taffy III, expected no surface ship attack, believing themselves protected by Oldendorf to the south and "Bull" Halsey to the north. Each "Taffy" detachment contained six carriers plus shepherding destroyers and destroyer escorts.

On the morning of the 25th, their crews busied themselves launching aircraft missions, mostly in support of the Surigao mop-up. Vice Admiral Fitzhugh Lee, aboard the Taffy III jeep carrier USS *Manila Bay*, described the situation in the brief dawn calm prior to the start of the Samar battle: "We just sent off planes engaged in close air support for the Army troops that were going ashore in routine unopposed amphibious landings. [...] we were in three circular carrier formations in a north-south line, with about 7 or 8 miles, maybe 10 miles, between groups. We could just see the group to the north of us, and we could not even see the third group, which was even farther north over the horizon." (Wooldridge, 1993, 206).

Taffy III consisted of six jeep carriers, including USS *Fanshaw Bay, Saint Lo, White Plains, Kalinin Bay, Kitkun Bay,* and *Gambier Bay;* three destroyers, *Hoel, Heermann,* and *Johnston;* and three tiny destroyer escorts, *Dennis, John C. Butler, Raymond,* and *Samuel B. Roberts.* None of the men aboard, including the overall commander Rear Admiral Clifton "Ziggy" Sprague, guessed they would soon enter the annals of U.S. naval history thanks to a desperately courageous last stand action.

The *Samuel B. Roberts*

The *Saint Lo* launched a six-airplane submarine recon detachment as a standard precaution that morning. Four Grumman TBF Avenger torpedo bombers and two Grumman F4F Wildcats left the deck and fanned out across the ocean in search of submarines running on the surface or other signs of enemy activity. One of the Avengers, piloted by William Brooks, flew northwest towards San Bernardino Strait.

Tom Van Brunt, an Avenger pilot scouting northeast, later reported the events that unfolded at 6:43 AM: "We hadn't been airborne more than fifteen minutes when Bill [Brooks] came on the net using our call sign. 'Derby Base, Derby Base, contact, contact. I have the Japanese navy in sight.' There was a pause and then a skeptical voice came back. 'How do you know they're Japanese?' Bill's response was slow, exasperated: 'I can see the biggest damn red meatball flag flying from the biggest pagoda mast I ever saw! They're shooting at me!'" (Sears, 2005, 127).

Brooks' astonishment at encountering a massive and instantly hostile Japanese fleet was matched by the surprise of the Japanese at encountering American aircraft and carriers on the Philippine Sea, not in Leyte Gulf. The flak batteries opened fire on the lone Avenger at the same time that lookouts spotted Taffy III to the southeast. The Americans floated in a loose defensive formation, the jeep carriers in the center, and the destroyers and destroyer escorts forming a ring around them to intercept submarines.

Brooks dropped his four depth charges in a futile effort to damage one of the cruisers, braving a whirlwind of flak to do so, then headed away south just 50 feet above the ocean surface, jinking unpredictably right and left. This maneuver, copied from the game birds he liked to hunt in the U.S., permitted his escape. He then set a course towards Taffy II to try to get a torpedo fitted to his Avenger.

On board the Japanese fleet, reactions ranged from dismay to jubilation. Kurita himself believed a stunning victory lay within his grasp. With the age-old tendency of human beings to see and hear what they wish to rather than what is actually in front of them, the Japanese officers identified the small *Casablanca*-class escort carriers as full-sized *Essex* carriers, the heart of the American naval juggernaut. With the jeep carriers inflated in their minds to the looming *Essex*-class, the Japanese also magnified the destroyers into battleships and the destroyer escorts into heavy cruisers in their imaginations. Kurita thought he had the chance to smash six carriers, three battleships, and four cruisers, perhaps enough on its own to bring the Americans to the negotiating table. The Admiral sent an exultant radio message back to Japan: "We are engaging enemy in gun battle [...] By heaven-sent opportunity we are dashing to attack the enemy carriers." (Hornfischer, 2004, 137).

Ranging shells began falling near Taffy III at extreme range. Looking northwest, the Americans could see the ominous towers of Imperial pagoda bridges looming darkly out of a rain squall as the gigantic force advanced to smash them. The main Japanese force headed straight towards Taffy III, while Vice Admiral Shiraishi Kazutaka led the six heavy cruisers eastward to outflank the Americans.

Unsettled weather prevailed during the action. Though the morning sun flashed and glistened at times on the tropical sea, cumulus clouds covered approximately 30% of the sky. Hazy conditions prevailed, with occasional rain showers under some of the cumulus clouds. As the morning warmed, periodic squalls developed over the Philippine Sea.

Moreover, the battle off Samar witnessed the first deployment of a weapons system soon to achieve permanent notoriety. One of the most fascinating aspects of World War II was Japan's use of suicide pilots, known around the globe as kamikazes, though the Japanese referred to them as Tokubetsu kōgekitai ("Special Attack Units"). Translated as "God Wind," "Divine Wind" and "God Spirit," kamikazes would sink 47 Allied vessels and damage over 300 by the end of the war, but the rise in the use of kamikaze attacks was evidence of the loss of Japan's air superiority and its waning industrial might. This method of fighting would become more common by the time Iwo Jima was fought over in early 1945, and it was especially prevalent during the invasion of Okinawa in April 1945.

The "privilege" of being selected as a kamikaze pilot played directly into the deep-seated Japanese mindset of "death before defeat." The pilot training manual assured each kamikaze candidate that when they eliminated all thoughts of life and death, fear of losing the earthly life can be easily overcome. Still, not all cases of those chosen to be kamikazes were equally noble. Recruits were trained with torturous regimens or corporal punishment, and stories of mental impairment caused by drugs or saki abound. Some were described as "tottering" and dazed, being carried to their planes by maintenance officers, and forcibly pushed in if they backed down. Pilots who could not find their targets were told to turn around and spare their own lives for another day, but if a pilot returned nine times, he was to be shot. At the moment of collision, he was instructed to keep his eyes open at all times, and to shout "Hissatsu" ("clear kill").

Altogether, nearly 4,000 kamikaze pilots died in combat between October 1944 and August 1945, and about one in seven managed to hit his target. At their peak, they did far more damage to the American navy than did conventional air attacks, and they undoubtedly placed a significant new obstacle in the path of the American forces slowly encircling the Japanese home islands. However, the widespread use of kamikaze tactics darkened and hardened attitudes toward Japan within the American military and helped to set the stage for the total war on Japanese civilians that the American military waged in the closing months of the war. *The Marine Corps Gazette* noted, "The ruthless atrocities by the Japanese throughout the war had already brought on an altered behavior (deemed so by traditional standards) by many Americans resulting in the desecration of Japanese remains, but the Japanese tactic of using the Okinawan people as human shields brought about a new aspect of terror and torment to the psychological capacity of the Americans." As one sailor aboard the USS *Miami* recalled about kamikaze attacks at Okinawa, "They came in swarms from all directions. The barrels of our ship's guns got so hot we had to use firehoses to cool them down."

The kamikazes were the most effective weapon the Japanese had in terms of sinking ships, but they only appeared in the final year of the war. The fact that Japan's military leadership concluded it was both necessary and justified to establish special units of pilots trained to sacrifice their own lives by crashing their planes into enemy vessels was a mark of their own desperation. In the heat of battle, individual soldiers occasionally risked certain or near-certain death to protect their comrades or advance their mission, but organized unites devoted to suicide tactics were virtually unknown before 1944. They appeared only once the course of the war had turned decidedly against the Japanese.

The concept in its modern form developed in the 1920s, with a history dating back to the deep thirst for self-destruction often shown by the samurai. One pilot, Shimamura Ataru, attempted to put the mood of the kamikaze pilots into words prior to leaving on his own fatal mission: "I shall fall, smiling and singing songs. Please visit and worship at Yasukuni Shrine this spring. There I shall be a cherry blossom, smiling, with many other colleagues. I died smiling, so please smile. Please do not cry. Make my death meaningful." (Rielly, 2010, 36).

Having lost the vast majority of its experienced flyers, and with demand for pilots higher than ever before, the Japanese Navy had no choice but to rush new recruits through highly abbreviated training programs. By 1944, American pilots received two years of training, including at least 300 hours of flight-time, before entering combat, but new Japanese pilots typically received 40 hours of in-flight training or less, and instead of learning navigation, they were simply instructed to tail their group leaders. Looking back, a flight instructor of the time wrote, "Everything was urgent. We were told to rush men through. We abandoned refinements, just tried to teach them how to fly and shoot. One after another, singly, in twos and threes, training planes smashed into the ground, gyrated wildly through the air. For long, tedious months, I tried to create fighter pilots. It was a hopeless task. Our resources were too meagre, the demand too great." (Sakai, 213).

As the U.S. forces steadily moved closer to Japan, the Japanese had neither the aircraft nor the trained pilots needed to mount carrier-based operations. Facing this dilemma, and called upon to stage a last-ditch defense of Japan's empire against the oncoming American advance, the Naval Air Service sought out a radical change in tactics. In fact, the desperate situation of Japanese aviators on and around the Philippines had already driven several to adopt haphazard kamikaze attacks. There were two unsuccessful attempts at suicide attacks on September 13, 1944, and another on October 15. On October 21, the same day that the first organized *Tokubetsu kōgekitai* strike took off from Luzon, a single Japanese aircraft, likely either an Aichi D3A dive-bomber or a Mitsubishi Ki-51, seemed to crash deliberately into the *HMAS Australia*, an Australian heavy cruiser, killing 30, wounding 64, and causing major damage. The unknown pilot apparently acted on his own initiative, and his attack was not part of an organized kamikaze strike.

If any officer in the Japanese Navy was qualified to oversee a radical departure in tactics, it was Vice Admiral Ōnishi Takijirō. He had served as a junior officer to Admiral Yamamoto Isoroku, architect of the Pearl Harbor attack, and like Yamamoto, Ōnishi had a forceful creative personality, a powerful bond with his men, and a reputation among his superiors as a maverick. He had a firm grasp of the practical details of naval aviation thanks to the fact that he had personally flown every type of Japanese aircraft, and he was courageous to the point of endangering himself without thinking about it. He was even the first officer in the Imperial Navy to practice parachuting.

Vice Admiral Ōnishi Takijirō

In October 1944, Ōnishi arrived in Manila to take command of the First Naval Air Fleet and was determined to keep the Philippines out of American hands. The islands had been an American territory since the 1898 Spanish-American War, and in 1935, the United States granted the Philippines commonwealth status and began preparations for full independence, but these plans were swept away in the weeks following the attack on Pearl Harbor. A Japanese invasion force landed on northern Luzon on December 10, 1945, and quickly advanced south, forcing General Douglas MacArthur, Commander of the United States Armed Forces in the Far East, into a humiliating and costly retreat. By late 1944, however, the Japanese occupiers were caught between a growing guerilla resistance movement and a looming American invasion. Ōnishi, his officers, and superiors all understood the importance of holding the islands, which served as a key midpoint in the transport of vital raw materials from Japan's new southeast Asian territories to the home islands.

The Philippines were crucial to Japan's war effort, and within days of his arrival, Ōnishi was promoting organized kamikaze tactics. As he told an October 19 meeting of officers at Mabalacat, headquarters of the 201st Air Group, "In my opinion, there is only one way of assuring that our meagre strength will be effective to a maximum degree. That is to organize attack units composed of Zero fighters armed with two-hundred-fifty kilogram bombs, with each place to crash-dive into an enemy carrier... What do you think?" (Inoguchi and Nakajima, 463). Ōnishi argued that suicide tactics could help to equalize the growing imbalance of forces, and by taking advantage of the unique spirit of discipline and self-sacrifice that he and other officers attributed to the Japanese military, relatively untrained pilots could deliver 500 pound bombs to their targets with far greater accuracy than conventional bombers. Furthermore, since the missions would be one-way by design, they could effectively double the ranges of their aircraft.

Despite the obviously radical nature of his suggestion, Ōnishi's fellow officers were largely open to the idea, which was indicative of their increasing desperation and their willingness to adopt any new tactic that might improve the odds. In fact, it was Captain Inoguchi Ren'ya who was responsible for their name. Officially, the group would be known as the *Tokubetsu kōgekitai*, "Special Attack Units," or *Tokkōtai*, but Captain Inoguchi suggested a more evocative title: *shinpū*. The name was a combination of two Chinese characters: *shin* (meaning "gods," "spirits," or "divine") and *fū* (meaning "wind"). Read in the classical Chinese fashion, the *on'yomi*, they yielded the compound *shinpū*, but when read in the native Japanese style, the *kun'yomi*, the same characters form the name *kamikaze*.

By 1945, the Naval Air Service would run short of volunteers for kamikaze missions, and of the nearly 4,000 kamikaze pilots who perished during the war, a considerable majority were conscripts who enrolled in the program under varying degrees of compulsion. At this early stage, however, Ōnishi's call for volunteers met with considerable enthusiasm among Japanese naval pilots in the Philippines. At a base in Cebu, all but two pilots on staff volunteered for kamikaze missions, and those two holdouts were laid up in the sick bay. One ardent volunteer, Lieutenant Seki Yukio of the 201st Air Group, was a newlywed who had been married for just three months to a woman he had been courting through the mail. "I'm doing this for my beloved wife," he explained to a war correspondent before departing on his final mission. Similarly, before his own final mission on October 28, 1944, Petty Officer Isao Matsuo addressed a letter to his father and mother: "Dear Parents, please congratulate me. I have been given a splendid opportunity to die. This is my last day."

Moreover, as the tide of the war turned decisively against Japan, and as casualty counts grew more and more lopsided, the distinction between suicide and conventional missions was not as clear as one might think. Japanese pilots were outnumbered, outgunned, undertrained, and underequipped, so they faced increasingly bleak odds when they flew into combat. For example, the second Japanese air strike of the Battle of the Philippine Sea (June 1944) was comprised of 107 attacking aircraft, and despite being a conventional operation, only 10 survived.

High casualties were not unusual for the Japanese in the latter stages of the war either. Of about 77,000 Japanese servicemen defending Okinawa between April and June of 1945, only about 7,000 survived. Increasingly, service in the Japanese military had itself become a sort of "suicide" mission. With the specter of death already hanging so closely over them, battle-weary Japanese pilots may not have regarded adoption of kamikaze tactics as the profound existential leap it appears to people today.

The first official *Tokkōtai* unit set off on its inaugural mission on October 21, and the night before the mission, Ōnishi addressed his men: "Japan is in grave danger. The salvation of our country is now beyond the power of the ministers of state, the general staff, and humble commanders like myself. It can come only from spirited young men like you. Thus, on behalf of your hundred million countrymen, I ask this sacrifice of you and pray for your success." (Ito, 37–38).However, this first mission ended in failure because the group was unable to locate a target and instead returned to base.

Ready for another attempt, two units of freshly minted kamikazes set out from Japanese airbases on the morning of the 25th to support Kurita's attack. The Americans had heard occasional rumors of suicide pilots, but they truly witnessed a sustained kamikaze attack for the first time at Samar.

This photograph shows the men of the first kamikaze unit. The men are being offered a ceremonial toast of water as a farewell. Yukio Seki, the leader of the first kamikaze unit, is shown with a cup in his hands, and Vice Admiral Ōnishi is in the middle of the photo facing the five men of the unit.

As the splashes of gunfire stalked towards them over the sea – brightly colored by the dye placed in Japanese shells so that observers could identify and correct the salvos of specific vessels – the escort carriers turned east into the light wind. This facing helped the aircraft still on their decks to take off, and explained why Vice Admiral Shiraishi's cruisers tried to move east of the American formation.

All the Grumman Avengers, F4F Wildcats, and other aircraft still aboard the jeep carriers launched with desperate speed. The American airmen gathered in squadrons and steered towards the pursuing Japanese fleet. The top speed for the American *Casablanca* carriers stood at 18 knots due to their engines, originally built for ore carriers on the Great Lakes hauling taconite iron ore from the "Twin Ports" of Duluth, Minnesota and Superior, Wisconsin. Conversely, many of Kurita's ships traveled at 35 knots, which meant that with about 15 miles still between them, every 5 minutes of sailing brought the Japanese a mile closer.

The mixed force of Avengers and F4Fs flew northwest to engage the Japanese. The pilots found motivation both in the ordinary aggression of fighting men and in sheer survival, since if the IJN forces sank the carriers, the airplanes might have nowhere to land, forcing them to ditch in the sea and most likely condemning their occupants to a lonely death in the waves.

Many of the aircraft had no ordnance loads but attempted to strafe the gigantic ships cleaving through the sea below them. Others carried bombs or torpedoes and managed to score hits on their targets. Tom Van Brunt dropped depth bombs on the cruiser *Suzuya.* Whether from his unorthodox depth charge attack or the unrecorded efforts of another plane, the cruiser suffered heavy damage, dropping out of formation and sinking hours later, though Van Brunt knew nothing of this until after the war: "I climbed and dived, but when I got through the cloud I realized I'd come in too shallow. I had to climb again and make a steeper dive [...] When I finally dropped the depth bombs and began to pull up I almost blacked out. [...] My gunner John South and my radioman Lester Frederickson told me two of the bombs straddled the cruiser. They saw explosions but couldn't give any damage assessment." (Sears, 2005, 147).

At approximately the same time that the American Avengers and F4Fs made their attack runs on Kurita's fleet, six kamikazes of the "Morning Sun" and "Floating Chrysanthemum" squadrons under First Flying Petty Officers Ueno Keeichi and Kato Toyobumi reached Taffy I from their base at Davao.

The Taffy I ships had just sent most of their remaining aircraft to aid Taffy III, leaving them with no effective air cover. In fact, live ordnance strewed the decks of the jeep carriers as the crews worked to rearm Avengers and other aircraft coming in singly after bombing the Japanese fleet.

The first kamikaze plunged into the deck of the USS *Santee*, a moment captured in an eerie photograph showing the air full of shrapnel and two American seamen crouching for cover behind a gun. 16 men died along with the kamikaze pilot, and dozens more were injured. The aircraft punched a hole in the deck and missed a pile of 1,000 lb bombs by a hairsbreadth.

A second kamikaze swooped at the USS *Sangamon* but a single impeccably aimed shot from the *Suwannee's* 5-inch gun smashed it out of the air just short of the *Sangamon*'s bow, though the debris killed one man and wounded two others on the deck. The flak guns on the USS *Petrof Bay* downed a third attacker.

The fourth kamikaze appeared hesitant to die now that the moment had actually arrived. He dodged through the clouds and squalls for nearly half an hour, moving back and forth over the ships, apparently unable to force himself to take his final plunge. However, an F6F Hellcat finally made the decision for him. When the American aircraft damaged the kamikaze's plane, he finally dived at the USS *Suwannee* at 8:04 AM and punched through the deck. Nevertheless, despite leaving a 20-foot hole in his wake, the kamikaze only slightly delayed the *Suwannee's* continued launching of aircraft. As a terse report to Taffy I's commander from the jeep carrier stated, "All we found of the Jap are bits of his flesh. We're ready for battle again." (Y'Blood, 1987, 296). The relative failure of the kamikazes lulled the Americans into a false sense of their ineffectuality, which would soon be dispelled by bitter subsequent experiences.

The USS *Suwannee* in the distance shortly after being hit by a kamikaze

Taffy III, in the meantime, enjoyed a brief piece of good fortune in the shape of a heavy rain squall that swept over them. The escort carriers plunged into the blinding gray curtains of rain, which sluiced in glistening rivers over their decks and pounded on their islands and catwalks in a frantic dance of exploding, silvery drops. Sprague ordered an immediate turn to the south, and the Japanese salvos began missing as the shadowy shapes of the CVEs blended into the squall.

For 15 minutes, the rain played havoc with the Japanese aim, then tailed off. Kurita, uttering an IJN aphorism – "A sighted enemy is the equivalent of a dead enemy" – ordered the pursuit to continue. As the rain swept away over the sea, leaving Taffy III relatively exposed to its enemies except for the volumes of smoke produced by the destroyers (DDs) and destroyer escorts (DEs), Sprague ordered the seven small escorts to attack the Japanese with their torpedoes.

Smoke coming from some of Taffy III's destroyers

Commander William Dow Thomas on the USS *Hoel* quickly organized the desperate attack against the vastly superior force of Japanese cruisers, battleships, and destroyers. The three destroyers would spearhead the charge, while the four lighter destroyer escorts would follow up, moving forward through the smoke laid by the destroyers during their attack run. Lieutenant Commander Robert Copeland of the Samuel B. Roberts used his megaphone to tell his crew they faced "a fight against overwhelming odds from which survival could not be expected." (Woodward, 1947, 175).

With courage equaling any Japanese banzai charge, the crews of the three destroyers *Hoel, Heermann,* and *Johnston* accelerated to flank speed and plowed through the seas straight towards the mighty Japanese armada, centered on the super-battleship *Yamato.* As they charged out of their own smokescreen, the IJN vessels opened fire. The air filled with the roar of incoming shells and the sea erupted into columns and curtains of varicolored spray as the dye-laden explosives tore into its surface.

Even as the first shells crashed through their structure, the plucky destroyers launched spreads of torpedoes and loosed salvos from their 5-inch guns, then wheeled away, back into the billows of white and black smoke lingering in the humid air. Aboard the *Johnston,* the captain of Turret Four, Robert Hollenbaugh, witnessed a devastating hit from a Japanese gun: "After the torpedo attack we made a sharp turn [...] Hauling ass, I mean we were going! [...] all of a sudden I heard this big 'Thump.' It was a shell hitting on the port side, just forward of mount four. It pierced the deck [...] and knocked out one of our engines. The stern just came up out of the water and slammed back down. [...] I heard Bobby Chastain, the trainer, and Sam Moody, the pointer, saying, 'Boats, we got no power.'" (Sears, 2005, 151).

The thin skins of the American destroyers, earning them their nickname of "tin cans," failed to set off the impact fuses of the Japanese shells, which passed through and detonated only when they struck the sea beyond. Nevertheless, the kinetic energy of the huge missiles still punched large holes in the destroyers, destroyed their equipment, and killed men or wounded them terribly.

The *Johnston* sat briefly, motionless and exposed to IJN fire, but almost immediately, a torrential rain squall swept over the vessel. This gave the crew time to start the engines again, make a few hasty repairs, and offer some treatment to the wounded. When the squall cleared, the *Johnston* could manage 17 knots again, returning to the attack.

"Stormed at with shot and shell," as the British had been on another October 25th long before at Balaclava, the seven small ships darted and wove, laying smoke, launching torpedoes, and firing at the Japanese ships with their 5-inch cannons and 40mm guns. As they did, the Japanese slowly shot them to pieces, reducing the upper works of the ships to torn rags of steel and butchering the crews. Headless bodies strewed the decks amid rivulets of blood, pieces of limbs and intestines, and pitifully wounded men.

However, the attack of the DD and DE squadron seriously hampered the Japanese. Many of the ships in Kurita's force found themselves compelled to turn and turn again, avoiding incoming torpedo wakes. Even the mighty *Yamato* made a lumbering turn to narrowly avoid a lethal spread of torpedoes, taking Kurita out of the center of the fight. The Japanese formation turned to a chaotic jumble, its advance greatly slowed, and Taffy III's few remaining aircraft continued to pound the IJN ships as well.

Inevitably, the American destroyers began to drop out of the fight. The *Hoel* sank first, with two-thirds of its crew slaughtered by the lethal fire. *Samuel B. Roberts* succumbed next, its hull blown open by a pair of massive 14 inch shells. Copeland ordered "abandon ship" at 9 AM. Men, many of them wounded or mangled, scrambled over the side to an emergency raft with boarding nets attached to its sides. As the skipper, medic, and other personnel swept the ship from stem to stern for survivors – with shells still plowing into the vessel, killing some of the men – they found Gunner's Mate Third Class Paul H. Carr fatally wounded by the rear 5-inch gun. Carr, dying from a huge wound in the guts, still held a 5-inch shell in his hands – the last of 325, the other 324 having already been fired. Carr asked the men to help him load and fire the shell.

When they left for a moment to fetch the medic, Copeland and his group returned to find Carr unsteadily on his feet, trying feebly to push the shell into the gun's smashed breech in order to fire it. The men administered first aid to Carr, but he soon died, and the remaining sailors abandoned ship immediately before it sank.

The ship's mascot, a black-furred 15-lb mixed breed dog named Sammy, swam to the raft and sat on it briefly. After a minute or two, however, he slipped into the water and swam back to the *Roberts* immediately before it sank. The men interpreted his action as a desire to "go down with the ship," though a more likely explanation is that Sammy held a strong attachment for one of the crew, and, finding the man absent from the raft, returned to the doomed ship to look for him.

With *Hoel* and *Roberts* gone, a ring of Japanese destroyers formed around *Johnston*, firing their guns unceasingly into the disintegrating American DD. Soon, the crew found themselves forced to abandon ship. As the destroyer sank prow-first, one of the IJN destroyers approached, slowing as it did. The burned, wounded, battered men floating in the sea watched nervously. Then they saw that the Japanese captain stood at the rail in his impeccable uniform, rigidly at attention, saluting the American destroyer and its crew.

Clint Carter noticed that most of the Japanese crew followed the example of their leader: "It appeared to me that every man on her deck was standing at attention, like a muster, giving us one big salute." (Hornfischer, 2005, 276). One man, however, thumbed his nose at the Americans, a gesture probably learned from the cinema. Another threw them a bulky can of tomatoes whose faded label still bore the legend "Product of Arkansas." Then the Japanese destroyer slid away in pursuit of Taffy III.

Despite the valor of the destroyermen, the escort carriers did not all escape. The Japanese cruisers shot *USS Gambier Bay*, sailing at the eastern end of the formation, to pieces during the course of the running battle. Finally holed below the waterline and devastated by internal explosions, the jeep carrier capsized and sank. Around 60 men died during the shelling and sinking; 800 lived to abandon ship, only to have sharks kill a number of them prior to rescue on October 27th.

Between them, however, the seven escorts (four of whom survived despite damage) and the small, mixed force of USN aircraft managed to sink four of Kurita's ships, all heavy cruisers – *Suzuya, Chokai, Chikuma,* and *Kumano*. Some historians of the battle think Kurita's *Yamato* was too far north to watch events, causing the admiral to temporarily recall his ships to re-form them. However, one of the surviving photographs of the *Gambier Bay's* last moments shows what strongly resembles a *Yamato*-class battleship in the background, perhaps a mile distant. If the photo does indeed show the super-battleship, Kurita made his decision to break off while on the scene.

Regardless of his exact location, the Japanese admiral gave a withdrawal order around 9 AM.

The Japanese ships sailed north for two hours, then to the west for an hour. At noon, Kurita turned south again as if to resume the attack, but then, 30 minutes later, changed his mind again and made the final decision to sail for San Bernardino Strait and escape. He later stated he did not believe the destroyers would attack so furiously without heavy ship support nearby, and that that the constant American radio chatter between various task forces made him fear being caught in a trap.

Thanks to that withdrawal, the attack of seven determined American destroyers and a handful of Avenger and F4F aircraft had effectively frightened off a 23-ship armada made up of battleships, heavy cruisers, and the exceptionally large, powerful destroyers of the Emperor's navy. he sacrificial courage of the destroyers and destroyer escorts had, to the amazement of the Americans, helped turn away Kurita's massed surface ships, and in at least one case won the grudging admiration of a Japanese captain. The final shots of the surface engagement ceased between 9:07 and 9:10 AM, as the USS *Heermann* and the IJN cruiser *Tone* hurled a few final, defiant parting shots at one another. Sprague heard a yell from one of his signalmen: "God damn it, boys, they're getting away!" (Hornfischer, 2004, 257). Whether that was yelled ironically or in actual frustration remains unclear.

Ziggy Sprague knew Taffy III remained in fatal danger, however, and took immediate steps to leave the area. Kurita's force could easily return, and other hazards might appear at any moment. At 9:17, Sprague issued the order to lay smoke on the port quarter of the escort carriers, raising a smoke screen between his ships and the retiring Japanese. Under cover of the artificial vapor, the American ships limped back into formation, then moved off to the south, increasing their distance from the enemy. Officers allowed many of the crewmen to leave their combat stations to eat quickly.

The carrier *Gambier Bay* laying a smokescreen

As it turned out, there was indeed another force bore down on the limping, battered escort carriers: the day's second detachment of kamikazes. The "Shikishima" kamikaze unit under Lieutenant Seki Yukio lifted off from the Mabalacat airfield at 7:25 AM, arriving near Taffy 3 at 10:30 AM. This unit consisted of five kamikazes, including Seki himself, plus four escort fighters. Seki spent around 15 minutes observing the American vessels, lurking in the rows and clusters of cumulus clouds knotted across the sky. At 10:49, he gave the attack signal by waggling his aircraft's wings, avoiding any telltale radio signal.

At 10:51, a sharp-eyed lookout on the USS *Raymond* spotted the aircraft and opened fire. This alerted the rest of the ships, which also poured torrents of flak upwards towards the diving Japanese. The first kamikaze, probably already dead at his controls, missed the *Kitkun Bay*'s island and instead tore away part of the port catwalk, killing one man, before plunging into the ocean. At the same time, the *Fanshaw Bay*, Ziggy Sprague's flagship, blew another kamikaze to pieces before the aircraft came anywhere near its target.

A sharp turn to port by *White Plains* made the kamikaze aiming for it smash into the ocean nearby, wounding 11 men with shrapnel thrown up by the water impact but causing no serious damage. At this moment, however, the attack took a fateful turn. A kamikaze approached *White Plains*, suffered a flak hit, and swerved abruptly to plunge towards *Saint Lo* instead. The pilot released his bomb to crash through the jeep carrier's flight deck, then plunged through himself somewhat farther on. Both explosions caused massive fires on the hangar deck, where several aircraft had just been refueled and rearmed with bombs and torpedoes. These aircraft caught fire and exploded.

Picture of a kamikaze attempting to hit the USS *White Plains*

Picture of the explosion on the *Saint Lo* after being hit by a kamikaze

The crew, responding quickly, could have put out the flames if not for a fatal design flaw present in the escort carriers, but not larger American carriers. The firefighting piping system used cast iron pipes, which fractured and leaked under the violent shock of the bomb and kamikaze impacts. Some of the sprinklers worked, while others failed, and the firefighting hoses lost pressure within a few minutes.

Captain Francis McKenna ordered the ship abandoned when it became clear no means for stopping the fire existed. The Captain himself left the ship last, half an hour after the kamikaze strike. Shortly after he slid down one of the prepared escape lines into the ocean, the *Saint Lo* suffered a catastrophic internal explosion that ripped its hull violently open. The remains of the ship sank quickly after the blast. 113 men died out of 889, with 30 more perishing from their injuries following rescue.

At this point, several additional kamikazes appeared, though their origin remains murky. They attacked the *Kitkun Bay* and *Kalinin Bay*, scoring several glancing hits on the latter that inflicted moderate damage. One pilot dived too steeply and, despite passing the flak unharmed, plunged straight into the sea rather than hitting his target.

As the kamikaze attacks ceased, Sprague ordered the retirement to the southeast to continue. He detached all of the four surviving escorts to pick up survivors from *Saint Lo*. Sprague, at the time and later also, expressed great bitterness at the failure of other help to materialize to rescue his men from the sea. Regarding the decision to use all his escorts to rescue *Saint Lo*'s crew, he remarked, "This desperate expedient which left the Task Unit without any screen for the next eight hours was made necessary by the absence of any rescue effort from other sources. [...] We had been through so much by then that it didn't seem to make any difference whether we had escorts with us or not." (Y'Blood, 1987, 307).

While Taffy III's remnants finally made their escape, dramatic events unfolded elsewhere in the American fleet in response to the battle off Samar. Sprague had broadcast a plain language appeal for help to Admiral Kinkaid in desperation at the height of the action. Learning of the apparent catastrophe unfolding in the Philippine Sea, and unable to understand how Kurita moved such a powerful armada through the San Bernardino Strait unopposed, Admiral Chester Nimitz sent a message to "Bull" Halsey at 10 AM. This message consisted of a single sentence betraying Nimitz's astonishment: "Where is, repeat, where is TF 34?"

However, the radioman on Halsey's flagship USS *New Jersey* left in the "padding" at the end of the message, intended to confuse Japanese codebreakers: "The world wonders." Halsey read the message – "Where is, repeat, where is TF 34? The world wonders" – and instantly flew into an aggrieved rage. He pulled the hat from his head and flung it to the deck, then began swearing and raving at a shout; some sources even suggest he sobbed in frustration. He interpreted the message as a piercing criticism from Nimitz, probably in part due to realization of how massively he had erred.

After Halsey's tantrum continued for several minutes, Rear Admiral Robert Carney barked at his superior, "Stop it! What the hell's the matter with you? Pull yourself together." (Hornfischer, 2004, 178). This had the effect of calming Halsey, though he dithered for over an hour before finally deciding to send the battleships back to aid Sprague at 11:15 AM. Their belated and ultimately futile race to help at Samar earned this maneuver the mocking title of "the Battle of Bull's Run," a clever pun playing off of Halsey's nickname and the first major land battle of the American Civil War.

Though Halsey later claimed ignorance of the situation to his south prior to receipt of the "world wonders" transmission, strong evidence suggests that he became aware of Taffy III's plight earlier and chose to ignore it. Admiral John S. "Slew" McCain, grandfather of 2008 presidential candidate John McCain, commanded Task Group 38.1, refueling at Ulithi on the morning of October 28th. At 7:25 AM, his radio operators intercepted a call from Kinkaid to Halsey describing the attack on Taffy 3 – which, unless Halsey failed to receive it, gave him almost real-time news of the potential disaster. "Slew" McCain immediately ordered an end to refueling and set Task Group 38.1 in motion towards Halsey's position, intending to support him against the Japanese carriers of the feint.

Then, at 9:40 AM, his radiomen picked up another Kincaid message, describing a massive Japanese fleet action against Taffy III. On his own initiative, McCain ordered Task Group 38.1

to alter course, sailing to the aid of Ziggy Sprague and his embattled flattops. At 10:30 AM, with a range of 330 miles still between his task group and Taffy III, McCain launched air attacks from his *Essex*-class carriers. Though the air groups failed to sink any more Japanese vessels, they achieved some bomb hits on Kurita's retiring forces, persuading them to continue on their way. As McCain later described the action, "The escort carriers put up a big fight, one of the biggest fights I've ever seen. I don't claim credit. [...] I went down to Leyte at 10:30 the morning of the 25th, a half hour before the Jap fleet turned around. It turned around for at least two reasons. Our escort carriers fought so furiously the Japs assumed they were a larger force. Also because we sent in carrier groups to help out." (Gilbert, 2006, 153-154).

Airstrikes from McCain's ships would sink a further cruiser in Kurita's retiring force the following day, October 26th. Altogether, Task Group 38.1 lost 18 aircraft during the Battle of Leyte Gulf, most of them to Japanese anti-aircraft fire. The surviving aircraft of the jeep carriers also aided in harassing the Japanese retreat during the ensuing days.

Throughout this time, Sprague radioed Kinkaid and asked for help in rescuing the men from the Taffy III escorts sunk during the action. Kinkaid sent a scout aircraft to find the men, which it did successfully. Unfortunately, the pilot radioed drastically incorrect coordinates, so when the ships sent by Kinkaid arrived at the designated location, they found only empty waves. The men from the sunken destroyers thus faced several grisly days in the water prior to rescue. Clinging to rafts too small to support all of them at once, the men suffered incredible hardships as they floated in the tepid tropical seas. The badly wounded died first, though a few, incredibly, survived only to die within minutes of being rescued.

On top of that, even those who were lightly injured or able-bodied soon found themselves marked for death. Sharks approached the rafts within a few hours of the sinking. Initially driven off by the men's shouts and splashing, they soon returned to circle in the clear water below the rafts. Survivors later claimed that some of the sharks measured 10 to 12 feet in length, and they began to attack their nearly helpless prey, taking bites out of limbs and bodies.

Desperately, the survivors tried hauling the injured out of the water in an effort to save them, but many quickly bled to death. One man, with a large bite taken out of his guts, screamed and begged with his comrades to kill him for around an hour before another sailor, unable to bear the sight and sound of his agony any longer, first attempted to shoot him with a waterlogged pistol, then opened the vein in his neck with a clasp knife.

Scorched by the sun, tortured by thirst, and frazzled by shark attacks, many of the men slipped into delirium. In a perhaps more merciful death than others suffered, these men spoke of their hallucinations of fountains of fresh water, beer, lemonade, beautiful women, and other marvels before swimming away to drown or simply diving straight down. Even those who survived began to experience frequent hallucinations, brought on by thirst, the slow hypothermia of the lukewarm tropical sea, and drinking seawater.

Lieutenant Everett Roberts of the *Samuel B. Roberts* found himself just as vulnerable to these curious visions as his crew: "As the currents propelled the survivors westward through the night, Roberts discerned a point of land that was dotted with fine homes. A gala dinner party was in progress, tuxedoed men and gloriously begowned women enjoying a high time by the sea." (Hornfischer, 2004, 304).

Even as the men had to endure all of that, the sharks continued to harry the survivors, often attacking in the night. The sleeping and half-sleeping men would awaken to frantic screams and the sight of a man being dragged off the raft by a shark. Despite their efforts to beat off the predatory fish, the victim usually vanished under the surface in a swirl of blood, never to be seen again. Other men, utterly exhausted, drowned when they fell asleep; the mild water entering their noses and mouths failed to wake them, and they died without ever realizing they were drowning.

Many of those who survived did so because they lost the energy and interest needed for the tempting phantoms of their imagination to lure them into the effort required to leave the raft. A few men actually reached the Philippine shore, where the Filipino guerillas gave them a very different welcome than they extended to the Japanese. The destroyermen were fed, given water and whatever medical care the local people had to offer, and found themselves hidden and protected by bands of fighters armed with machetes and submachine guns. When they recovered sufficiently, the Filipinos took them to American intelligence outposts or the rapidly advancing American front lines.

Most, however, remained at sea until the 27th, when an LCI (Landing Craft Infantry) found the clusters of survivors and picked them up off their rafts. Most proved unable to eat, throwing up anything they consumed, but they drank large quantities of water. Crammed into any belowdecks spaces available, they slept for extended periods as the LCI took them to a location where a hospital ship awaited.

Ziggy Sprague eventually arranged for their return to the United States for recuperation aboard commandeered cruise ships, and the survivors of the desperate Samar destroyer charge found themselves returning "Stateside" in luxury suites and well-appointed cabins that accommodated tourists in more peaceful times. Sprague later offered his own interpretation of the Samar action and the remarkable survival of Taffy III when confronted by one of the most powerful concentrations of Japanese non-carrier warships ever assembled: "In summation, the failure of the enemy main body and encircling light forces to completely wipe out all vessels of this Task Unit can be attributed to our successful smoke screen, our torpedo counterattack, continuous harassment of enemy by bomb, torpedo, and strafing air attacks, timely maneuvers, and the definite partiality of Almighty God." (Hornfischer, 2004, 322).

The Battle at Cape Engaño

The final major action of the Battle of Leyte Gulf occurred near Cape Engaño, where elements of Halsey's task force clashed with Vice Admiral Ozawa Jisaburo's decoy Northern Force. Ozawa, a gaunt figure 6 feet 7 inches tall, acquired the nickname "Onigawara" – roughly "ogre-gargoyle" – due to his combined height and supposed ugliness, but his intelligence, professionalism, and concern for his men's welfare won him considerable popularity among them.

The battle at Cape Engaño, one-sided from the beginning, could only end in disaster for Ozawa. His entire purpose consisted of serving as a sacrificial pawn drawing Halsey's force away from San Bernardino, in which he succeeded admirably. However, it remained necessary to persuade the Americans that the decoy force presented enough of a threat to prevent "Bull" from turning back too soon.

With just 108 aircraft available, Ozawa and his men prepared to fight, and Ozawa himself described this strategy following the war: "A decoy, that was our first primary mission, to act as a decoy. My fleet could not very well give direct protection to Kurita's force because we were very weak, so I tried to attack as many American carriers as possible [...] The main mission was all sacrifice. An attack with a very weak force of planes comes under the heading of sacrifice of planes and ships." (Woodward, 1947, 149).

The Northern Force sent 80 of its 108 aircraft to launch a strike on Halsey's task force to sting him into action. The other 28 aircraft provided a meager fighter cover to Ozawa's carrier, three light carriers, two hybrid battleship carriers, three light cruisers, and ten destroyers. Of these aircraft, approximately 40 survived to land on Luzon airfields.

On the night of the 25th, Halsey sped north around midnight and, as he approached Ozawa's slowly retiring force, formed his battleships, cruisers, and destroyers into Task Force 34. This surface fleet pushed out ahead of the carriers. Bull Halsey's plan consisted of devastating the IJN armada with airstrikes, at which time Task Force 34 would arrive to blow the survivors to pieces with direct gunfire.

Scouting aircraft kept Halsey apprised of his opponents' position in the ocean from 1 AM onward in the early morning of the 26th. Eventually, the Americans lost contact with the Japanese for a time. Regardless, the American carriers sent off their first strike groups at 6 AM, keeping them "orbiting" ahead of the fleet until scouts reestablished contact. The scouts continued probing north, but found nothing. Two junior lieutenants serving as part of the fleet's intelligence section, Lt. Byron White and Lt. Calvert Cheston, pored over charts and decided the Japanese fleet probably lay in an easterly direction. They argued passionately with their superiors, and the admirals eventually gave them permission to send a squadron of four fighters to the east.

At 7:35, under a brilliantly sunny sky, the fighter pilots bore out White's and Cheston's hunch by finding Ozawa's entire force northeast of Halsey's task forces. With this information in hand, Halsey released the full strength of Task Force 38's strike units against the Japanese.

The first massed formations brushed aside the tiny fighter umbrella of 28 aircraft, shooting down some and forcing the rest to retreat. The first raid sank one of the Japanese light carriers, the *Chiyoda*, and immobilized another, the *Chitose*. Though this represented a triumph, the American pilots concentrated on the already damaged ships rather than picking fresh targets. Rear Admiral Carney, soon to snap Halsey out of his rage with a well-chosen rebuke, ascribed this fact scathingly to "an inherent mammalian tendency to jump on cripples." (Woodward, 1947, 142).

During this attack, one of the bombs caused damage that may have accidentally saved Admiral Ozawa's life. This bomb struck the *Zuikaku*, Ozawa's only full-sized carrier and his flagship. The explosion completely destroyed the carrier's radio equipment. A modern commander without a radio is utterly useless, so Ozawa found himself compelled to move his headquarters to *Oyoda*, a nearby light cruiser.

American strikes continued through the day, and in all, 527 sorties pounded Ozawa's Northern Force. In the late morning, Kinkaid's and Nimitz's communications intervened, impelling Halsey to take his fast battleships and many other ships south to deal with Taffy III's critical situation. Perhaps characteristically, Halsey stripped Task Force 38 of most of its heavy ships, including all the battleships, leaving the carriers relatively vulnerable despite their screen of destroyers and heavy cruisers.

Vice Admiral Marc Mitscher commanded Task Force 38 following Halsey's exit, continuing the pressure on Ozawa's force. At 1:30 PM, under a light cover of cumulus clouds, the American aircraft, including Helldiver torpedo planes, located and attacked the carrier *Zuikaku* and the light carrier *Zuiho*, setting both afire. Repeated attacks continued, until the *Zuikaku* developed a heavy list. A surviving photograph from on board the famous carrier during its final moments shows a crowd of men standing on the violently canted deck, saluting the Japanese flag.

At 2:30 PM, the *Zuikaku* rolled over and sank, taking half of its crew to the bottom with it. At 3 PM, the *Zuiho* also sank as torpedo attacks and bombing continued. At this point, Mitscher loosed his cruisers and destroyers to finish off the Japanese ships, as well as search for downed pilots. Mitscher always showed great solicitude towards American airmen shot down in action, putting forth major efforts to locate and rescue them.

The cruisers attacked and sank the crippled light carrier *Chitose,* then looked for further targets. At the same time, Ozawa learned of the exposed position of these relatively light American warships and sent his two battleships south again, hoping to destroy some *Essex* carriers or at least a few destroyers and cruisers. Ultimately, the two forces missed each other on the vast expanses of the Philippine Sea. Airstrikes petered out during the late afternoon, and the surviving ships of Ozawa withdrew northward, having lost the remaining Japanese carriers plus a destroyer.

The final blow in the battle of Cape Engaño went to SS-368, the USS *Jallao,* a submarine of the tough *Balao*-class built in Manitowoc, Wisconsin. Captained by Lieutenant Commander Joseph Icenhower, the *Jallao* detected Ozawa's retreating ships and moved in, seeking a kill on its first combat patrol. As radarman Jack B. Weinstein, later a U.S. federal judge, described in an interview: "As we closed in, I noticed two pips on the radar. He asked what it was [...] I had never seen that phenomenon, but I said, 'Captain, it looks like a large destroyer or a small cruiser,' which was kind of nervy, I suppose. It turned out to be a small cruiser. [...] We made an attack, half-submerged with a spread of four torpedoes, as I recall, and the ship sunk immediately." (US Courts, 2014, online).

The *Jallao* sank the cruiser *Tama,* which broke in half when struck by the torpedoes with the loss of its full complement of 450 men. This event, at 11:10 PM, represented the final sinking during the main action at Leyte Gulf.

The Philippines Campaign of 1944-1945

The Results of the Battle of Leyte Gulf

The American naval victory in Leyte Gulf allowed for an amphibious invasion of Leyte Island itself, and over the course of two months worth of fighting, the Allies eventually established themselves on the island and mostly wiped out the Japanese contingent, killing an estimated 50,000 Japanese. It was also at Leyte that the iconic picture of MacArthur wading ashore was taken, an image that has become closely associated with his return to the Philippines.

Picture of the amphibious invasion of Leyte

American soldiers fighting on Leyte

MacArthur walking ashore onto Leyte Island during the 1945 Philippines campaign

As MacArthur's campaign was progressing on Leyte, Allied forces began their attack on the Philippines with a landing at Mindoro, from which they planned to provide developed airfields that would allow them to give air cover to ships moving toward the Lingayen Gulf at Luzon. Secondarily, these airfields at Mindoro would give the Allies more options from which to contest Japanese air power in the region. American planners estimated the Japanese garrison on Mindoro to be roughly 1,000 men made up of a mix of the Japanese 8th Division and the 105th Division.

MacArthur assigned the American Sixth Army under General Krueger to carry out operations on Mindoro, and he would be supported by both air and naval units. Krueger delegated the task to Brigadier General William Dunckel, who utilized the 19th Regimental Combat Team of the 24th Division and the 503d Parachute RCT to carry out the mission. The ground forces began moving toward Mindoro on December 12, 1944 aboard the ships of Task Group 77.12. The Task Group moved unopposed through the Mindanao Sea until the next day, December 13, when they were spotted by Japanese surveillance. Japanese commanders held off attacking the Allied ships because they wanted to figure out the destination of the Task Group before engaging it, but by the middle of that afternoon, 10 Japanese plans, including three kamikaze planes, attacked the Task Group, with one kamikaze crashing into the flagship *Nashville*. With roughly 190 wounded sailors to deal with, some ships picked up survivors and returned to Leyte, while the command staff was transferred to the *Dashiell* to continue the mission.

Picture of a Japanese kamikaze plane during the campaign

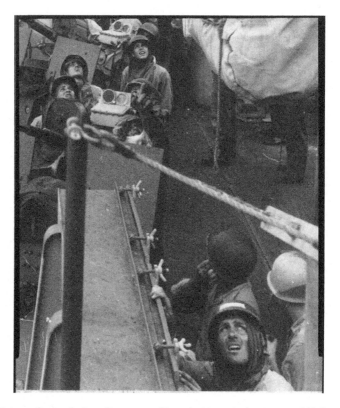

Picture of an anti-aircraft crew on a Navy destroyer trying to cover Mindoro

By this time, the Japanese military believed the Task Group was headed toward either Panay, Cebu, or Negros, and in the course of searching for it near those areas, they wasted valuable time in which they could have continued their attacks. Meanwhile, on the morning of December 15, the Task Group reached Mindoro and began preparations for beach landings. As the landing units were disembarking, Japanese air operations attempted to aid ground troops in repelling the Allied forces. Although much of the Japanese air power was destroyed by Allied planes, kamikazes did manage to sink two landing ships, as well as the destroyer *Moale*. Japanese planes also damaged one other landing ship, the destroyer *Howorth*, and the CVE *Marcus Island*. In the air attacks, the Allies suffered 27 casualties, but aside from that, the troops of the 19th and 503d were able to land with little resistance, and this allowed some of the naval vessels of the Task Group to withdraw from the operation and move to support units in other locations.

As this was occurring, Allied planes attacked Luzon on December 16th, and the aircraft carriers designated for the Philippines campaign withdrew to the east for refueling before beginning a second series of attacks that took place on December 19th. Over the course of the next few days, naval and aerial engagements with Japanese aircraft destroyed an estimated 450 enemy planes, leaving the Allies with almost complete air superiority over the Philippines until the Japanese called in reinforcements from Formosa and the home islands.

By December 15th, the 19th and 503d had created a beachhead seven miles inland at Mindoro and had taken the airfield at the town of San Jose. Army engineers who had accompanied the landing parties then began building new airstrips roughly three miles south of the airfield at San Jose. The new airstrips, at a site they called Hill Drome, became operational on December 20th, and on that day American P-38s and P-61s began arriving from elsewhere in the Pacific. These airfields would be important in opposing a Japanese counterattack, which began on December 20th when 50 Japanese planes flew in to reinforce the existing 15 planes the Japanese Army Air Force had at Mindoro. Air attacks on December 21st destroyed two more landing craft, and ground units stationed on Mindoro were also attacked, causing roughly 70 casualties.

To counter the Allies, Japanese commanders ordered their Southwestern Area Fleet, which was comprised of two cruisers and six destroyers and was stationed at Manila, to Mindoro on a raiding mission to try to sink Allied ships off the coast. However, the Southwester Area Fleet was spotted in the South China Sea by Allied submarines, and 105 planes were sent from Mindoro to engage with the fleet. Although the Southwestern Fleet was attacked from the air, they managed to make their way to the beachhead, where they shelled the beach and airfields for roughly 40 minutes before withdrawing. In total, the Southwestern Area Fleet managed to destroy 26 planes and damage some Allied installations on Mindoro, while suffering the loss of one destroyer and sustaining damage to nearly all of the ships in the fleet.

On December 28th, Japanese air attacks resumed against Allied naval units near Mindoro, where they sunk three ships, along with a tanker and two landing vessels. Although these were heavy losses for the Allied naval presence at Mindoro, the Japanese lost 50 aircraft between December 28th and January 4th, and with no more reinforcements forthcoming, Japanese air power in the region was once again basically nullified.

Meanwhile, on Mindoro proper, Allied ground units began patrols on December 19th, where they searched for Japanese troops and guarded areas that might be landing spots for reinforcements for the Japanese garrisons on Luzon. Mindoro guerrillas also worked with Allied troops by helping to guide the patrols and engaging some of the remaining Japanese soldiers in mopping-up operations across the island. Reinforcing the 19th and 503d, General Krueger sent the 21st Division to Mindoro after the Southwestern Fleet Raid just in case a ground-based attack was being planned by Japan.

Army engineers continued building on Mindoro, and MacArthur sent additional bombers and fighters to the air bases there in preparation for later missions. He also had engineers build airfields for heavy bombers that would target areas in the southern Philippines and Formosa. Work on these heavy bomber airfields began on January 2nd, but they would not be ready for heavy bomber support in time for the invasion of Luzon. Nonetheless, by the middle of January, Allied Air Forces had three fighter groups, two medium bomber groups, two night fighter squadrons, three tactical reconnaissance squadrons, a photographic squadron, and an air-sea rescue squadron. With this air power mustered at Mindoro, the principal goal of the invasion of the island of Mindoro was complete, as the Allies now had their air bases in which to launch further air attacks. They now also had a base close to Luzon that put pressure on the Japanese to defend multiple possible entry points onto that island.

A map of action around Mindoro

Moving Toward Luzon

With southern Mindoro under Allied control, MacArthur began a series of three feints to confuse Japanese forces on Luzon. First, he sent the Western Visayan Task Force to seize northeastern Mindoro and Marinduque Island, which he hoped would lead the Japanese to believe that the two areas would be bases from which the Allies would try to launch an invasion on southern Luzon. Then, naval units would begin fake maneuvers along the southern coast of Luzon, while guerrillas operating on Luzon would work with Allied forces in destroying infrastructure like railroads, bridges and communications lines in southern Luzon. Finally, Allied forces throughout the Pacific would maneuver to give the impression that Formosa, and not Luzon, was the next target for their operations.

On January 1st, the Western Visayan Task Force began its part of the operation by moving from its base in southern Mindoro toward northeastern Mindoro, which took them roughly 30 days to complete. As this was occurring, guerrilla operations in Mindoro had neutralized the remainder of the Japanese garrison on the island. These guerrillas killed 50 soldiers, and the remaining 300 stationed there fled into the interior.

However, the rest of the planned deception did not go as planned. The delays that the Western Visayan Task Force faced in moving to the north of the island meant that they did not arrive in time to put their part of the plan in place, but they did succeed in freeing groups of Filipinos on Mindoro. Nonetheless, Japanese commanders were well aware that Luzon was the next target of Allied operations, and that an attack would not occur in the southern region but instead would focus on the Lingayen Gulf, which was the same invasion point that the Japanese had used for its invasion back in 1941.

A map indicating the Japanese invasion points on Luzon in 1941

A picture of Filipino guerrillas on Mindoro

Allied aerial bombard of Luzon had begun in the fall of 1944, and they had already knocked out key military installations. Naval units also began to move on Luzon, with Admiral Halsey's carrier group and Admiral Kinkaid's surface forces nearing the Lingayen Gulf. In fact, during the beginning of the assault on Lingayen, military officials had problems coordinating staging activities between ground troops, naval vessels, and landing craft between the various launch and landing points. The initial landing at Lingayen Gulf involved two ground units, the XIV Corps and the I Corps. Along with these two ground units, the ships of the II and III Amphibious Force had the task of ferrying these units to their landing locations.

American battleships heading towards Lingayen Gulf

The landing units were designated the Luzon Attack Force, with the first group, consisting of screening and support ships, leaving from Leyte Gulf on January 2, 1945. Between January 4th and 5th, a second group left Leyte Gulf, this time consisting of three light cruisers, six destroyers, as well as smaller covering vessels. Finally, on January 6th, the ships carrying ground forces began making their way to the Lingayen Gulf.

To support this convoy of ships moving toward Lingayen Gulf, Mindoro-based planes began increasingly heavy attacks on Japanese targets in late December and early January. They especially targeted defensive installations at the Lingayen beaches, as well as Japanese transports bringing reinforcements to Luzon. The Third Fleet's fast carriers also moved into the region, and by January 3rd, they were in position to begin operations targeting Japanese air bases within range of Luzon: Formosa, the Ryukyu Islands, and the Pescadores. By January 6th, the fast carriers moved again, this time to the coast of Luzon, where they would provide cover over North Luzon (with Allied Air Force planes from Mindoro covering the Lingayen Gulf and Clark Field).

Picture of the Third Fleet moving towards the Philippines

In terms of the Japanese presence at Luzon by early January, 1945, when air attacks against island accelerated, they had only a minimal air presence remaining to contest the skies, so military leaders in Japan began to devote their resources to consolidating air power for the home islands rather than spreading out their remaining planes in an attempt to protect territories like the Philippines. The remaining Japanese planes at Luzon attempted a series of attacks on American naval units. They attacked a mine sweeping group off the coast of Mindoro and a kamikaze crashed into one ship, killing 95 men and wounding another 65. As these operations made clear, Japanese air tactics in their defense of the Philippines increasingly centered on the use of kamikazes, and on January 5th, planes attacked the Third Fleet, which was preparing for a new set of strikes on Luzon. Kamikaze planes hit two CVE, two heavy cruisers, three destroyers, a destroyer transport, and a mine sweeper, with total casualties for the day within the Third Fleet amounting to 65 dead and 195 wounded. On the other hand, the Japanese lost nearly all of the 45 planes that began the attacks, further depleting their already weak air forces.

At the same time, Japanese naval units also attempted to engage Allied forces. During the afternoon of January 5th, Allied ships spotted two Japanese destroyers that were attempting to attack a mine sweeper group near Manila Bay. A mixed group of two Australian frigates and an American destroyer attempted to intercept these ships, but when they were unable to get within firing range, they had to call off their attack plans and return to Manila Bay. Japanese submarines harassed other Allied naval vessels, with one group, which included the *Boise*, MacArthur's command ship, being fired upon by torpedoes. The torpedoes missed their marks, and one Japanese submarine was sunk by return fire.

At Lingayen Gulf, kamikaze planes were a major problem for Allied naval vessels. Admiral Jesse Oldendorf noted the problems he had in defending against kamikaze planes, as it only took one or two planes escaping away from Allied air cover to deal heavy damage to his ships. Anti-aircraft weapons were also problematic because their 5-inch antiaircraft weapons equipped with proximity fuses had problems tracking the erratic flight techniques of kamikaze pilots. Meanwhile, their 40 mm and 20 mm automatic batteries often did not deal enough damage to halt the heavily armored kamikaze planes. Fortunately, even though Allied forces had trouble dealing with kamikaze planes, the problem was lessened by the lack of aircraft that the Japanese on Luzon possessed. By January 6th, they had only a small number of operational planes remaining.

Oldendorf

Luzon

A picture of the initial landings on Luzon

Allied soldiers advancing on Luzon

The plan for the Lingayen landings was to have 6th Army establish beachheads and then secure a base from which supplies and reinforcements could come ashore. They would then coordinate offensive maneuvers against the Japanese 14th Area Army. Thus, on January 9th, 1945, or S-day, the naval vessels positioned off the coast began their bombardment of potential Japanese positions at 0700. After half an hour, assault troops from the XIV Corps began coming ashore and were followed by the 37th Infantry Division, which landed to the XIV Corps' left, while the 40th Division landed on the right. The Japanese defenders did not contest the beaches here, and in fact, Filipino guerrillas began coming toward the American troops to help them.

By the evening of the 9th, some units had made their way as far as four miles into the interior of the island, but the next day, January 10th, saw some resistance from Japanese forces when a platoon of Japanese infantry attacked the 160th Division, which suffered 15 casualties, the most of any regiment in the first three days on Luzon. As they continued to move away from the beaches, with the 185th Infantry moving to the west and the 160th moving toward the south, a gap began to open between them. General Rapp Brush therefore moved the 108th Infantry to close this gap and stop a potential weak point in case of a Japanese counterattack.

Meanwhile, the 148th Infantry moved to the southeast, and with no resistance against it, quickly moved into its designated zone by the afternoon of January 10th. Nearby, the 129th Infantry made contact with Filipino guerrillas at the town of Malasiqui, and then later were attacked by Japanese units, forcing them to halt for the remainder of the day. Even with some slight delays, by January 11th, nearly all Allied assault units had reached their designated Army Beachhead Line zones, except on the right flank, where a series of hills and rough terrain made movement difficult.

The I Corps, which landed to the left of XIV Corps, was also able to complete their landings without any engagement by Japanese forces. The units that made up the I Corps included the 172nd Infantry, 1st and 3rd Battalions of the 43rd Division, and the 20th Infantry, along with the 6th Division being held in reserve, and they were able to move an average of three and a half miles in the first day. The 43rd Division of the I Corps had the most difficulty moving out from the beaches at Lingayen, as they had to travel over a series of hills whose compactness provided Japanese troops with natural cover from which to attack the Americans. As the 43rd Division's 169th Infantry moved to the southeast, they were attacked by Japanese mortar and artillery fire. The 169th Infantry was ordered to take Hill 470, one of the largest of the hill structure, but reconnaissance showed that the Japanese had strong defensive positions on that hill.

The 172nd Infantry also encountered artillery and mortar fire as it moved away from its landing location. Although harassed, they were able to quickly move away from the beaches and take their objective of Hill 247. On the next day, January 9th, the 103rd Infantry, was ordered to take Hill 200, a small cluster of hills on which the Japanese had built some defensive positions. Hill 200 was relatively geographically unimportant, but it blocked the most direct path to Route 3, a major north-south highway that led to Manila. The 103rd Infantry encountered sporadic attacks by small groups of Japanese troops that delayed their advance, and they were forced to halt for the night near the town of San Jacinto.

On January 10th, the 6th Division moved four miles inland, and by the time they stopped as night fell, they too had faced skirmishes with Japanese troops. Because of the harassment from Japanese units, these units within I Corps had fallen behind the scheduled pace, and now a gap appeared between XIV Corps and the I Corps. Another potential problem sprang up when the 103rd Infantry pursued and cleared nearby Japanese artillery pieces. This was an important task that neutralized their shelling of American troops in the area, but it opened another gap when the 103rd Infantry lost contact with the 6th Division on its right and the 169th Infantry, which was positioned to the left.

Also on the 10th, the 169th Infantry continued their attempt to take Hill 470, where they faced heavy resistance from Japanese units stationed there. The 169th battled their way forward and took the hill by the afternoon, and they were then ordered to take another area designated Hill 318, where they were pinned down by mortar and artillery fire. The 169th Infantry spent the rest of January 10th and January 11th dealing with the Japanese company that had dug in at Hill 318.

Another unit that was having problems advancing was the 172nd Infantry, also positioned on the left of the I Corps. Like the 169th, the 172nd had to face entrenched Japanese positions on hills that gave them the high ground on which to see American movements and position their artillery and mortars. While the Japanese soldiers did not directly engage the 172nd, they did target them with heavy shelling that made it difficult for the unit to progress. In fact, the 172nd Infantry was halted by Japanese shelling and had to be relieved by members of the Sixth Army Reserve on January 11th.

At MacArthur's headquarters, army commanders decided to commit the bulk of the Sixth Army Reserve to the I Corps, and to place them on the left flank, the only zone in which American troops were facing strong resistance from the Japanese. MacArthur came to believe that the Japanese had decided not to contest the beach landings and had withdrawn into the interior in an attempt to lure the Americans into a false sense of security and to overextend them, which would allow for a counterattack by Japanese units. He felt that on the left of I Corps, his troops had made contact with the forward Japanese defensive lines, and that they would have to be careful in advancing from this point on.

As MacArthur focused his attention on the left, he sent reconnaissance missions and made contact with Filipino guerrillas who provided information on Japanese troop movements. These sources painted a picture of the Japanese holding positions to the north and east of the I Corps landing sites, and the engagements that had occurred on January 10th and 11th were designed to slow the American drive to give Japanese forces from elsewhere on the island time to gather and prepare for a counterattack.

The Japanese 14th Area Army, under the command of General Tomoyuki Yamashita, was aware of the imminent American invasion, and that it would occur through Lingayen Gulf, but the Japanese did not expect it to occur as soon as it did. Japanese commanders had originally planned to make a decisive stand at Luzon, but when the Americans invaded Leyte, they decided to commit to a major engagement there. Leyte was a complete disaster for the Japanese, and the significant losses they faced there directly impacted their ability to defend Luzon later on in the war. Three divisions were diverted from Leyte in late fall of 1944 to aid in the defense of Luzon, but Allied air and naval attacks sunk transports that cost the Japanese nearly a third of their reinforcements and a large quantity of supplies. Yamashita had been planning to use his reinforcements to mount a counterattack shortly after the Americans landed, but with the losses that these divisions faced in transport to Luzon, he decided instead on drawing up defensive lines and holding out for as long as possible.

Yamashita

Like the American defense of Luzon in 1941, Yamashita and the 14th Area Army faced shortages of food, ammunition and medical supplies that would greatly impact their ability to hold out. In fact, by mid-November 1944, even before the American landings, food shortages were so dire that many soldiers had their rations cut by one-third. Also mirroring the American defense of Luzon, Yamashita decided against defending Manila and instead moved supplies away from the city for a more decentralized defense of the island. Japanese troop strength was very poor, as divisions were hastily formed from garrison units, as well as sailors stationed on the island and even Japanese civilians. Regular units were also in poor condition and lacked equipment. This would play a heavy role in Yamashita's ability to defend Luzon in the face of the American advance.

Unlike MacArthur in 1941-1942, Yamashita did not plan to withdraw into the Bataan peninsula, which he felt was too compact an area in which to mount a defense with the 275,000 soldiers that were available to him. Instead, he decided to leave the southern portion of the Lingayen Gulf undefended, where the terrain was too flat to mount a serious defense, so he gathered his troops to the north and east, where the hills and mountains that made up that zone would allow him to create strong defensive positions. For this, he created a special force called the Shobu Group, whose 152,000 troops were ordered to hold the hills and mountains in the area.

Yamashita also decided to defend a second area, a mountainous region near Clark Field in the Central Plains. His goal here was to stop Allied forces from being able to use the main airfield in Luzon for as long as possible. The soldiers sent to this area were called the Kembu Group, and numbered roughly 30,000 men, but were composed of a mix of army engineers, airplane ground crews, and antiaircraft units, in addition to experienced soldiers.

Yamashita set up a third major force called the Shimbu Group, which was ordered to defend the mountains to the north and east of Manila. The Shimbu Group was supposed to help facilitate the removal of supplies from Manila, and once this had been accomplished, they were ordered to destroy major roads and bridges surrounding the city. The Shimbu Group consisted of roughly 80,000 men.

A map indicating the defense zones for different Japanese groups on Luzon

The Japanese soldiers who made contact with American troops after the Lingayen landings were members of the Shobu Group, and these soldiers had created a triangular defensive perimeter among the mountains of northern Luzon. Their goal was to hold the roads leading to the Cagayan Valley until the Japanese could move supplies out of the valley. Yamashita deployed reconnaissance units to patrol along the southern shores of the Lingayen Gulf with orders to withdraw if they encountered any resistance, but some units were caught out of position during the Allied landings, and these were the Japanese soldiers who the American I Corps first made contact with.

On January 11th, the I Corps began moving north hoping to capture the junction of Routes 3 and 11, which would secure the left flank and would allow the Sixth Army to begin its drive toward Manila without fear of counterattacks from this area. This important junction was defended by the Japanese 58th IMB, which had taken the high ground and had constructed a number of trenches and tunnels along the area's hills. There were 6,900 soldiers in the 58th IMB, and they also had 15 75 mm guns and 12 artillery pieces to help them in their defense. The American advance troops, composed of the 158th RCT with about 4,500 men, were tasked with making contact with the 58th IMB and would then have the help of nearby planes and ships, which would bombard the Japanese positions before a ground assault.

On January 12th, the 172nd Infantry began an attack on Hill 580, which was a Japanese advanced position located four miles away from the junction. Their first attempt on the hill was unsuccessful, and it would take until the next day before they were able to overcome the Japanese troops defending it. Once Hill 580 was captured, the 172nd continued forward with help from the 43rd Division's 103rd Field Artillery Battalion, and they captured Hill 565 before moving to within two and a half miles of the main Japanese position at the junction of Routes 3 and 11. A second operation involving the 63rd and 158th Infantry Regiments engaged nearby Japanese fortified positions, but problems with their artillery support delayed their movement, and the 63rd Infantry had problems linking up with the 158th Infantry at the designated point near Routes 3 and 11.

On January 14th, the 158th Infantry was surprised by the Japanese 58th IMB, allowing the Japanese to deal heavy damage with their artillery pieces. Japanese troops had also been able to hide from American patrols in the network of caves and tunnels they had dug, and since the Americans had no idea that this Japanese position stood in their way, they inflicted 85 more casualties. The next day, the 158th called in air and naval support, which allowed them to advance about 1,000 yards. At the same time, the 63rd Infantry, positioned to the east of the 158th, was also taking heavy fire from Japanese artillery positions.

By January 15th, American commanders realized that both the 158th and 63rd were facing much stronger Japanese positions than they had originally believed, and therefore General Leonard Wing redirected the 172nd Infantry to flank the Japanese by coming through the town of Rosario and then attacking Japanese artillery positions on the north of Route 3 from behind. He also sent some troops from the 169th Infantry to bolster these forces. However, even with the new troops moving into the area, Allied forces were unable to dislodge the Japanese from their strong defensive positions among the hills near the Route 3 and 11 junction, and a stalemate developed that halted all progress along the 43rd Division's left.

Along the right, the 103rd and 169th Infantry Regiments were driving eastward. By January 13th, they had reached the Japanese 23rd Division's outer defense perimeter, and they began operations to take two major points along this outer perimeter: Hill 319 and Hill 355. The 169th Infantry attacked the Japanese 64th Infantry, whose orders were to hold the western approaches to

Route 3. The 64th Infantry held the high ground on Hill 318, which allowed them to observe all activities by the Allied forces and utilize excellent artillery placement for their defense of the hill. The 169th Infantry was ordered to embark on a frontal assault of Hill 318, which they accomplished at the cost of 70 casualties. From the first few days on Luzon, American commanders realized that the time-consuming nature of assaults on dug-in Japanese hill-top positions meant that a rapid advance onto Route 3 was probably impossible, and so General Wing ordered the 169th Infantry to go around Hill 355 rather than attack it and instead move through the town of Palacpalac.

The 103rd Infantry was ordered to take a Japanese position south of the 169th's position called Hill 200. Hill 200 was another Japanese perimeter position in which they linked a series of hills by building tunnels and caves. As at other similar locations, aerial bombardment did little damage to these positions because Japanese troops could hide in the caves to avoid most bombs. This meant that the 103rd had to painstakingly clear Hill 200, beginning on January 12th. Hill 200 was only manned by 400 Japanese soldiers, but it took about four days to completely take the hill, and by the night of January 16th, the Americans had just concluded mopping up operations when they were attacked by a force of Japanese tanks moving in from the east. The Japanese counterattack was not a large-scale concerted effort to push out against Allied troops but merely consisted of a series of smaller counterattacks that Yamashita allowed his subordinates to engage in. Yamashita wanted to avoid the possibility of losing a large number of soldiers in one engagement, but he also wanted to delay the Allied advance.

In this series of counterattacks, the Japanese 71st Infantry attacked the rear of the Allied 172nd and 169th Infantry Regiments, while the Japanese 72nd Infantry attacked the rear of the Allied 169th and 103rd Infantry Regiments. As this was occurring, the 23rd Division sent a tank-infantry force to stop the advance of the Allied 103rd Infantry. Although the Japanese 71st and 72nd were able to get to the rear of the Allied positions, they were quickly pushed back.

At Palacpalac, 200 Japanese soldiers came into contact with the 1st Battalion of the 169th Infantry during the night of January 16th. Both groups were surprised by the attack, as the Japanese did not expect to see American soldiers at that location. The ensuing engagement lasted until the night of the 17th, and the 169th suffered 30 casualties in the fighting. The largest of the series of counterattacks occurred with the Shigemi Detachment attacking the 3rd Battalion of the 103rd Infantry. During nighttime on January 16th, Japanese tanks and infantry attacked an American position near the town of Potpot, and two Japanese tanks broke through the perimeter while a third was destroyed by antitank fire. The accompanying Japanese infantry then engaged in a two-hour battle with American soldiers before finally withdrawing. The two tanks that had broken through the line later returned in the early morning hours of January 17th, where they were engaged by American troops and destroyed. In this battle, the Americans suffered 12 casualties and lost one 37 mm antitank gun, a jeep, a scout car, and a tank. The Japanese lost 11 tanks in the engagement, as well as 50 soldiers killed.

By sunrise on January 17th, the Japanese counterattacks had ended and American commanders began reinforcing their forward positions (the 169th and 103rd Infantry Regiments). On the 17th, American forces held a 25 mile wide front that included some important Japanese perimeter defense positions, but even with these gains, the 43rd Division still had important work to do in its sector of the front. They needed to take the junction connecting Routes 3 and 11, and then they needed to push through to the southern portion of Route 3, which was an important road for Japanese movements of supplies and troops. Making things more difficult, as of January 17th, the 43rd Division had seen the bulk of fighting against the Japanese and had suffered roughly 800 casualties up to that point.

The 43rd Division, along with its reinforcements from the 158th and 63rd Infantry Regiments, began moving toward the Route 3 and 11 junction, which was being defended by the Japanese 58th IMB and 23rd Division, which held territory south of the junction. Japanese forces observed as American troops began moving toward their positions and did not engage as the Americans took control of the junction; instead, they allowed American forces to continue moving south of the junction to a defensive complex called Hill 35-Mt. Alava, which they had heavily fortified. The American 169th Infantry, meanwhile, probed the area for new approaches to Hill 355 and Mt. Alava while one battalion was posted near Hill 355 in order to keep Japanese units from counterattacking from that position.

The 169th Infantry spent January 17th and 18th preparing to attack Mt. Alava from the east and southeast. On the 18th the 2nd Battalion scouted new approaches to the Japanese position before moving past the town of Sison by midday, but in the late afternoon, Japanese forces began firing mortars and artillery at the 169th, pinning the American troops down near the town. On the 19th, some units of the Japanese 64th Infantry began withdrawing to Mt. Alava to attack the 169th Infantry's 2nd Battalion from the southwest, and by midday on the 19th, Japanese artillery and ground troops forced American troops to withdraw in the face of heavy fire. Since the Americans had to withdraw on flat land with no protection, they faced casualties of nearly half their troop strength (350 combat-ready men out of an initial force of 1,000), but they were eventually able to link up with the 716th Tank Battalion near Route 3, which forced the Japanese to call off their pursuit. The Japanese 64th Infantry at Mt. Alava also took heavy losses in the engagement, as they had compromised their defensive positions in the attack and roughly 400 of their men had been killed in the process of forcing an American retreat. Mt. Alava was now in a precarious position, and when the Americans launched an attack on Japanese defenses there on January 20th, they were able to overcome the small force still stationed there, taking the crest of the mountain by late afternoon and finishing up operations by the 21st.

Having taken one of the key points in the area, American forces now began preparations to take Hill 355, which they had initially isolated and bypassed. During January 22nd and 23rd, American troops engaged in a series of assaults on the hill against dogged resistance from Japanese soldiers, but by late on the 24th, American troops had finally taken most of Hill 355, killing 500 Japanese soldiers from the 64th Infantry in the process. Mopping up operations continued until January 28th as American units continued to engage the last remaining clusters of Japanese troops on Hill 355, killing 150 and capturing an assortment of artillery and antitank guns. By January 29th, after having wiped out Japanese troops at both Hill 355 and Mt. Alava, the 169th Infantry returned to join up with the other American forces in the area.

As the 169th Infantry was engaging Japanese troops on Mt. Alava and Hill 355, the 103rd Infantry began operations nearby at Pozorrubio. The 103rd began by attacking Hill 600, an elevated area between Pozorrubio and the Routes 3 and 11 junction. The 103rd attacked through frontal assaults on the Japanese positions, gaining some ground on the hill, but they were unable to overcome Japanese defenses. On January 22nd, after the attack had been ongoing for a few days, a group of officers was meeting at a forward area on Hill 600 when they were hit by Japanese artillery fire. The unit lost four company commanders and 2 other officers, as well as 7 enlisted men, with 33 other soldiers injured in the attack. This forced the 103rd Infantry to retreat from their positions on Hill 600, and American strategists decided to regroup and plan a new strategy against Hill 600 and other nearby hills.

General Wing began by deploying the 103rd Infantry to attack Hill 600 from the northwest before moving on to Hill 800. The 169th Infantry moved up to the north of the 103rd, where they would take Question Mark Hill, located near Hill 800. Finally, the 63rd Infantry, which had previously been held back as I Corps reserves, was deployed to take Benchmark Hill, located northwest of Question Mark Hill. The operation began on January 25th and continued until January 27th as American troops engaged in a series of frontal assaults on Japanese positions. The 3rd Battalion, 63rd Infantry attacked from the west side of Benchmark Hill and were able to secure it after taking 36 casualties. They then joined the rest of the 63rd Infantry to clear Hill 1500.

The 169th Infantry attacked Question Mark Hill and were able to take most of the hill, but they could not dislodge the Japanese soldiers fighting on the eastern side of the hill. On the 27th, they changed tactics and brought artillery and bombers to attack the remaining Japanese troops on that hill. The 103rd Infantry moved against Japanese positions on Hill 700 and Hill 600 on January 25th, but they were pushed back by intense Japanese fire against their attacks. Late in the afternoon, members of the 103rd found an undefended area connecting the two hills, and they were able to use this area to launch renewed attacks that surprised the Japanese defenders, allowing the Americans to take both hills.

As I Corps was pushing forward, XIV Corps was moving through the Central Plains, where up to January 18th they had suffered few casualties. General Oscar Griswold, XIV Corps commander planned to push his troops forward in a series of controlled advances to make sure they kept their supply line secured and did not outrun I Corps. Their continued lack of engagement with Japanese forces meant that the XIV Corps moved quickly through January 21st until its forward elements created a perimeter line south of the towns of Victoria and Tarlac. Tarlac especially had been an important railroad junction for the Japanese, who had stored a large quantity of supplies there, and Allied bombers had hit Tarlac heavily in the buildup to the landings, so when the forward units of the XIV Corps arrived, the Japanese garrison had withdrawn into the interior of Luzon and the town itself was badly damaged.

Griswold

Encountering no resistance from Japanese troops, the XIV Corps advanced past the Victoria-Tarlac line, and with the speed at which they were advancing, General Griswold was instructed to take Clark Air Field. Even though his troops had not faced significant Japanese opposition, Griswold was worried about the speed with which the XIV Corps was advancing. At one level, he believed he was stretching his supply lines thin, which would be a big problem if his troops later faced Japanese counterattacks, and he was also concerned that a gap had opened between the XIV Corps and the I Corps, which meant his left flank was exposed between the towns of Cuyapo and La Paz. Griswold had received vague reports of Japanese troops movements near Cabanatuan, 15 miles east of La Paz, and American patrols in the following days came into contact with Japanese troops at Moncada and La Paz. During the night of January 21-22, a platoon of Japanese infantry, in concert with one tank, attacked the 148th Infantry's perimeter one mile west of La Paz. The Japanese withdrew after destroying a bridge in the area.

American commanders decided to shore up the area between I Corps and XIV Corps by having the 37th Division and 40th Division move into the XIV Corps' left, where they would also float into the I Corps sector, thus filling the gap between the two forces. During the evening of January 22nd, the advanced elements of the 160th Infantry, along with the 40th Reconnaissance Troop, reached Capas, where they nearly came upon the Japanese garrison stationed there. The Japanese just managed to evade an attack, hurriedly escaping while leaving supplies behind. The next day, on the 40th Reconnaissance's left, the 108th Infantry came across some Japanese soldiers who had not retreated in time from the towns surrounding Capas and engaged them. On the right, the bulk of the 160th Infantry advanced unopposed to take Bamban Airfield, while one battalion of the 160th was tasked with securing the town of Bamban, where they fought with Japanese soldiers defending the town. It took them most of the day to secure the town, but once this was accomplished, they rejoined with the rest of the 160th and moved toward a network of ridges to the west of the town, where they were engaged by Japanese positions utilizing small arms fire and mortars.

This strong Japanese position surprised American commanders, who believed that the main Japanese defense of the area would be centered on Clark Field. After halting and gathering his forces, General Griswold had the 160th Infantry engage the Japanese defenses while the 40th Division probed for Japanese positions to the west and southwest, the direction of Clark Field. He also kept the 37th Division and 129th RCT in reserve to help in the push forward if needed. The problem Griswold faced in confronting Japanese defenses was that the Americans had little information about Japanese troops strength in this area. War planners estimated that there were between 4,000 and 8,000 Japanese soldiers around Clark Field, and American intelligence believed most of these troops were members of the Air Force, meaning only a few soldiers would be experienced in ground combat. American military officials therefore believed that there would only be weak resistance to the American advance at Clark Field.

In actuality, the Japanese stationed the Kembu Group at Clark Field, which was composed of 15,000 men from the Army and Navy. Of these 15,000 men, roughly 8,500 were experienced ground combat soldiers split into four units defending the area surrounding Clark Field, and the Japanese defenses protected not only Clark Field but also the route south toward Manila. The American 40th Division, which probed Japanese defenses to the west and southwest, made contact with enemy positions on January 23rd and then began an attack against them, but American soldiers encountered problems with the landscape as they had to climb hills devoid of any kind of protection while facing machine gun and mortar fire. The unit attacking what was called Hill 1800 was able to overcome Japanese defenses, but on the next hill, Hill 500, American soldiers were unable make any progress up the slope against intense Japanese fire.

Even with a detachment of the 40th Division being stopped at Hill 500, American commanders still believed that they were encountering a small defensive force rather than the Kembu Group's defensive perimeter, so they believed American forces could quickly overcome the defenses and take Clark Field. On January 25th, the 160th Infantry attacked Hill 636, overcoming one defensive position before meeting heavy resistance halfway up the hill. To the north, other members of the

160th attacked other hills in the area, first taking Hill E before attacking Japanese defenses on Hill G. Even though Japanese defenses were much heavier than the Americans had planned for, their attacks took a heavy toll on the Japanese center and the 160th Infantry was threatening to outflank Japanese positions on their right. While the Japanese expected their defenses to hold for at least a week, they were already in danger of being overrun in the first few days of fighting.

Griswold next ordered the 160th and 108th Infantry Regiments to move toward the south and attack Hill 636, which blocked the path to Clark Field. Once they overcame defenses at Hill 636, they could secure Clark Field and then move toward nearby Fort Stotsenburg. As was the case in nearly all American attacks on Japanese hilltop defensive positions, Japanese troops fired machine gun, artillery, and mortar rounds at American soldiers, pinning them down and forcing them to call for mortar and artillery support. American fire then allowed the ground troops to move forward a bit at a time until they could take a Japanese machine gun or artillery position before having to repeat the process. This meant that the process of overcoming Japanese defenses was painstaking and slow, with each American battalion involved in the fighting losing an average of 20 casualties per day. At the same time, while Japanese soldiers slowly wore down American units, they were unable to halt the slow and steady gains that American troops made day after day.

On January 26th, the 160th Infantry made a big push on the Japanese right, taking Hill 636 and Hill 600 against soldiers who were unable to hold their positions and had to retreat in the face of the American attack. Meanwhile, the 108th Infantry attacked closer to the center, where Japanese defenses held and stalled their progress. By this time, American commanders had realized they were up against strong Japanese defenses and scrapped their plans for a quick victory at Clark Field. Even though their progress was slowed by the stronger Japanese defenses, as of January 27th, they had dealt damage to Japanese positions and had also captured major transportation points at the Manila Railroad and Route 3 near the town of Bamban. Japanese forces were also suffering heavy losses, with the Takayama Detachment of the Kembu Group alone losing nearly 1,000 men killed in the fighting up to this point.

On January 28th, the 40th Division began a new attack against the Kembu Group's positions, with the 129th Infantry coming in from the west with support from the 754th Tank Battalion. To the north, the 160th Infantry gained quite a bit of territory near Hill 620 before getting pinned down by gunfire and artillery. They were later hit by a counterattack that pushed them backward. On the 29th, the 160th Infantry regrouped and broke through the center of the Takaya Detachment's position.

The 129th Infantry also saw major action when they were ordered to take a Japanese hill-position called Top of the World. This location was a strongly defended, 1,000 foot high hill that was the major objective in the area. The 1st Battalion, 129th Infantry began the attack on the morning of January 31st, where they were quickly pinned down by enemy fire, but the 1st

Battalion was ultimately able to make some headway during the afternoon, and by nightfall, they had gained a precarious foothold halfway up the hill. On February 1st, more units of the 129th climbed the hill, and after fierce fighting, they were able to take the crest by midday.

The result of these engagements on the right led to huge losses for the Kembu Group. American troops had penetrated areas along the flanks and center of their position and had also effectively destroyed the armored units that were attached to the group. Over 2,500 Japanese soldiers had been killed or injured, and a further 750 casualties had occurred among reinforcements that had been sent to aid the Kembu Group. By early February, the XIV Corps had taken Clark Field and had secured critical areas of Route 3 and the Manila Railroad. This meant that while the Kembu Group was still a threat, they had been sufficiently weakened that the Americans could begin to turn their attention toward Manila.

Pictures of abandoned Japanese planes at Clark Field

Advancing to Manila

At San Jose, roughly 100 miles north of Manila, along with the towns of Lupao and Munoz, Japanese commanders placed the 10th and 105th Divisions, along with the 2nd Tank Division. These units were reinforced by the 7th and 10th Tank regiments and the 2nd Mobile Infantry. These would be the troops tasked with opposing the I Corps as it moved south. For the I Corps, their plan of attack against San Jose involved a pincer maneuver, with an attack from the northeast through Munoz being carried out by the 6th Division while the 25th Division would attack from the southeast through Lupao.

The drive toward San Jose began on February 1st, and the I Corps would have to cross flat land with little cover against a defense that consisted of dug-in Japanese medium tanks, with support from infantry units and machine gun positions. The 3rd Battalion, 20th Infantry led the line, and they were confronted by Japanese tanks and artillery south of Route 99, the road leading into Munoz. On the 2nd, the 1st Battalion, 20th Infantry again was halted by the Japanese defense, while the 2nd Battalion also failed to make much headway against Japanese defenses near Route 5. The 1st Battalion, 35th Infantry advanced close to Lupao before taking artillery, mortar and machine gun fire from Japanese defenses in the town. This forced the 1st Battalion to retreat, and on the next day they resumed the attack but were unable to make gains, and like the 20th Infantry, were unable to take their town.

Because of the slow progress, American commanders decided to bypass both towns, thus sending reinforcements to keep Japanese forces confined within Lupao and Munoz while the main body of troops moved forward toward their objectives. The 35th Infantry, along with the 6th Division, advanced near San Jose, and on February 4th, they were able to take the town almost unopposed. With that, American commanders realized that the Japanese had committed the bulk of their forces to defending the paths leading into San Jose at Munoz and Lupao, and had virtually no remaining troops to defend San Jose proper. The Japanese troops remaining in these towns were increasingly isolated and surrounded by American units, and the Japanese defenders at Munoz attempted to break out on February 7th. They failed to realize that Route 5, their escape path away from town, was in the hands of the Americans, and they were quickly engaged by strong American positions along the road that virtually wiped them out.

At Lupao, the 35th Infantry advanced, pushing Japanese troops further and further back until they too decided to attempt a break out. A group of 11 tanks attempted to break through the 35th Infantry's line, and five of them were able to get away. Their crews left the tanks in the foothills near town and retreated on foot. Japanese infantrymen also retreated away from the town, and by February 8th, American troops held Lupao.

Across the Central Plains, the 40th Division continued fighting the Kembu Group in mid-February, and American units continued to deal with the difficult task of assaulting dug-in Japanese troops. The XIV Corps had taken Clark Field and controlled an important point in the Japanese defenses at Top of the World, but the Kembu Group still had roughly 25,000 soldiers holding strong positions in the foothills near the Bamban River. For General Krueger and the XIV Corps, the task of defeating the Kembu Group would involve coordinated attacks involving air support and artillery fire that would force the Japanese troops into their trenches and caves for protection, which would be followed by American infantry operations.

On February 6th, General Kruger ordered the XIV Corps to re-engage the Kembu Group. The plan of attack involved the 185th and 160th Infantry Regiments attacking the center of the Kembu Group's position, while the 108th moved on the right and the 129th on the left. On February 6th, the 160th Infantry began operations against McSevney Point, a major defensive position for Japanese troops. The 160th was aided by support from tanks, planes, and artillery, which pinned down Japanese troops in their foxholes and caves as American infantry advanced behind them to attack the enemy troops as they emerged from their shelters. It took three days for the 160th to take the summit of McSevney Point, followed by a series of ferocious Japanese night counterattacks. On the morning of February 10th, the 160th realized that the Japanese had withdrawn from the position following their last unsuccessful counterattack.

The loss of McSevney Point convinced the commander of the Kembu Group to withdraw from that portion of the defense perimeter to their last-stand positions, which created a gap in the defensive line that isolated the two wings. The gaps created by this maneuver allowed American units on both flanks to drive the Japanese troops back. On the Japanese right, the Eguchi-Yanagimoto Detachment held out for nearly a week, but by February 12th, they had lost everything except Hill 7. With that detachment defeated at Hill 7 on the afternoon of the 12th, the 108th Infantry had overcome the Japanese right.

On the left, the 185th Infantry was making important gains against the Japanese defenses, while in the center the 160th Infantry had pushed forward into the Japanese's last-stand line. American units continued moving forward in the painstaking task of taking hill after hill, and between February 10 and 12, American troops took three of the last major Japanese hill positions. On February 15th, with continued American advances on the left, right and center, and with heavy casualties among its soldiers, the Kembu Group was effectively destroyed. Isolated units of the Kembu Group still remained, but the XIV Corps now only needed to engage in mop-up operations, and American commanders could fully turn their attention to the drive to Manila. Overall, the XIV Corps lost 285 men killed and 1,180 wounded, while the Kembu Group suffered 12,000 deaths (Smith, p.206)

The rest of XIV Corps had been moving toward Manila since late January. While they were harassed by Japanese units during this time, they were not appreciably slowed in their drive toward the capital, and by early February, American commanders had planned for a pincer maneuver involving the XIV Corps from the north and the 11th Airborne Division moving in from the south. The 11th Airborne landed in southern Luzon on January 31st at Nasugbu, a site that allowed them to isolate Japanese forces in southern Luzon (so they would not be able to reinforce defenses at Manila) and position themselves for the drive north to that city.

After landing, the 11th Airborne's 511th Infantry led the line in moving north to Manila, but they were delayed when they had to fight a series of actions against small Japanese units defending the bridges leading to the capital city. In fact, the major obstacle for the 11th Airborne involved the logistics of their movement, as Japanese destruction (and attempted destruction) of bridges challenged their ability to move men and supplies to their staging points for the attack on Manila. Army engineers had to work quickly, using pontoons and reinforcing roads and undamaged bridges to keep the 11th Airborne moving.

Taking Manila

There were roughly 10,000 Japanese troops stationed at Manila, and they were broken up into three combat groups that defended the north, south, and center of the city. However, aside from breaking their troops up into these groups, the plan for defending the city was not well-conceived, with Japanese officers looking to inflict heavy casualties on American troops and to stop them from controlling Manila for as long as possible. They also planned to demolish infrastructure that could be useful to the Americans, such as the port area, bridges, water supply system and power grid. Japanese troops cannibalized guns from wrecked aircraft and ships, and many of their heavier weapons were 20-mm and 25-mm airplane guns that were modified for use on the ground.

The XIV Corps reached the outskirts of Manila on February 3rd and promptly began operations against the suburb of Santo Tomas, where the 8th Cavalry experienced the first instance of close-quarter city fighting in Manila when they were attacked by Japanese troops hiding in buildings at the intersection of Quezon Boulevard. The Japanese hid among numerous buildings, including Bilibid Prison and Far Eastern University. The 8th Cavalry was able to retreat away from the intersection, and while there was potential for heavy fighting at Santo Tomas, this did not materialize because Japanese troops stationed there were surprised by the American advance and had not expected their arrival for another two weeks. Thus, the Japanese units stationed there retreated following the engagement at Quezon Boulevard and the Americans were able to take control of the suburb.

Along with the 8th Cavalry, the 37th Division made its way into the city from the north, and its 145th Infantry began clearing the Tonto District, which they accomplished on the morning of February 9th. To the left of the Tonto District, the 148th Infantry cleared the Binondo District before moving on to the Santa Cruz District. As this was occurring, Japanese troops in the area blew up the Pasig-Jones and Santa Cruz Bridges, the two western bridges into the city. The Japanese Northern Force also began destroying military stores and installations along the northern entrance to the city, setting off large-scale fires that were intensified by strong winds. These fires lasted until February 6th before they were finally brought under control by American troops and Filipino citizens.

Aside from the fires, the 37th Division and 1st Cavalry Division had little problem clearing the northern suburbs of Japanese forces. In fact, the Northern Force had executed its orders to destroy certain key points and had withdrawn south over the Pasig River, where they destroyed the bridges after they had crossed. American troops killed roughly 1,500 Japanese soldiers in various engagements throughout the northern sector prior to the withdrawal, and this had given the Americans experience in what to expect in the fighting to follow.

On the morning of February 7th, the 37th Division was ordered across the Pasig River, where they would engage the Central Force's 1st Naval Battalion in the western portion of Paco District, and especially Provisor Island. The 37th Division had no problems making their way to Paco District, but upon reaching the Paco Railroad Station, they faced heavy fighting from Japanese troops stationed there, as well as those in the nearby buildings of Concordia College and Paco

School. On the night of February 9th, most of the Japanese troops withdrew from these positions, and when the 148th Infantry stormed the Japanese positions the next day, they faced a much smaller force than expected.

Meanwhile, the 129th Infantry crossed the Pasig on February 8th and then moved west toward Provisor Island. A small force in two boats tried to sneak across the river to the island to take one of the outbuildings and create a landing spot for the invasion of the island, but they were quickly attacked by Japanese troops and were only saved from being wiped out because of mortar support that kept Japanese troops from surrounding them. That night, they were evacuated off the island, but the force had sustained 17 casualties in the aborted mission. The next day, the 129th fired artillery and mortar rounds at the island to soften up defenses for another attempted amphibious landing, this time involving 90 men. Three boats were sunk by machine gun and mortar fire, but the rest were able to make it to the island, where they took the boiler building while mortar and artillery fire pounded the rest of the island. The mortar and artillery fire dealt heavy damage to Japanese positions, and American troops were able to secure the island on February 11th. Their goal in taking the island was to control the power plant located there to provide power for the city, but the Japanese troops had destroyed some of the equipment prior to the American landings, so they were unable to use the power plant.

The 1st Cavalry was ordered across the Pasig River around the same time as the 37th Division, and as it moved to into the Santa Ana District, it encountered little resistance and quickly set up patrols to secure the area. Thus, by February 10th, the XIV Corps had secured two sectors across the Pasig River, and along with the 11th Airborne to the south, they now had the ability to deploy their forces to encircle the city and cut off withdrawal routes for the Japanese soldiers stationed there. The 5th Cavalry moved from the west, taking the strategic area of Nielson Field, while the 8th Cavalry, and later the 12th Cavalry (which relieved the 8th Cavalry), made its way to Manila Bay. Furthermore, the 37th Division made contact with the 11th Airborne coming up from the south, completing the encirclement of Japanese forces in Manila.

The Japanese commander tasked with defending Manila, Admiral Sanji Iwabuchi, had originally planned to defend the city until the end, but as American forces began moving toward the city, Iwabuchi decided that the situation was so dire that he began planning for a withdrawal. First, he moved his headquarters to Fort McKinley, a few miles outside of the city, and then began planning a more general retreat.

As this was occurring, General Yokoyama of the Shimbu Group was planning for a counterattack against American forces near Manila. Yokoyama believed there was only one regiment of American troops near Manila and believed he had an opportunity to cut them off from the main attack force on Luzon. With Iwabuchi away from the city, Yokoyama halted the Manila Naval Defense Force from retreating out of Manila and had them hold their position in Manila pending the outcome of the Shimbu Group's counterattack.

The counterattack would consist of two columns. The northern column would attack across the Markina River, aiming for Novaliches Dam and Route 3 north of the city, while the southern column would also move across the Markina, then through the Balara Water Filters, before establishing contact with the northern wing at Grace Park. The 112th Cavalry, which had replaced the 12th Cavalry, faced the brunt of the northern column's counterattack between February 15th and 18th. After a series of skirmishes in which 300 Japanese soldiers were killed, the counterattack fell apart and the northern column retreated, and the southern column was caught as it was crossing the Marikina River when American artillery units attacked it on February 16th. For the next three days, the 7th and 8th Cavalry fought off their attempts to break through American lines, and when the southern column finally withdrew on the 19th, American troops had killed roughly 650 enemy soldiers. With the failure of the counterattacks, there was no hope of Japanese forces opening a gap in the American circle, and from that point on, the Shimbu Group had no further contact with the Manila Naval Defense Force, which was left on its own to attempt to repel American forces at Manila.

After stopping the Shimbu Group's counterattack, American forces turned their attention back to taking Manila. As the XIV Corps pushed in from the north and west, the 11th Airborne held their lines around Manila and also cut off the Abe Battalion of the Southern Luzon Force at Mabato Point. Between February 18th and 23rd, three infantry battalions, with support from artillery and tanks, attacked the Abe Battalion, killing 750 men while suffering only 60 casualties.

Within Manila, engagements between American and Japanese troops took the form of street fighting, with American troops being forced to slowly push forward and clear buildings and streets one at a time. As this was occurring, American artillery units and bombers took out most of the remaining Japanese mortars and artillery, reducing them to using light weapons, grenades and machine guns against the oncoming Americans.

Filipino citizens running from the fighting in Manila in February 1945

The Allied push against Manila

American troops pushed Japanese forces back block by block, finally leading up to the last stand by Japanese forces at the cluster of governmental buildings known as the Walled City. The Americans resorted to artillery bombardments for several days because American commanders believed Japanese troops had constructed a series of tunnels and bunkers in the Walled City that would be difficult for American infantry to assault without heavy bombardments before the final attack. On February 23rd, the ground assault began with the infantry advancing into the Walled City while being supported by tanks, artillery and mortars. Much of the subsequent fighting occurred between American infantry units and isolated pockets of Japanese troops who had sought cover from the artillery fire.

It took a little more than a day to finish clearing Japanese troops from the Walled City, and by late on the 24th, they had finished operations at the Walled City and nearby Fort Santiago. In total, the battle of Manila cost the XIV Corps 1,000 men killed and 5,500 wounded. The Japanese lost 16,000 men killed in the area around Manila, and the Manila Defense Force itself lost 12,500 men killed, with the rest being members of the Shimbu Group who had engaged

American troops either during the failed counterattack or in skirmishes around periphery of Manila.

In addition to the military casualties, large portions of the city were destroyed by the fighting, and the damage done to Filipino civilians was extensive. The Japanese had fought to the death across Manila, and Admiral Iwabuchi and his men had also presided over the systematic murder and rape of Filipino civilians. MacArthur had refused outright to countenance tactical airstrikes in support of his own troops for fear of killing civilians, which slowed the advance and increased American casualties. While this presented a classic moral-military conundrum, nobody can deny the moral integrity of MacArthur's command, but when the city fell at the end of February, an estimated 100,000 civilians were dead.

American troops in the Walled City on February 27, 1945

An aerial view of the devastated ruins of Manila in May 1945

Mopping Up

As Manila was falling, Japanese commanders on Luzon had a decision to make regarding how to proceed with their defense of that island. Their main remaining goal was to deny the Americans the use of Manila Bay, a port that could be used as a staging area for an assault on the Japanese home islands. They could either deny the use of the bay by holding out at the Bataan peninsula, as the Americans had done in 1941-1942, or they could position themselves in northern Luzon and attempt to hold out there.

After securing Manila, the Sixth Army began moving to engage and destroy the Shobu and Shimbu Groups, the two largest Japanese troop concentrations remaining on Luzon. While the XIV Corps was fighting in Manila, the I Corps had positioned itself along the northern portion of the Central Plains, and after its victory against the Manila Defense Force, both portions of the Sixth Army were now ready for the next part of the operation. However, after the victory at Manila, MacArthur shifted tactics in a way that hampered the Sixth Army's ability to quickly engage and defeat the remaining Japanese soldiers on Luzon. With Japanese defeat at Luzon seemingly assured, MacArthur ordered a garrison force to be established in Manila and also siphoned off troops from Luzon to help retake central and southern Philippine islands that had been bypassed in the initial invasion of the nation.

Given the reduction in troop strength, the attacks against the Shimbu and Shobu Groups would be more difficult than had been originally anticipated. The Shimbu Group consisted of roughly

30,000 soldiers, and they were deployed along a defensive line that was aided by rugged, mountainous terrain. American operations against the Shimbu Group commenced on February 20th, when the 7th Cavalry marched through the Marikina Valley that led up to the Shimbu Group's positions. Behind the 7th Cavalry was the 8th Cavalry, which secured the town of Tagig and then also made its way through the Marikina Valley.

On February 23rd, the 7th Cavalry made contact with the forward elements of the Shimbu Group's defensive line and came under attack near Antipolo. The 7th and 8th Cavalry faced heavy fighting for the next week, during which they were barely able to gain any ground. The fighting was made more difficult by the fact that Japanese soldiers based their defense around a series of caves that were difficult for artillery to hit, forcing American troops to engage each cave and bunker and either kill or drive out the Japanese soldiers stationed within them.

The 6th Division also began marching toward the Shimbu Group's positions on February 22nd. They headed toward the northern section of the Japanese defenses, where they attacked positions located at Mount Pacawagan and Mount Mataba. Under fierce fighting, they were unable to dislodge Japanese soldiers from these locations, and by March 4th, American commanders decided to revise their plans. In their new plans, American forces would concentrate their efforts against the Shimbu Group's left, where they hoped to outflank Japanese positions. If this was successful, American troops could then get around Japanese defenses and attack their most fortified positions from behind.

On March 8th, the 1st Cavalry and 6th Infantry began their attack, while to the south, the 20th Infantry and 1st Infantry cleared what were believed to be the Shimbu Group's main supply route. The 1st Infantry was able to force its way a mile and a half forward, and by March 11, they had created a gap in the Japanese defenses. The 20th Infantry then moved in behind the 1st Infantry before heading to the east to attack a second section of the defense.

The Shimbu Group's commanding officer, General Yokoyama, became concerned about the penetration into his defenses and ordered that section of the perimeter to fall back to its secondary defense lines. He then ordered a counterattack on March 12th that involved a three-pronged assault by seven infantry battalions. Even in the beginning, this counterattack seemed destined to fail as American artillery quickly knocked out communication and command post positions that were crucial to coordinating the elements of the attack. The counterattack then devolved into isolated endeavors by Japanese units, and Yokoyama called it off on March 15th after having suffered losses amounting to two battalions of soldiers.

In the aftermath of the counterattack, American troops put renewed pressure on Japanese defenses. While their progress continued to be slow, American units advanced at four points along the defense perimeter, and they also drove a deep wedge along the Japanese left. American forces were unable to make further gains in the next few days, but General Yokoyama, believing that his situation was precarious, decided to pull his units on the left back across the Bosoboso

River. However, due to communication problems along the line, these units did not begin their retreat until March 22nd, and on that day, an attack by American 6th and 43rd Division units coincided with the retreat. The Americans therefore encountered little resistance as they pushed forward and gained important positions at Mounts Baytangan, Yabang, and Caymayuman.

With the withdrawal and loss on their left, Japanese forces in that area were able, in the short-term, to remain in the field, but they now faced the possibility of being flanked and encircled, thus destabilizing the entire Japanese defense perimeter. As this was occurring, a renewed push against the center of the Japanese line in late March further weakened their position. Although fighting would be slow as American troops advanced, the defense had been compromised, and after taking Ipo Dam, the center of the Japanese line had collapsed. Thanks to the strength of the Japanese defense along hill and mountain positions, coupled with their use of caves, trenches and tunnels, continued fighting would occur through late May, but the Shimbu Group had lost cohesiveness, and their ability to mount a serious threat to American troops had been negated. From this point forward, American units engaged in mopping up operations that involved slowly moving forward and killing or driving out isolated groups of Japanese soldiers who remained in the field.

The Shobu Group was the second major Japanese force remaining in the field in Luzon, and unlike the Shimbu Group, they had planned to withdraw into northern Luzon, where they would attempt to hold out for as long as possible against American forces. The Shobu Group deployed its units to create a triangle, with its points at Baguio, Bontoc, and Bambang, and with a fourth sector in the Cagayan Valley which supplied Japanese forces. The 32nd Division was ordered to attack the Shobu Group, and they began moving out in early February where they reached the town of Santa Maria and then continued further on toward the entrances of the Arboredo and Agno River Valleys. For the next week, the 32nd Division engaged Japanese a series of outpost defenses before finally coming across the main Japanese defensive line in the area on the Villa Verde Trail.

Like the 32nd Division, the 25th Division also began operations in northern Luzon in early February. During reconnaissance operations, the 25th Division found that Japanese troops had concentrated in their area, meaning that they had positioned troops to defend the approaches to their defensive triangle from this direction as well. Aerial reconnaissance during this period also discovered the Baguio-Aritao supply road, which connected Japanese troops at Bagui and Bambang. American commanders realized that if they could take the supply road, they would be able to isolate Japanese troops at the two locations, so they decided to target the supply road in their attacks against the Shobu Group.

Aside from the two American divisions, Filipino guerrilla units (known as the USAFIP) also operated in tandem with the Americans in northern Luzon. Guerrilla units were tasked with reconnaissance operations and attacking Japanese patrols. Over time, their operations expanded to the point that Filipino guerrillas comprised roughly one division of combat troops against the Shobu Group.

American commanders chose to begin their efforts in northern Luzon against Bambang. The 25th and 32nd Divisions would be involved in these efforts, while the 44th Division would occupy Japanese forces at Baguio to keep them from reinforcing Bambang.

During late February and early March, the 33rd Division probed Japanese defenses. On the east side, 33rd Division troops were able to take Japanese positions in a ridged area that was referred to as the Hill 600-1500 line. Elsewhere, American troops had problems gaining traction against entrenched defenses, such as along Route 11, where the 71st Infantry was only able to get within a mile and a half of its stated objective of an area called Camp 2.

Meanwhile, the 33rd Division commander, Major General Percy Clarkson, was upset that his forces were only being used to hold Japanese forces in place at Baguio during this initial phase of the mission. When he realized that Japanese forces were engaging in a withdrawal all along its line, he argued that he should be allowed to push his troops forward to take a more forward position. 33rd Division reconnaissance units moved forward beginning on March 7th, and they were surprised to find almost no resistance along the western portion of the Japanese defenses, which allowed them to take Aringay and Caba. Other units pushed Japanese troops back from the hills at the entrance to the Tuba Trail. The seeming lack of defenses in this area convinced Clarkson to focus on this area, and by mid-March, he had made plans to utilize both regular troops and guerrilla units to make a push on Baguio. American forces first took the port town of San Fernando against a 3,000 man defense force, and this cleared the way along Route 9 for the drive on Baguio.

Aside from losing territory leading up to Baguio, Japanese forces had the added problems of supply difficulties, with American air strikes on supply roads restricting the supplies that made it to Japanese troops. Before the end of March, front-line troops were receiving less than a quarter of their daily rations, and starvation and diet-related diseases were taking its toll on Japanese troop-strength. Yamashita, realizing the precarious position that his forces at Baguio were in, ordered Japanese civilians and governmental officials to evacuate the city. For his soldiers, however, he ordered them to remain to defend the city for as long as possible.

In early April, American forces made their push for Baguio. The 129th Infantry broke through at Sablan in a battle involving artillery and medium tanks. The 148th Infantry then secured Route 9 through the town of Calot, and other American units secured supply depots along the area that Japanese troops were retreating from. Finally, between April 11th and 15th, American artillery, airplanes, and tank units targeted and destroyed nearly all artillery pieces that Japanese forces in the area had at their disposal. In order to try to shore up his position, General Sato, commander of Japanese troops at Baguio, sent two infantry companies to a barrio two miles southeast of Calot, but before they arrived, American troops had passed that point and had taken the town of

Yagyagan. This episode highlighted the dysfunction that Japanese commanders were experiencing by this point.

Beyond Yagyagan, Japanese forces had created a defensive position at the Irisan gorge, an area with defensible high ground positions that were well positioned to fire down into Route 9, which passed through the gorge. Elements of the 148th Infantry began the assault by engaging in a frontal attack on the Japanese positions, while other units made an enveloping maneuver from the sides. After heavy fighting, the 148th was able to secure the area. American units continued to push forward, where they overcame a series of hill positions leading into Baguio, and by April 22nd, they were ready to make their final push into the town.

On April 22nd, two battalions from the 130th Infantry moved in from the west, while a battalion from the 75th Infantry came in from the south. These units met heavy resistance from Japanese troops, but elsewhere the 123rd Infantry was able to make important gains that triggered a withdrawal by some sections of the defense. The speed of the American advance forced a general Japanese withdrawal at this location as well, and by April 24th, the 33rd Division held most of Baguio. While losing this important location was a blow to the Japanese, they were able to get 10,000 troops out ahead of the American advance, which they could subsequently use to reinforce other sections of the their defensive perimeter.

The 25th and 32nd Divisions on the Bambang front they quickly made contact with Japanese troops and then began assessing plans for an assault on Bambang. In late February, the 126th Infantry of the 32nd Division attacked two Japanese delaying positions, while American patrols in the nearby Agno Valley found no sign of Japanese troops. To the west. in the Arboredo Valley, American units found the opposite: Japanese forces had set up strong outposts here to stop an advance. Units attacking from three directions compressed the defense line, and after heavy fighting accompanied by artillery support, elements of the 127th Infantry were able to break through the outpost line on February 24th. As Japanese troops from the 10th Reconnaissance division (which had been manning the outpost) retreated, they were pursued by the 127th, which continued forcing contact with the retreating troops and harassing them. Finally, as the 10th Reconnaissance withdrew to the Salacsac Pass area, they were reinforced by two companies of infantry and one under-strength artillery battalion. As the Japanese units were being reinforced, the 127th Infantry was joined by the 2nd Tank Battalion to increase their troop-strength in that vicinity.

Since Salacsac Pass was a strong defensive position, it seemed as though the opposing forces were headed toward a stalemate, and much of the month of March involved American attempts to dislodge Japanese troops from their high-ground positions, while Japanese troops made use of their terrain advantage to repulse American attacks. The 10th Reconnaissance and their reinforcements also were able to fall back to secondary and tertiary defense positions at Salacsac Pass, giving them an increased ability to delay and harass the American advance. In fact, the

128th Infantry and 2nd Tank Battalion had not yet broken through by April 5th, and between the 5th and 17th, American soldiers at Salacsac Pass were suffering large numbers of casualties.

After more reinforcements, American troops spent the month of April attacking a series of Japanese hill positions. Japanese soldiers delayed the push as long as possible, and in late April they sent a counterattack that failed to allow them to gain territory against the Americans. American forces finally began to make headway in early May as they engaged in an enveloping movement involving battalions from the 127th and 128th Infantry as the 126th Infantry engaged troops in adjacent areas. The attack was successful and occurred so quickly that American forces reached the Villa Verde Trail.

It was at this point that the 32nd Division was close to linking up with the 25th Division near Santa Fe. With that, the last obstacle for American forces before Bambang was Balete Pass, which the 27th Infantry began attacking on April 27th. Aiding the 27th Infantry was the 35th Infantry, and these two units fought their way up Kapintalan Ridge while the 161st Infantry came in from the west to begin an enveloping movement against Japanese positions. This movement surprised the Japanese troops, and by May 4th, the Americans had captured Balete Pass and had moved beyond it. Helping the troops engaged on the Bambang Front was that at this point, Baguio had been secured, and reinforcements could now help bolster the American troop-strength.

The last major action along the Bambang Front occurred at Santa Fe. From May 14-22, the 27th Infantry cleared enemy troops around Kanami Ridge while the 161th Infantry took a strong enemy position at Mount Haruna. Continued fighting occurred along the Bambang Front, but this mainly took the form of invading pockets of Japanese forces. By May 29th, American units were in the process of surrounding Japanese troops at Bambang when Yamashita sent orders for a withdrawal from that location. The fighting had been extremely costly for both sides, as the 2nd Tank Division and 10th Division suffered casualties amounting to 13,500 men, while roughly two-thirds of the 20,750 soldiers at the Bambang Front were killed. (Smith, p.538)

The withdrawal at Bambang, coupled with the losses at Baguio, forced General Yamashita to order a general withdrawal of the Shobu Group to their last-stand positions, known to American commanders as the Kiangan Pocket, on June 15th. At the Kiangan Pocket, the American 6th Division moved up Route 4 before quickly breaking through a portion of the perimeter that was being manned by the Japanese 105th Division. As this was occurring, UFAIP guerrillas attacked from the direction of the Cagayan Valley. The situation for Japanese troops was one of extreme disorganization. Some troops were still trying to make their way to the last-stand position, while others were trapped by American forces.

General Krueger took advantage of the confusion among Japanese units by pressing his advantage, looking to move his forces quickly forward with the 37th Division moving up Route 5 through Santa Fe and Bagabag while the 6th Division would move in a more northerly direction through Route 4. This movement would surround and restrict the retreating Japanese troops. Between June 1st and 4th, Japanese antitank units tried to slow the American pursuit, but although they engaged the 775th Tank Battalion which was reinforcing the 129th Infantry, they were unable to do enough damage to delay their progress. Within the next few days American troops secured the towns of Aritao, Bayombong, and Bagabag.

The American advance continued through mid-June, where they reached the Cagayan Valley. Fighting within the valley occurred when the American 37th Division engaged with Japanese soldiers from the Yuguchi Detachment, who were retreating up Route 5. The 37th Division killed 600 Japanese soldiers and captured another 285 (Smith, p.569). By this time, Krueger believed that Japanese forces were on the verge of defeat, so he sent additional troops in the form of the 11th Infantry of the USAFIP.

By the end of June, Japanese troops, who had been harried and harassed for the majority of their retreat, had reached their final positions. American units had penetrated into northern Luzon to the point that there were two separate elements of the Shobu Group. One, comprised of 13,000 soldiers, was located at Sierra Madre. Meanwhile, the main body of 52,000 troops was positioned at the Japanese last-stand area. Although in raw numbers it seemed that Japanese troops still had the ability to threaten American forces, most of these soldiers were ill-equipped and were suffering from starvation and disease. As it turned out, a final confrontation in northern Luzon never occurred. Instead, American troops focused on containing Japanese forces, and the remaining Shobu Group units actually stayed in the field until the end of the war, at which point they finally surrendered. Mopping up operations also occurred on islands in the central and southern Philippines, but with the capture of Luzon, American forces were now prepared to begin building the military infrastructure for bombing missions and a possible invasion of the Japanese home islands.

Iwo Jima

The Strategic Importance of Iwo Jima

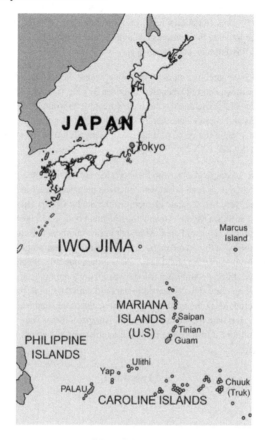

Map of the region

Iwo Jima is more officially known as "Sulfur Island," and it lies in a chain of volcanic islands south of the Ogasawara Islands. In total, the area is known as the Ogasawara Archipelago or the Bonin Islands, and it was critically important because Iwo Jima is situated approximately 650 nautical miles south of Tokyo. For U.S. naval and air forces, the island had tremendous strategic importance as an air base for fighter escorts in support of long-range bombers hitting the mainland, and as an emergency landing strip for B-29s returning from raids. The B-29 was essential to movement toward and eventual victory over the Empire. The B-29 "Superfortress," built by Boeing, possessed superior technology such as remote control machine gun turrets and pressurized cabins for high altitude work, and two of them would eventually carry the atomic bombs to the Japanese mainland. Of equal importance were the fighter escorts, such as the P-51 Mustangs, though these single seat fighters saw less action in the Pacific than they had in Europe. In the entire war, they shot down almost 5,000 enemy aircraft.

The B-29 "Superfortress"

P-51 Mustangs

These raids fell under the operative name of "Operation Scavenger," and Iwo Jima would not only hasten "Operation Downfall" (the ultimate destruction of the Japanese homeland), but would figure into logistics for delivery of the two atomic bombs ultimately dropped on the Japanese cities of Hiroshima and Nagasaki in the following months. Iwo Jima allowed blockades from both the sea and air, and from its location, aerial attacks could be conducted on enemy air and naval forces. In addition, Japanese kamikaze pilots, who had proven themselves an incredibly deadly threat to the American navy, would have to operate out of Okinawa or Kyushu if Iwo Jima was lost to them.

Japanese military commanders were fully aware that if Iwo Jima was lost, invasions of the mainland would soon follow, and even though this small patch of land in the sea covered an area of only 8 square miles, the Japanese had other reasons for defending it so passionately. It is commonly thought that the Japanese leadership did not want the Empire to be seen as an "easy" enemy, and furthermore, the island sat on the flight path of American B-29 bombing raids. If the Americans were able to use Iwo Jima, the distance and fuel requirements would be shortened, not to mention that emergency landings would require a much shorter distance. Japan needed the island airfields for its own planes, which were still conducting almost daily attacks on B-29s in the Marianas to the southeast, and Japanese planes had succeeded in destroying a healthy number of B-29s on the ground. Finally, the Japanese had an important radar station on the island that could signal ahead with news of American raids two hours in advance.

Initial raids against Iwo Jima were carried out from aircraft carriers that would distinguish themselves in the overall move toward Japan itself, commencing in June 1944 and comprised chiefly of B-24 bombers from the 7th Air Force in the Marianas. The island would be bombarded for over 70 days ahead of the actual amphibious invasion of Iwo Jima, which would not occur until over half a year after the first bombardment. The number of days spent bombarding the island was the most in the Pacific during the war.

When the actual invasion did commence, the offensive was on an epic scale. Over 800 warships, including six battleships, were involved, and after a lengthy bombardment during which 6,000 tons of shells and bombs were launched against the island by noon of the first day, an extra 10 days of naval bombardment was requested by Marines involved in the projected landing. As the U.S. Navy's website put it, "Prior to the invasion, the 8-square mile island would suffer the longest, most intensive shelling of any Pacific island during the war."[7]

The USS *New York* bombarding Iwo Jima on February 16, 1945

However, due to unfavorable weather conditions and the heavy aerial bombardment already accomplished, the Marines were granted only three extra days of bombardment, forcing them to

---

[7] Battle for Iwo Jima, 1945, The Navy Department Library – http://www.history.navy.mil/library/online/battleofiwojima.htm

prepare for the set date of February 19 as landing day. Unfortunately, the prolonged bombardment, although certainly softening the Japanese positions to some degree, did not have the far-reaching effects that the Americans expected or hoped for, given the use of such heavy ordnance. In fact, many Marines mistakenly believed that the bulk of Japanese soldiers on the island had been killed by the bombardment. In reality, once the landings were complete, there would be about 100,000 men fighting within an area 1/3 the size of Manhattan. While American planners optimistically thought Iwo Jima could be taken in a week, the island would be one of the most densely populated spots on the planet for 36 days.

A strategy briefing before the invasion of Iwo Jima

The Japanese Defense of Iwo Jima

In 1945, the Allies would quickly understand and fear just how ferociously the Japanese were willing to fight, and much of that was a result of the Battle of Iwo Jima. In fact, the Japanese defending the island had no illusions about victory and did not even consider it a realistic option. They merely hoped to bloody the enemy so badly that the Allies would reconsider invading Japan. As Japanese military officers reported after the war:

> "In the light of the above situation, seeing that it was impossible to conduct our air, sea, and ground operations on Iwo Island [Jima] toward ultimate victory, it was decided that to gain time necessary for the preparation of the Homeland defense,

our forces should rely solely upon the established defensive equipment in that area, checking the enemy by delaying tactics. Even the suicidal attacks by small groups of our Army and Navy airplanes, the surprise attacks by our submarines, and the actions of parachute units, although effective, could be regarded only as a strategical ruse on our part. It was a most depressing thought that we had no available means left for the exploitation of the strategical opportunities which might from time to time occur in the course of these operations."

In command of Japanese forces on the island was General Tadamichi Kuribayashi, and he arranged a defensive scheme for Iwo Jima that flew in the face of all previous Japanese viewpoints on defense, particularly island defense. While the previous commander, General Hideyoshi Obata, had arranged artillery close to the beach and had positioned infantry to defend an island from the very water's edge, Kuribayashi decided instead to turn the inner island, from the back of the beach line inward, into an impenetrable and invisible fortress. The first Japanese troop reinforcements for Iwo Jima began to arrive well before the American bombardment from sites such as the naval base at Yokosuka and Chichi Jima.

Kuribayashi

Kuribayashi had the benefit of having traveled in the United States, and he had even attended Harvard for a short time. In his travels, he learned that American industry could be militarized at the touch of a button, and that American popular opinion was sensitive to high casualties in conflicts. If anything, his openly stated view that the U.S. should not be engaged as a military enemy may have contributed to his being given the task of defending Iwo Jima by leadership who may have viewed the defense of the island as a suicide mission. Once assigned his post, however, he took on the matter of American sensitivity to casualties as a tangible strategy – "If American casualties are high enough, Washington will think twice before launching another invasion against Japanese territory."[8] As for the Japanese view of casualties, a different mindset altogether was predominant: the strategy of sacrifice with no survivors.

---

[8] IwoJima.com – Japanese Iwo Jima Strategy

When the new General arrived on Iwo Jima on June 8, 1944 to relieve Obata, 80 fighters were positioned there. By the next month, all but a few were gone, and those remaining were destroyed in the American naval bombardment. Kuribayashi's first step was to evacuate all civilians from the island, and in direct opposition of General Obata's positioning, his beach strategy was based on an intention not to have one aside from minimal light-arms fire from infantry. The amphibious invaders would not face significant fire for the first 500 yards after landing. Meanwhile, Japanese artillery was positioned on high ground, particularly that over the Chidori Airfield and on the slopes of Mount Suribachi, the highest point of land on the island at 560 feet high. This included all artillery pieces, rockets and mortars.

In the next phase of arranging the defense, an extensive network of caves and tunnels were created, in full knowledge that no structure built above ground could stand up against the naval bombardment. Kuribayashi and his Japanese defenders were eventually in possession of 361 artillery pieces of 75mm or larger, 5 anti-tank battalions, a dozen 320mm mortars, 65 mortars of 150mm and 81mm, 33 naval guns and 94 anti-aircraft guns. Standard weapons included a small detachment of the Type 95 light tanks (employing three crewmen and 37mm guns), field guns in and around caves, Arisaka 7.7mm bolt action rifles with attachable bayonets, Nambu 8mm automatic, magazine-fed pistols, machine guns, knee mortars and standard issue grenades, not of the pin type but those that required striking to activate. Tank defenses were originally intended to be mobile, easily switching from firefight to firefight, but given the difficult terrain, Kuribayashi decided to install them in static positions and bury them, with turrets that were camouflaged to the point of virtual invisibility from the air.

The black ash that inundated the island was suitable for a superior quality of concrete, and the resulting caves, bunkers, pillboxes and large rooms were elaborate. Up to one quarter of the entire garrison was enlisted in the tunneling, and while some of the caves were suitable for two to three men with gear, others could hold up to 400, with multiple entrances and exits to prevent forces from becoming trapped. Ventilation systems were engineered to contend with the danger of sulfur fumes common to the island. On Mount Suribachi itself, the 60 foot-deep crater with a 20 foot ledge on which one could walk the entire circumference of the rim was particularly well-developed as a fortress. The Japanese had constructed elaborate caves all the way around the crater, and according to one of the 28th Marines who took the summit, "It was down in the crater that the Japanese were honey-combed."[9] Approximately 800 of the so-called "pillbox" structures were erected in a short amount of time, an impressive and rare feat of engineering given the distance from supplies and the time available. Men of the 28th found the crater to be naturally warm, but not nearly so much as the north end of the island, as one noted, "some of our boys received burns just from sleeping on the ground."[10] It was said that Marines who preferred hot food could have it simply by burying it for a short time throughout much of the island.

---

[9] Oral History: Iwo Jima, the Flag Raising: John Bradley Interview – www.history.navy.mil/flags/faq87-31.htm
[10] Oral History: Iwo Jima, the Flag Raising: John Bradley Interview

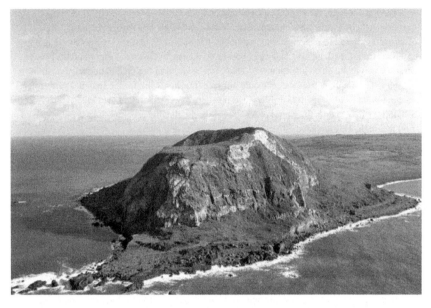

Mount Suribachi on the southern end of Iwo Jima

On the other hand, the black ash, according to accounts of veterans who were there, made advances particularly difficult. This "black sand" is described as large-grained, like coffee or BB shot, and climbing any slope was far more difficult than climbing in sand. Where one might sink to the top of the shoes in sand, advancing Marines sank from the ankles to the knees depending on the particular terrain. Vehicles also sank to hubcap height.

Kuribayashi's command post was installed on the north side of the island, northeast of Kita village and south of Kitano Point, and it was built 20 yards underground and connected to over 150 yards of tunnels. The enormous chamber featured a complete war room. On the second highest point of the island, Hill 382, a radio and weather station was established, and Colonel Chosaku Kaido, the artillery commander, occupied an enormous blockhouse nearby. The main communications center was over 50 yards in length, 20 yards in width, and far underground. An underground passage was to connect all major installations and comprise approximately 17 miles in length, but by the time the American bombardment began, only 11 miles had been completed.

In order to protect the two operating airfields, Kuribayashi ordered the construction of anti-tank ditches along all airstrips, and Japanese forces mined every conceivable ground approach. On January 2, 1945, B-24 Liberator bombers inflicted heavy damage on one of the fields, but Kuribayashi took 600 men from their units to repair the damage quickly. Using 11 trucks and a handful of bulldozers, the field was operational again within 12 hours, with 2,000 men filling the bomb craters.

In terms of strategy, Kuribayashi's plan included not only allowing enemy forces to cross the beach with minimal to no opposition but also not to return fire against American naval vessels. This was mostly to avoid divulging the locations of Japanese positions. The only light-arms resistance by the Japanese defenders would be over occupied areas above the Motoyama Airfield, the north beaches and Mount Suribachi. Once artillery was first deployed, pieces would be moved to the ground above the Chidori Airfield. This kind of operation required enormous stockpiles of ammunition, food and supplies, and even though many transport ships had been sunk before reaching Iwo Jima, the island's occupiers were well-entrenched in time for the attack. As late as February 1945, personnel continued to arrive before the island was encircled.

On August 10, 1944, almost six months prior to the amphibious invasion, Rear Admiral Toshinosuke Ichimaru arrived with over 2,000 additional personnel, many of them aviators and ground crews (Ichimaru himself was a famed aviator). While Iwo Jima's airfields had been used for conventional purposes, they would also be used for the notorious kamikaze attacks, which truly began to increase as a Japanese strategy in October 1944. Translated as "God Wind," "Divine Wind" and "God Spirit," kamikazes would sink 47 Allied vessels and damage over 300 by the end of the war, but the rise in the use of kamikaze attacks correlated the loss of the Empire's air superiority and its waning industrial might. This method of fighting would become more common by the time Iwo Jima was fought over, and it was especially prevalent during the invasion of Okinawa. The "privilege" of being selected as a kamikaze pilot played directly into the deep-seated Japanese mindset of "death before defeat." The pilot training manual assured each kamikaze candidate that when they eliminated all thoughts of life and death, fear of losing the earthly life can be easily overcome.

Still, not all cases of those chosen to be kamikazes were equally noble. Recruits were trained with torturous regimens or corporal punishment, and stories of mental impairment caused by drugs or saki abound. Some were described as "tottering" and dazed, being carried to their planes by maintenance officers, and forcibly pushed in if they backed down. Pilots who could not find their targets were told to turn around and spare their own lives for another day, but if a pilot returned nine times, he was to be shot. At the moment of collision, he was instructed to keep his eyes open at all times, and to shout "Hissatsu" ("clear kill").

In January 1945, Ichimaru informed troops on Iwo Jima that the Philippines had been lost and the Japanese fleet largely destroyed, leading to a high likelihood that Iwo Jima would be attacked soon. 127 American ships were reportedly heading northeast from Saipan toward Iwo Jima in an apparently unexpected change of American tactics, and anticipating that the assault would come sooner than it did, defenders on Iwo Jima were prepared, with the exception of the central tunnel's completion.

These defenses would have to contend with U.S. soldiers who were likely to carry an M1 Garmand, Thompson M1 or M1Carbine. Flamethrowers were well-designed for dealing with this kind of defense and would be used throughout the battle. American aircraft over Iwo Jima were predominantly Vought F4U Corsairs, and the landing craft included LCTs (Landing Craft Tanks that carried four), LSTs (Landing Ship Tanks that carried 20 in the U.S. version) and LVTs (Landing Vehicle Tracked, an amphibious, sometimes armored personnel carrier commanded by Army personnel, not Navy. American soldiers were commonly equipped with satchel charges and backpack explosives as well.

A Marine equipped with a flame-thrower at Iwo Jima

In sum, the strategic intent of the overall defensive scheme, no matter what was to occur, called for "strong, mutually supporting positions…defended to the death. Neither large-scale counterattacks, withdrawals nor bonsai charges were contemplated."[11]

---

[11] *Battle of Iwo Jima: Japanese Defense* – http://www.battle-fleet.com/pw/his/Battle-Iwo-Jima-Defense.htm

Aerial photo of Iwo Jima in 1945. The airstrips are visible

The Opening Phase

LVTs approaching Iwo Jima

At 2:00 a.m. on the 19th of February, battleship guns announced the beginning of the Iwo Jima offensive, also called D-Day like its more famous European counterpart. Soon after, over 100 bombers assaulted the island, followed by more bombs dropped by carrier aircraft. At 8:59 a.m., a minute ahead of schedule, the first of 30,000 men from the 3rd, 4th and 5th Marines began to land, and they would be followed by 40,000 more later in the day. The first aim was to neutralize and capture Mount Suribachi, and though these landing forces weren't fought on the beach by Japanese infantry, they had to deal with heavy artillery being fired at them by well-hidden units. The Japanese would open the steel doors to let their artillery pieces fire, close the door while reloading, and fire again. Kuribayashi also wisely waited for as many Marines as possible to land on the beach, thus offering more targets for the Japanese artillery.

Thanks to Kuribayashi's strategy of offering light resistance (at least from Japanese infantry), the Marines quickly found their landing zones congested, so much so that the 21st Marine regiment was boated and prepared to land but couldn't due to lack of space. With space so limited, some troops re-embarked onto their respective ships and landed later in the afternoon. When the Marines who landed encountered no Japanese forces, they mistakenly thought most of them had been killed in the bombardment. In fact, the Japanese were merely waiting for their approach, and the first lines of Marines that did approach on the 19th were quickly mowed down by machine gun fire once they got within range of the hidden Japanese positions.

Marines burrowing in on the beach

While the Marines had to contend with artillery on Mount Suribachi, important naval actions took place around the area and mitigated the potential damage. On February 18, the U.S. carrier *Enterprise* task groups 58.5, 58.4 and 58.1 separated from the main group, and headed for a refueling rendezvous to the southwest of Iwo Jima. The next morning (D-Day for the Marines), *Enterprise* refueled and set course 60 miles northwest of Iwo Jima. *Enterprise's* primary responsibility on the 19th was to protect amphibious forces from air attacks, and at 1630, she launched six Night Air Group 90 Hellcats to cover the forces at dusk. Two hours later, four VF (N)-90 fighters encountered eight interceptions, but most of the Japanese planes turned away and declined to engage. Before 1930, an enemy "Helen" (twin-engine heavy bomber) was knocked out of the sky (or as the Navy and Air Force was fond of saying, "they splashed it.").

On the 20th, the Marines advanced from the south of Mount Suribachi, north of the airfield, and satchel charges and flame throwers were used to reach entrenched Japanese forces on the mountain, all while cruisers and destroyers bombarded Japanese positions. Furthermore, ravines were set with gasoline fires to force the enemy out of entrenched positions. However, the elaborate tunnels dug by the Japanese allowed their men to flee further inward from the use of fire instead of being smoked out, and when the attacks would stop, the Japanese defenders could simply move right back into position. Another problem hampering the Marines was that the use of tanks in this theater of operations had a major disadvantage; a Sherman tank was difficult to disable, often requiring that Japanese attackers come out in the open, but the terrain throughout most of the island was not suited for armored movement.

A Sherman tank equipped with a flame-thrower attacks Japanese positions on Iwo Jima

At 0830 on the morning of the 20th, the 23rd advanced after a 15 minute period of shelling, naval bombardment and air preparation, and at the appointed "King" hour, the artillery was lifted approximately 400 yards and fired continuously for five minutes, supported by the 4th Tank. This advance was met with machine gun, mortar and artillery fire, but by noon, the northern limits of the airfield had been taken after "a series of well-concealed pillboxes and infantry strong points [were] reduced."[12] For the rest of the day, little progress was made by the 23rd, as they formed a seaward wall of defense against the airfield.

The 24th Marines took moderate to heavy losses on the second day, from after midnight to dawn. The 3rd and 4th Platoons of Regimental Weapons Company were ordered not to land until the beach's condition had been improved, a large enemy mine field was cleared, and a road for the tanks was "taped" through the field. For the 5th Marines, the day was marked by a series of counterattacks and Japanese attempts at infiltrating American lines. They were shelled by artillery and mortar fire throughout the night, and when "K-Hour" came, advances were slow, with "extreme difficulty in completing proper re-supply and reorganization of front line units on time."[13] Supply and evacuation problems persisted on the beaches, and LTVs were used primarily for bringing in supplies. In the late afternoon, an enemy air strike brought 50 caliber strafing, rockets and bombs to the top of the quarry, and the distance was so near that the markings were clear. Five were killed, with six wounded. Only 200-300 yards had been gained in

[12] *Iwojimahistory.com* – http://www.iwojimahistory.com/content/view/13/35/1/0/
[13] *Iwojimahistory.com*

two hours, and the Americans' left flank was mostly unable to move throughout the day. Orders were received to consolidate, dig in and establish firm contact.

For the 26th Marines, few supplies or equipment could be received from the beach, but they managed to defend against a morning Japanese counterattack with help from artillery fire. Advance was all but impossible given the abundance of mines; the Japanese had planted yardstick mines tied to 63kg bombs. Two or three of the enemy artillery pieces had been destroyed by naval guns, and an enemy dog-tag identified the Japanese unit opposing them as the 145th Infantry Regiment. A captured enemy document identified a second Japanese unit as well: the 312th Independent Infantry Battalion. Where the advanced stopped, 300-400 enemy dead were counted.

The 28th Marines, as they did every night, received a heavy barrage of shelling from Mount Suribachi, which by now had already been appropriately dubbed "Meatgrinder Hill." In the early morning, an enemy barge landed on the west beach, and 39 enemy soldiers were killed trying to reach shore. The Marines were fearful of "banzai" attacks at night, a tactic frequently used by the Japanese that simply attempted to overwhelm Allied positions with massive numbers of men, so they were alert at all hours. To help prevent such attacks, the American navy would shell the island throughout the night in an effort to actually brighten the night sky and prevent Japanese soldiers from sneaking up on the American lines. At 0800, the 28th was ordered to attack, seize Suribachi, and mop up the west beach. Tanks arrived, and the advance went through 200 yards of reinforced concrete pillboxes, but Major Allen and Captain Young of D and I Company were severely wounded and evacuated.

Meanwhile, the 21st Marines were in the boats by 0800, and landed at Beaches Yellow 1 and 2 at 1345. A warning was issued that friendly Marines of the 4th Division were moving through on that day. Recon was limited by darkness, and there was heavy artillery and mortar fire on the assembly area, although no casualties were reported. Three enemy tanks were spotted on the airstrip by the 23rd Marines. Naval artillery destroyed one, and the other two retreated. At 0045, orders were received for continuation of the attack, after pre-arranged strikes at selected targets. With the advance came increased resistance, and removal of mines slowed progress. Due to the number of casualties, units began to merge with others, and contact with adjacent units was lost during daylight hours only to be reestablished at night.

Tanks, once thought to be essential in all advances, were maintained at the rear with terrain and mines continuing to pose significant problems: "the mere appearance of a tank forward with the infantry during the attack resulted in heavy artillery and mortar fire."[14] Employment of half-track, 75mms became impractical, and they were returned to the rear, where their absence was keenly felt. The 24th endured heavy fire from throughout the night, and a half-track platoon of Regimental Weapons Company landed on "Yellow" Beach 1 on the morning of the 21st. The

---

[14] Iwojimahistory.com

entire day was spent scanning advanced routes and removing mines.

Supplies landing at Iwo Jima

While the Marines inched their way toward Mount Suribachi and the airfield on the southern end of Iwo Jima, the navy was attempting to prevent attacks by Japanese planes taking off from nearby islands. After 0900 on the 21st of February, the *Enterprise* and the *Saratoga* CV-3 split up. *Saratoga* and her three escort destroyers went to join Task Group 52.2, Rear Admiral Calvin Durgin's forces of escort carriers to the northeast of Iwo Jima. *Saratoga* operated in tandem with *Lexington* CV-16 and *Hancock* CV-19. "Saratoga was now 'Queen of the Jeeps" (escort carriers), but her reign was short-lived."[15] Before 1600, she picked up a large "bogey" on radar that turned out to be a mass of 20-25 planes at a distance of approximately 75 miles. They were first identified as friendly due to the belief that American air patrols were returning, but when planes were sent aloft to confirm it, they shot down two Zeroes. The body of enemy planes emerged from the low fog and descended on *Saratoga*, which took three direct hits from the planes' bombs, while two enemy planes fell off the starboard side and one crashed directly into the flight deck. The crew fought the fires for 90 minutes as the carrier sped up to 25 knots, but a second attack began four hours later and *Saratoga* was targeted by five suicide planes. In the

---

[15] USS Enterprise: 1945 Iwo Jima

attack, the *Saratoga* was badly damaged, and the USS *Bismarck Sea* was sunk, making it the last carrier to sink during World War II.

Enterprise turned to the north rather than follow the route of *Saratoga*, to strike at the airfields that supported the suicide missions over Iwo Jima. She was now the only fleet carrier operating at Iwo Jima, and her added mission was now to inflict as much damage as possible on the enemy airfields of the region. Instead of a full-out launching of fighters, she launched pockets of 4-8 Hellcats on the hour around the clock. Outright kills were few, but many potential threats were turned away, and the carrier inflicted significant damage on the airfields and the harbor of Chichi Jima. Many Japanese cargo ships were sunk, along with other important structural and resource damage. The USS *Gregory* joined *Enterprise* at Chichi Jima to assist in the rescue of ditched pilots, and before leaving, *Enterprise* targeted the airfield at Susaki and the seaplane base at Futami. By the beginning of March, enough of Iwo Jima was controlled that landings and take-offs could be maintained without fear of suicide attacks, and *Enterprise* remained off the island until March 9. "If the [USS Carrier] Enterprise and Task Group 58.5 had played a secondary role during the Tokyo raids, they made up for it at Iwo Jima."[16]

Two hours before dawn on the 21st, an attack by approximately 100 Japanese soldiers was repelled, but explosions occurred in the rear area and two fires erupted on the beach "Blue" 1 in ammunition dumps. Lieutenant Colonel Mustain was killed in action, and Major Fenton Mee took command, and in the course of the confusion, an unintended gap formed between elements of 1/25 and 2/25. All units were ordered to consolidate for the night. Thousands of Marines had to shift position that night, all while small enemy groups remained active on the beach after dark. Making matters worse, the American supply lines from the beach were poor, at a time when flame-thrower servicing was needed and supply materials such as radio battery replacements would have been helpful. Several Marines of the 27th were stabbed in the night, and general rules of combat as a tactical code did not exist for either side. Japanese who spoke English continued to call for help, then shoot whichever American responded.

The Americans' right flank also dealt with heavy resistance early on the 21st. The right flank met heavy resistance and had to deal with increasing artillery, even as naval gunfire destroyed two pieces. Tanks and infantry reported cases of booby-trapped saki bottles and terra cotta mines, also found in shell holes and foxholes. One of the most harrowing incidents of the day involved 24 Japanese soldiers committing mass suicide by jumping together off of a cliff around airfield I.

---

[16] USS Enterprise: 1945 Iwo Jima – http://www.cv6.org/1945/iwo-2.htm

Raising the Flag on Mount Suribachi

The flag atop Mount Suribachi

During the 21st, pyrotechnics were set off atop Suribachi over the heads of the 28th Marines, the unit charged with the taking of Suribachi, and if that wasn't enough for the Marines to sit through, a 40 plane strike was called in before the K-hour advance only 100 yards from the Marines' position. For the advance itself, both tank and air support would soon become impossible, and the tanks were ultimately unable to make it by K-hour, so there would be no advance until they arrived. When they did, multiple pillboxes and blockhouses were knocked out, and the armor was able to "bore through the main defenses in front of the mountain."[17]

---

[17] Iwojimahistory.com

There were multiple incidents of cave attacks before the 28th reached the base of the mountain, but the various units consolidated at late afternoon.

All told, the enemy dead for the day totaled 508, and despite all the difficulties, the Marines achieved a major milestone in successfully encircling Mount Suribachi by the 22nd of February. The 21st Marines were ordered to relieve the 23rd by 0730, and this was accomplished under cover of darkness, although the First Battalion received heavy enemy fire that resulted in severe casualties as they made their way across a stretch of Airfield I. They were not able to be in position at the appointed time, so a request was offered to have the 2nd Battalion of the 24th Marines attached to initiate the next attack on schedule. However, that request was inevitably canceled. The right flank gained only about 50 yards of ground, with 250 on the left for the entire day, but many enemy fortifications were compromised.

Members of the 24th Marines

February 23rd would go down as perhaps the most auspicious day in the overall invasion of Iwo Jima, as it was on this day that Marines reached the top of Suribachi after non-stop heavy fighting. At 1020, a patrol under command of Lieutenant Harold Schreir of the 28th Marines reached the top and raised a small flag on the summit. That flag was raised by five Marines atop the same mountain as part of a 40 man patrol and was hoisted by Platoon Sergeant Ernest I. "Boots" Thomas of Tallahassee, Florida. A Marine Corps photographer captured the first raising on film, just as an enemy grenade caused him to fall over the crater edge and tumble 50 feet. The lens of his camera was shattered, but the film and soldier were safe. Historian James Bradley described in *Flags of Our Fathers* why this would not end up being the iconic moment of the battle:

> "The Secretary of the Navy, James Forrestal, had decided the previous night that he wanted to go ashore and witness the final stage of the fight for the mountain. Now, under a stern commitment to take orders from Howlin' Mad Smith, the secretary was churning ashore in the company of the blunt, earthy general. Their boat touched the beach just after the flag went up, and the mood among the high command turned jubilant. Gazing upward, at the red, white, and blue speck, Forrestal remarked to Smith: 'Holland, the raising of that flag on Suribachi means a Marine Corps for the next five hundred years.'
>
> Forrestal was so taken with fervor of the moment that he decided he wanted the Suribachi flag as a souvenir. The news of this wish did not sit well with 2nd Battalion Commander Chandler Johnson, whose temperament was every bit as fiery as Howlin Mad's. "To hell with that!" the colonel spat when the message reached him. The flag belonged to the battalion, as far as Johnson was concerned. He decided to secure it as soon as possible, and dispatched his assistant operations officer, Lieutenant Ted Tuttle, to the beach to obtain a replacement flag. As an afterthought, Johnson called after Tuttle: 'And make it a bigger one.'"

Picture of the first flag-raising atop Mount Suribachi

A larger flag would be brought by an LST, and when that flag was raised, the iconic photograph of Joe Rosenthal taken. Rosenthal noted, "Out of the corner of my eye, I had seen the men start the flag up. I swung my camera and shot the scene. That is how the picture was taken, and when you take a picture like that, you don't come away saying you got a great shot. You don't know."

As it turned out, Rosenthal had taken a picture that would win a Pulitzer, but initially, a lot of people assumed it was a staged shot. As one writer asserted, "Rosenthal climbed Suribachi after the flag had already been planted. ... Like most photographers [he] could not resist reposing his characters in historic fashion." Rosenthal would be forced to argue for decades that he had spontaneously captured the flag-raising, insisting, "I don't think it is in me to do much more of this sort of thing ... I don't know how to get across to anybody what 50 years of constant repetition means." Thankfully, a film of the very same moment, shot by Bill Genaust, proved that Rosenthal hadn't staged the iconic picture.

A 1945 stamp commemorated the flag-raising atop Iwo Jima

The second flag raised by Marines atop Mount Suribachi. Photo by Mark Pellegrini

The first platoon to reach the top stayed for three days before being relieved, and the flag always flew throughout the Iwo Jima offensive. Unlike certain mythologies that were constructed around famous historical events elsewhere, the flag-raisings of Iwo Jima occurred during a month of stark reality and were not documented for cinematic glorification. The raising of the flag on Suribachi created a national "ecstatic moment…a quintessential moment of American heroic triumph, and a celebration of the virtues of the common soldier."[18]

After the colors were raised, elements of the different Marine units met at the southernmost point as ordered. Congratulations were sent from Lt. General Smith, Vice Admiral Turner and Maj. General Rockey of the 5th Marines. The rest of the day was spent demolishing caves and mopping up the remaining pockets of resistance, and a night defense of just 40 men from E Company was left on the summit.

Although every American now remembers Rosenthal's picture and associates it with Iwo Jima, there was still plenty of work to do. While that moment unfolded atop Mount Suribachi, Marines were advancing toward the second airfield at the island's opposite end. At the same time, the Marines had to strengthen their own defensive positions during February 24th and 25th because enemy units attempted night infiltrations in groups of two and three.

---

[18] Edward T. Linenthal: Review of "Iwo Jima in American Memory," Karal Ann Marling, John Wetenhall, p. 9

Accurate and intense enemy fire fell on the 25th Marines throughout the night, and such a bombardment became more the rule than the exception. All the while, enemy patrols that harassed front lines were repelled, but these attacks still inflicted American casualties, and just as importantly, they slowed the American advance. The 25th Marines made only moderate advances over these few days, but when they fired two rocket barrages against the hill, it drove a bunch of Japanese out of the structures and out into the open, where most were immediately killed. The total enemy dead in that action was 200. When the 25th Marines were counterattacked at mid-day by 100 Japanese soldiers following a heavy mortar barrage, they pushed back that attack but suffered even more casualties. As if the fighting wasn't miserable enough, a cold rain began to fall on the island during February 26 as well.

Thus, the 5th Tank of the 26th Marines moved out at daybreak through February 27th in a steady rain and under heavy fire, but the unit managed to extend 200 yards into the 4th Marines' zone, and the attack managed to advance 400 yards. This was considered an enormous gain in perspective, but the right flank was unable to advance at all. A bluff to the right stymied their progress, and fire from the top pinned down the advance. This bluff would end up harassing and delaying the entire invasion of Iwo Jima for a number of days, since the effectiveness of the tanks was largely negated by the Japanese positions on this higher ground.

As the progress was halted, uncoordinated counterattacks came from the left and somewhat in the center, but both were repelled by the Japanese on the afternoon of the 27th. A couple of units reached ground in advance of the main lines but were forced to withdraw, and due to conditions on the beach, with the rain and volcanic ash mixing, it was even harder for supply items to reach the front. On top of that, the 27th Marines' beach defenses reported a counter-landing of 50 Japanese during the day, with another 400 landing during the night. These were repelled by a combination of beach defenses and naval fire. No offensive enemy action was reported during the morning hours, but the Marines were shelled consistently. The total enemy dead for February 27 came to 515.

During the early morning hours of February 28, flares from Suribachi were again sent up by night over the 28th Marines, the closest unit to the mountain's base. This helped the Marines defend against any nighttime attacks, and enemy swimmers were killed coming ashore on the west beach. During daylight hours, the forward advance continued, with three teams landing abreast, but since the rain had mixed with volcanic dust, almost all automatic weaponry was reduced to single-shot weaponry.

The attack on Iwo Jima was only supposed to take a week, but Marines had been on the ground for 10 days and still had plenty of work to do.

Fighting on the Northern End of the Island

Marine machine-gunners attacking Japanese positions

As symbolic and encouraging as the taking of Suribachi might have been, the mountain made up only one point of the island and one mission. The northern end, with its airfield and Japanese fortifications, was equally defended and arguably possessed a heavier arsenal of resources, including eight infantry battalions, a tank regiment, two artillery and three heavy mortar battalions. The fight for Iwo Jima was far from complete after Suribachi.

Likewise, the center of the island offered a strong resistance and was dubbed the "meat grinder" by attacking forces. The highest point of this area was Hill 382, also known as "Turkey Knob," which housed a large Japanese communication center. The southern extension of Hill 382 was known as the "the Amphitheater." Toward the northern tip, Marines did experience one minimal "banzai" charge, which contradicted direct orders of General Kubayashi, and the desperate act was a deadly mistake. The 700 Japanese dead spelled the end of organized resistance in the center of the island.

On the northern end, the 22nd Marines continued attacks on known targets with artillery and tank support. The First Battalion "jumped off" on time, but the 2nd found itself in an intense firefight, with no advances made until mid-morning. By early afternoon, after Suribachi had been taken on the 23rd, American units had reached the southwest edge of Airfield II. Some of the men crossed the runways before being driven back, and ultimately, by the end of February 23, no change of position had been gained due to heavy incoming fire. Meanwhile, the beach and rear sections were shelled, and by early evening, a Condition Red alert was issued to all units. Soon after, enemy planes appeared, but their subsequent bombing was ineffective.

As different Marine units prepared to advance on the morning 24th, The 27th Marines were held in Division Reserve, and even before the advance they reported that tactical maps distributed among the officers had been compromised due to copies lost in battle. Sure enough, at 0300, enemy infiltrations began along the west coast. Pull-type booby traps were found tied to saki bottles, helmets, and even dead Japanese soldiers. The heaviest concentration of enemy fire was directed at roads to the west of Airfield I, but the Americans held out, and enemy dead for the day was listed at 645. Failed enemy infiltrations against the 28th were attempted throughout the night, but to no avail.

February 24th's daily advance began at 0730 with a friendly air strike along the front lines, and about two hours later, the entire line moved forward under heavy fire and bad terrain. A gap developed between the Marines during the day, and heavy fire was received from Airfield II, but at 1700, all units consolidated for the night. The furthest units had advanced about 400 yards with the support of two airstrikes and artillery, and they maintained contact with the enemy throughout. By now, the Marines had grown accustomed to the Japanese's constant attempts at infiltration in the darkness, which were supported by heavy artillery and mortar fire, but the forward units managed to repulse those attacks during the early morning hours of February 25. The forward units were relieved at 0900, and the day was spent reviewing the Division front.

Beginning the next northern advance on the 24th of February, following 75 minutes of naval bombardment, the 4th and 5th Marine Divisions attacked again in the north, supported by tanks. The Japanese were successful at stopping the tanks with anti-tank guns and mines, and throughout the entire day, the 5th Division gained only 500 yards. However, the 21st Marines fared better. The 2nd Battalion of the 21st Marines sighted enemies behind their lines at 0630, and the infiltrators were killed immediately. Excellent progress was made in the day's advance, with the 3rd Battalion gaining 600 yards against well-organized pillboxes and other entrenchments. Attacks continued at 1330, and at 1445, twelve "Blue" Tanks were at last operational on the second airfield. Enemy fire and mines produced heavy tank casualties, but the 2nd Battalion circled west of the airfield, and by 1545, two companies had crossed it. The high ground above changed hands several times, with much hand-to-hand fighting, and at 2145, units were consolidated for the night. The 21st Marines could be proud of their accomplishments on February 24.

Not all of the Marines were so fortunate. The 23rd Marines drew heavy shelling during the night of the 24th, and although attempts were made to pinpoint the origin of fire, success was minimal. The 24th had to content itself marking mines during the day. Meanwhile, the 3rd

Marines advanced along the troublesome bluff to the right of the central invasion, which helped to suppress Japanese fire being rained down on Americans from that position. The 3rd advanced 500 yards throughout the afternoon, far enough that contact was lost for a time between the 3rd and the other Marines.

At the end of February 24, the 27th continued as a reserve unit. 30 enemy dead were found in a sulfur hole, and several had committed suicide, including three officers. This was a sight encountered with increasing frequency as the month wore on. New mine fields were discovered, overrun mortar positions were found to be booby-trapped, and roads around the airfield received concentrated enemy fire. Enemy dead totaled 645, and well over 100 enemy infiltrators had been killed, with many of the Japanese soldiers tied to crude demolition as booby-traps. The early daylight hours were spent mopping up on and around Suribachi.

At 0930 on the morning of the 25th, the 3rd Marines began their attack to the north, and as with the day before, movement was slow and casualties high. The 9th Marines saw their first action in the Iwo Jima offensive on the 25th. They were passed through the 21st and commenced their attack at mid-morning, but the source of enemy fire was difficult to locate even at 25 yards. Progress was slow against enemy fire, and tanks received heavy resistance around the Airfield II area. The 1st Battalion of the 9th Marines managed to cross the runways toward Hill 200-P and gain a foothold on the hill, but they suffered heavy casualties. The 2nd Battalion tank support was a good deal more effective; since the area was small in dimensions, two or three tanks wielded enormous influence. The 2nd Battalion advanced 400 yards before being stopped abruptly under heavy fire.

After a 95 minute artillery barrage, the 23rd advanced and flanked Airfield II, an objective that would be denied them until late afternoon, but ultimately, the Japanese defense of the field was weakened by aggressive infantry and tank attacks. All Marine units consolidated on favorable ground in late afternoon, and orders were issued for attacks the following day. Small groups of enemy infiltrators were spotted by night, and elements of the 24th were ordered to the assembly area. They were pinned down for the day and requested two airstrikes, neither of which ever came. With the continued enemy strength on the bluff line right continuing to stymie progress, all advances were halted until it could be neutralized.

The 23rd Marines, also in the vicinity of Airfield II, continued the attack during the early morning of the 25th against pillboxes, bunkers, emplacements and caves. Mine fields were discovered on the airfield runway and in the area of the Radio Weather station on TA 200W and heavy enemy tank fire was received from Hill 382, but by the afternoon, the southwest slopes were taken, with American units consolidating by dusk. Tanks were brought up, but their presence drew much heavier fire, exacerbating the situation. The center of the line gained 75-150 yards but sustained heavy casualties, and the Marines were forced to withdraw from its positions below the cliff line under cover of smoke screens.

By February 26, the Marines had still failed to take the bluff line that was causing them so many problems as they advanced, but enemy fire from that position had decreased. They had also managed to destroy a large number of pillboxes by now, and a group of 20 Japanese were killed in a cave on the northwest slope of Suribachi.

The second airfield was finally taken by the 3rd Marines on the 27th of February, and the 9th Marines were still in the vicinity of Airfield II. Tanks increased in importance as the Marines' advance was almost immediately blocked by caves and pillboxes to the front and at the flanks. Heavy fire came from the right, and only small gains were made in the morning. The Japanese continued trying to infiltrate the American lines that night, in tandem with artillery bombardment, but the 28th Marines again fought them off. 103 enemy dead were confirmed.

During the 27th, the 25th Marines advanced after dawn with the cliff line to the right. The advance went 150 yards before immediately halting as the Marines found themselves in an open area with no cover. They took heavy casualties, and two of the three tanks in support were destroyed. By evening, it was decided that the objective ground could not be reached, so the 25th withdrew through the lines back to the positions of the preceding night. The center and right gained 200-300 yards, and all units halted the advance on favorable ground to consolidate as night fell. The 26th Marines withdrew into the assembly area for "reorganization, salvage and evacuation of the dead."[19] Almost all enemy dead were recovered under cover of darkness, with the 27th Marines using phosphorous to camouflage the troop movements. The total Japanese dead for February 27 was listed at 840.

Securing Iwo Jima and the Aftermath of the Battle

By the last day of February, the third airfield was occupied by Marines, but the surrounding hills were still held by the Japanese. Soon after, Marines assaulted the hills, 362A and 382, successfully taking and holding them by the 1st of March. The following night, an after-dusk attack was staged by Marines on Hill 362A, but the hill would not be secured until the 8th of March. On March 4th, a damaged B-29 landed on the island during the fighting, an important sign that Marines were sufficiently in control of the airfield to make landings possible. The first P-51s would arrive at the island as air support for Marines by March 6th, and Task Force 58 was relieved in preparation for a subsequent assault against Okinawa.

By the end of the first week of March, the southern airfield was fully operational for the Americans, and evacuation of the wounded proceeded without interruption. Since Iwo Jima was interconnected with so many simultaneous actions proceeding in the South Pacific, the bombing of the airfields in Chichi Jima was of great parallel importance, and attacks on Paulus and Yap in the western Carolines ensured that the strategic air importance of Iwo Jima would not simply be transferred to another site by the Japanese. Somewhat symbolically, of all the flag-raisings on

---

[19] www.Iwojimahistory.com

Suribachi, the final one was hoisted by the U.S. Combat Team 28 on March 14, 1945, near the end of the conflict.

Over the course of March, the Japanese continued desperately attacking, including mounting a counterattack on the 23rd and 24th Marine Regiments, but that assault was stopped by artillery, and 650 of the enemy were killed. Resistance continued throughout the following days as Japanese units repeatedly penetrated American lines in attempts to sever communication, but the defense had just about reached its last gasp. The final Japanese resistance was overcome at Kitano Point on March 25th, and the last Japanese unit to attempt a penetration of the American lines was allegedly led by Kuribayashi himself. The result of that action left 250 more Japanese dead, including Kuribayashi. At 8:00 a.m. on March 26, the island was declared secure, although a lengthy time would go by before final resistance was rooted out of the caves. Either way, the 147th U.S. Army Infantry arrived for garrison duty on Iwo Jima by March 20 and would have full control of the island by the 4th of April. By April 7, 100 P-51s were able to land on the island and subsequently escort a B-29 bombing raid against the Japanese mainland. It would be incorrect to assume that once the island came under American control, the fighting stopped or the environment became safe. It was clearly operational, but not necessarily safe, and casualties were suffered through the last day of American occupation.

The island of Iwo Jima remained under American control for several years even after the war, until it was eventually returned to the Japanese in 1968. In the last months of the war, the aircraft carrier USS *Iwo Jima* was under construction at Newport News, Virginia, but she was canceled on August 12, 1945 and her partial hull was scrapped. Her namesake, however, was launched from Bremerton, Washington in 1960 and commissioned in 1961. Today, no civilians are allowed on the island, and the Japanese operate a naval base there. American carriers still use it for landing training, and nuclear weapons are said to have been located at one time or another on Iwo Jima, Ton Chichi, Okinawa and other Japanese sites.

Final casualties for the entire Iwo Jima offensive have been estimated at 6,821 American dead and 19,189 wounded, compared to 20,000 Japanese dead and 1,083 wounded and/or captured. Clearly, fighting to the death and committing suicide were prevalent among the Japanese ranks. In this strategy of sacrifice, the Japanese remained true to their word, and of the few prisoners taken, many were conscripted Korean laborers. It has even been estimated that up to 6,000 Japanese fighters are still entombed within the network of caves.

Cyril O'Brien recalls that of the 3,400 soldiers of the 28th who came ashore with him, the unit that would scale the summit of Suribachi first, only 600 were standing when the battle was ended. In his words, Iwo Jima was a battlefield "with no front lines, no rear, every inch a battleground...the enemy was nowhere and everywhere...the Japanese were not on Iwo Jima. They were in it!"[20] This small island, only a few miles in length, inflicted about 33% of all

---

[20] Cyril O'Brien, Iwo Jima Retrospective – www.military.com

Marine casualties during World War II, and it was the first major Pacific battle in which American casualties exceeded those of the Japanese. According to O'Brien and others who have fought in multiple theaters, the Iwo Jima experience could only be measured by itself.

That assertion is also supported by the fact that Iwo Jima stands as one of the most highly decorated engagements in modern American history. The Medal of Honor, created during the Civil War and often awarded posthumously, was bestowed on 27 heroic men who participated in the battle, 22 of whom were Marines and 5 of whom were Navy men. The Medals of Honor received for service at Iwo Jima comprised a quarter of the total awards given for the entire war. Half of the Iwo Jima Medals of Honor were granted posthumously, and the last living recipient, Herschel "Woody" Williams, was invited aboard the USS *Iwo Jima* in 2011 to participate in a remembrance ceremony. The youngest of the recipients, to whom the award was given posthumously, was Jacklyn Lucas, who had turned 17 on Valentine's Day, days before the offensive. Upon his recruitment, he was actually 14 but effectively hid the fact.

Iwo Jima was so important to the men who fought there that the 133rd Naval Construction Battalion is still seeking a unit citation for their work alongside the invading Marines, and the 31st Naval Construction Battalion and their comrades stormed the beaches, "fought alongside their Marine counterparts, and provided essential resupply efforts during the invasion. They provided staging areas for supplies, transported wounded back to our ships and helped bury the dead. They established a base camp to provide food and shelter to those on the island, built a road up Suribachi, and a runway that would be used for forward refueling and repair of B-29s headed for Japan."[21]

---

[21] 31st Navy Seabee's Association – www.31st-Seabees.com/iwo%20jima.htm

The memorial atop Mount Suribachi. The inscription reads, "'Among the Americans who served on Iwo Jima, uncommon valor was a common virtue.' - Nimitz"

Iwo Jima was also notable for the participation of Native American code-talkers, particularly the Navajo, who served in every major Marine action from 1942-1945. Some Native American languages had been used effectively in the First World War, and Navajo was perfectly suited to work against the Japanese because the language was oral, not written, and consisted of multiple dialects, all of tremendous complexity. It was thought that only 30 or so non-Navajos understood the language, and that none of them were Japanese. "Navajos could encode, transmit, and decode a three-line English message in 20 seconds. Machines of the time required 30 minutes."[22]

Six Navajos worked around the clock during the first two days of the assault on Iwo Jima, and in that time, they sent and received approximately 800 messages. The Japanese, adept code-breakers, nonetheless remained baffled by the Navajo language and never came close to cracking it. As one soldier at Iwo Jima put it, "Were it not for the Navajo, we would never have taken Iwo Jima."[23] Several members of the code-talkers unit were decorated for their actions in September

---

[22] www.history.navy.mil/faq61-2.htm

1992.

Naturally, the Battle of Iwo Jima instantly became a source of pride among Americans, and it was almost immediately glorified in the 1949 movie *Sands of Iwo Jima*, starring John Wayne and including cameos of a few of the Marines who had famously raised the flag on Iwo Jima. However, a lot of historians have second-guessed the need for fighting the battle of Iwo Jima at all, and the question of whether it was truly necessary is still debated by modern scholars. Considering the horrific casualties suffered as a result of "the bloodiest fight in Marine history,"[24] it is a sensitive question for Americans, particularly the families of Marines, but it is known that leading officers debated each other on the subject at the time. By April 1945, just a few weeks after the battle had ended, retired Chief of Naval Operations William V. Pratt openly questioned in *Newsweek* magazine the "expenditure of manpower to acquire a small, God-forsaken island, useless to the Army as a staging base and useless to the Navy as a fleet base..." Pratt went on to openly wonder "if the same sort of airbase could not have been reached by acquiring other strategic localities at lower cost."

Some historians have asserted that the battle took place in part due to rivalry between the service branches. Historian Robert S. Burrell argued that the Battle of Iwo Jima was only justified in hindsight and that it could have been avoided entirely, writing, "This justification became prominent only after the Marines seized the island and incurred high casualties. The tragic cost of Operation Detachment pressured veterans, journalists, and commanders to fixate on the most visible rationalization for the battle. The sight of the enormous, costly, and technologically sophisticated B-29 landing on the island's small airfield most clearly linked Iwo Jima to the strategic bombing campaign. As the myths about the flag raisings on Mount Suribachi reached legendary proportions, so did the emergency landing theory in order to justify the need to raise that flag."

Occasionally, Burrell and others have argued that in making the decision to go ahead, larger mission objectives, local plans and dates were altered, the same sort of questions that plagued the aftermath of the Battle of the Bulge. As Burrell noted, "The Marine Corps, which paid the heaviest price, remained completely excluded from the decision-making process."[25] These theories purport that the Navy moved strategically on its own behalf, as it did by not waiting for the Army to complete the Philippines mission and free up troops for an invasion of Formosa, by conspiring with the Air Force to create stronger post-war departments for themselves at the expense of the Army in going ahead with Iwo Jima.

Conversely, those who argue Iwo Jima was essential point to several facts. For example, when Admiral Spruance asked Curtis LeMay directly, "What do you think about the value of Iwo

[23] www.history.navy.mil/faq61-2.htm
[24] Robert S. Burrell, "Breaking the Cycle of Iwo Jima Mythology: A Strategic Study of Operation Detachment", in Journal of Military History, Vol. 68 No. 4 (Oct. 2004) p. 1143
[25] Robert S. Burrell, p. 1144

Jima?"[26], Le May is said to have responded that it would "...be a tremendous value to me. Without Iwo Jima, I couldn't bomb Japan effectively."[27] Taken at face value, this would appear to be an authentic response. Furthermore, Burrell's argument, according to Officer Brian Hanley, is "disabled by an impaired understanding of historical analysis and weakened further by a tendency to disparage beyond reason the motives and judgment of Navy and United States Air Force leaders."[28] While Hanley admits that inter-service rivalry is omnipresent in joint actions, the Battle of Iwo Jima (as in most cases) was based on less than perfect intelligence, and the results were not profound in relation to hopes and expectations, leading Hanley to conclude that "one conspicuous defect of Burrell's argument is the absence of sound strategic analysis."[29]

Today, of course, the Battle of Iwo Jima is almost synonymous with the famous photograph of servicemen raising the flag atop Mount Suribachi. Rosenthal's iconic photo of the flag raising was able to identify the soldiers who participated, which included Marines Ira Hayes, Mike Strank, Rene Gagnon, Harlon Block, Franklin Sousley, and U.S. Navy Corpsman John Bradley. The flag was raised during the fourth day of the Battle of Iwo Jima, and it would win the Pulitzer Prize for Photography. The tragic postscript that's often forgotten is that the picture did not capture the end of the campaign; in fact, three of the soldiers pictured in the photo died over the course of the next month on Iwo Jima.

So inspired was sculptor Felix de Weldon by Rosenthal's photo that he recreated it in a life-sized model, casting it in bronze and having it erected across the Potomac River by the Arlington Cemetery in September 1954. During the 179th anniversary of the United States Marine Corps (which was founded in 1775), the memorial was dedicated to then President Eisenhower. The 32 foot figures hoisting a 60 foot flag stand upon a 10x3 base, upon which all major engagements in Marine history are inscribed.

Bibliography

Battle of Iwo Jima: Japanese Defense – www.battle-fleet.com/pw/his/Battle-Iwo-Jima-Defenses.htm

Burrell, Robert S., "Breaking the Cycle of Iwo Jima Mythology: A Strategic Study of Operation Detachment", in *Journal of Military History*, Vol. 68 No. 4 (October, 2004)

Christ, James F. *Iwo, Assault on Hell*, Battleground Publishing: Chandler, 2010

Hanley, Brian, "The Myth of Iwo Jima: A Rebuttal", in *The Journal of Military History*, Vol. 69 No. 3 (July 2005)

---

[26] Robert S. Burrell, p. 1145
[27] Robert S. Burrell, p. 1145
[28] Brian Hanley, "The Myth of Iwo Jima: A Rebuttal", in The Journal of Military History, Vol. 69 No. 3 (July 2005), p. 802
[29] Brian Hanley, p. 802

Iwo Jima.com – *Japanese Iwo Jima Strategy*

Linenthal, Edward T.: Review of "Iwo Jima in American Memory" of Karal Ann Marling, John Wetenhall

O'Brien, Cyril, *Iwo Jima Retrospective* – www.military.com

Oral History, *Iwo Jima: The Flag Raising, John Bradley Interview* – www.history.navy.mil/flags/faq87-31.htm

Oral History – www.history.navy.mil/faq61-2.htm

The Battle for Iwo Jima: Military Service Records – www.myheritage.com/MilitaryRecords

The Navy Department Library, *Battle for Iwo Jima, 1945.* – www. history.navy.mil/library/online/battleofiwojima.htm

31st Navy Seabee's Association – www. 31st-Seabees.com/iwo%20jima.htm

USS Enterprise: 1945 Iwo Jima – www.cv6.org/1945/iwo-2.htm

Okinawa

Planning for Okinawa

Okinawa was home to 450,000 people, and along with Formosa, "formed a kind of eastern protective barrier for preserving Japan's lifelines through the East China Sea as well as the last barrier to an invasion of the homeland up through southern Japan" (Gow, p. 21). As American forces moved closer and closer, and especially after their victory at Saipan, Japanese military planners began to see Okinawa as the site of a potential attack, so they sent 100,000 soldiers to the Ryukyu islands and began constructing fortifications, all while moving thousands of civilians off the islands.

The Ryuku islands and Allied (blue) plans for operations.

Aerial view of Okinawa

In terms of Japanese airpower, a directive initiated on March 1, 1945, called Operation Ten-Go, featured kamikaze units as important avenues of attack, a strategy the Japanese increasingly relied on starting around the end of 1944. Translated as "God Wind," "Divine Wind" and "God Spirit," kamikazes would sink 47 Allied vessels and damage over 300 by the end of the war, but the rise in the use of kamikaze attacks was correlated to the loss of the Empire's air superiority and its waning industrial might; due to the growing lack of experienced pilots, the Japanese military turned to kamikaze pilots who were able to deal large amounts of damage even with their lack of training. Not surprisingly, Allied leaders and soldiers who fought against kamikazes were amazed by the pilots' determination and bravery, as Vice Admiral C.R. Brown noted, "There was a hypnotic fascination to the sight so alien to our Western philosophy. We watched each plunging kamikaze with the detached horror of one witnessing a terrible spectacle rather than as the intended victim. We forgot self for the moment as we groped hopelessly for the thought of that other man up there."

Earlier in the war, kamikaze units were voluntary, but by 1945 they were compulsory, and

Kikisui, or massed attacks by kamikaze pilots, would be the method used by the Japanese to attack Allied vessels off the coast of Okinawa. The "privilege" of being selected as a kamikaze pilot played directly into the deep-seated Japanese mindset of "death before defeat." The pilot training manual assured each kamikaze candidate that when they eliminated all thoughts of life and death, fear of losing the earthly life can be easily overcome. Still, not all cases of those chosen to be kamikazes were equally noble. Recruits were trained with torturous regimens or corporal punishment, and stories of mental impairment caused by drugs or saki abound. Some were described as "tottering" and dazed, being carried to their planes by maintenance officers, and forcibly pushed in if they backed down. Pilots who could not find their targets were told to turn around and spare their own lives for another day, but if a pilot returned nine times, he was to be shot. At the moment of collision, he was instructed to keep his eyes open at all times, and to shout "Hissatsu" ("clear kill").

The American plan for seizing Okinawa was very ambitious, in part because the military did not anticipate the maniacal resistance put up by Japanese defenders, but an ambitious campaign was also a necessity for logistical reasons. They not only planned to invade and defeat Japanese forces concentrated there but then also quickly develop the infrastructure with which to create the military bases that would be so important in attacking the Japanese home islands. Since Japan was not engaged in any other military operations in the Pacific at the time, and because they were cut off from their forces in the south, the bulk of Japan's military manpower and machinery would be focused on the Ryukyus during the campaign. Adding to the difficulty of the operation was the fact that Okinawa was far from Allied bases in the Pacific. American strategists believed the Japanese would respond to the attack by launching all available aircraft in both Formosa and the Chinese mainland, and if the Japanese managed to overwhelm American airpower, the ground forces fighting on Okinawa would then be isolated and in danger of being overwhelmed by Japanese forces. In order to combat the airpower at Japan's disposal, American military leaders believed Allied aircraft carriers would have to stay in the combat zone for a long period of time, where they would be attacked by an estimated 3,000-4,000 land-based Japanese aircraft (Gow, p. 24)

Crucial to American efforts was the need to gather intelligence about the island, a difficult prospect considering Okinawa was still roughly 1,200 miles away from the nearest American air base in late 1944. During the early part of 1945, the Americans focused on gaining intelligence on Okinawa, and that January, they estimated that there were 55,000 Japanese soldiers on the island. Military planners also assumed the Japanese would send further troops to the island, and that the defense force would probably be in the region of 66,000 by the time of an attack.

The plan that came together for Okinawa, called Operation Iceberg, set the invasion date for April 1, 1945, and the plan called for taking other Ryukyu islands such as Okina Daito, Kume, Miyako and Kika by April 8. From there, American forces would quickly move to attack Kyushu, the southernmost of Japan's home islands. The responsibility for the attack on Okinawa would be given to the Central Pacific Task Force, a joint army-navy force that was headed by Vice Admiral Spruance. Spruance would also have command over Task Force 50, which was made up of naval covering forces and special groups, along with Task Group 58 and Task Force 57, which consisted of an American fast carrier force and a British air carrier force. In terms of naval operations around Okinawa, the fast carriers would strike Okinawa, Kyushu, and other nearby islands in order to neutralize Japanese air power. The carriers of this group would then station themselves to the east of Okinawa and engage in support duties after American troops landed and began their attack. Meanwhile, the British carrier group would continue with strikes and patrols and would also be ready for any further operations against Kyushu (Frank, p. 29).

In terms of ground troops, Operation Iceberg relied on the element of surprise. One week before the planned invasion, the 77th Division would attack Kerama Retto, an island to the west of the home islands, which would then subsequently be used as a base for supplying ammunition and fuel for the forces engaging in the attack. They would then begin a diversionary attack on southeast Okinawa and then attack the beaches of western Okinawa near the island's two main airfields. Then, the XXIV Corps would take the southern portion of the island as well as any islands that would be needed for navy installations.

The Beginning of the Battle of Okinawa

As Allied troops began the campaign, they quickly took the Kerama islands, which Japan had failed to fortify because they did not believe the islands possessed sufficient importance to be targeted by an American attack. American forces occupied all of the islands by March 29th, while the British Task Force 57 reached its position for the attack on Okinawa on March 26th. As American naval vessels moved on Okinawa, the last task before the attack was to clear the waters off the coast of mines. In the last week of March, 5,182 tons of shells were fired at the Ryukyus to soften their defenses. The next part of the plan would involve landing ground troops on Okinawa.

Allied soldiers landing on the Kerama islands.

The ground invasion was set to begin on April 1, 1945, and on that day, over 1,300 ships were involved in landing soldiers on the island. American forces had gained plenty of experience in amphibious landings over the past two years, but unlike at Guadalcanal or the Marianas, the Japanese did not contest the beach areas, allowing 60,000 troops to come ashore by the end of the first day. As they moved toward Okinawa's two main airfields, they experienced little resistance and quickly captured them.

The invasion plan on April 1.

The USS *Idaho* shelling Okinawa on April 1.

Marines coming ashore on April 1.

American forces moving on the beaches of Okinawa, April 1.

Unlike American ground troops on day 1 of the assault, naval forces positioned off the coast were attacked. Admiral Spruance's flagship, the *Indianapolis*, as well as the battleship *West Virginia*, two transports, and one landing ship were all hit by suicide attacks. The British carrier *Indefatigable* was also hit by a kamikaze plane, but it remained able to continue launching and recovering planes. As the first day came to an end, casualties were much lighter than military estimates had assumed, and it was a surprise that American forces had captured the airfields so quickly. However, Allied officials understood that the Japanese would not simply capitulate, especially not on an island so close to the home islands.

Ahead of the invasion of Okinawa, the Japanese commander at Okinawa, Lieutenant General Ushijima of the 32nd Army, positioned his troops to execute the commands that had been given to him: to hold Okinawa until the end and exact as heavy a price as possible on the Allied forces invading the island. The 32nd Army had been weakened when its 9th Division was sent to Formosa, but they still possessed an important artillery arsenal greater than any the Americans had faced in the Pacific so far. In fact, Ushijima's decision not to contest Okinawa's beaches probably stemmed from his desire to keep his artillery from being attacked by American warplanes and naval guns. Instead, he positioned them inland where they would be safer, a similar tactic to the one the Japanese used at Iwo Jima. Ushijima also conceded the airfields as indefensible and opted to position his troops in fortifications around the island.

Ushijima

A picture of Japanese commanders on Okinawa in February 1945. (1) Admiral Minoru Ota, (2) Lt. Gen. Mitsuru Ushijima, (3) Lt. Gen. Isamu Cho, (4) Col. Hitoshi Kanayama, (5) Col. Kikuji Hongo, and (6) Col. Hiromichi Yahara.

On the second day of their attack, the invading forces altered the plan due to the ease with which they had captured the airfields. Instead of first attacking the southern portion of the island before moving to the north, American troops would now simultaneously take both areas of the island. From the beginning of their advances, however, both thrusts, made up of Lieutenant General Simon Bolivar Buckner, Jr.'s Tenth Army (moving north) and Major General John R. Hodge's XXIV Corps (moving south), began to encounter resistance in the form of camouflaged Japanese positions surrounded by minefields.

Hodge

Bolivar, Jr.

Spruance, Nimitz, and Buckner

On Hodge's drive south, the 7th Division, which was positioned along the left flank, fell behind the 96th Division when they were engaged by Japanese forces positioned along a ridge parallel to the coastline near the town of Kuba. After an aerial bombardment of the Japanese position, the 7th Division engaged in a frontal assault that was turned back by the Japanese units. A second aerial bombardment was followed by a second frontal assault, but that attack also failed. On their third attempt, the men of the 7th Division again proceeded with a frontal assault, but this time the division's Company C broke off and flanked the Japanese position. The Japanese were completely surprised by this maneuver, and Japanese soldiers defending the ridge were wiped out when Company C brought the brunt of their grenades and flamethrowers on them. This would establish a pattern in American engagement with Japanese troops on Okinawa, because while the Japanese were very skilled at defending against a frontal assault, they were constantly unable to cope with flanking maneuvers. After gaining the sightline of the ridge, American reconnaissance could start to determine the positions of Japanese forces in the defensive zone around the town of Shuri (Frank, p. 70).

Meanwhile, the 96th Division was also facing stronger resistance from Japanese forces as it moved south. When the Americans came up to a ridge near Mashiki, they faced Japanese defenses that included a tank moat, barbed wire, and minefields. After aerial bombardment of the Japanese position, the American 2nd Battalion, 383rd Infantry charged, forcing the Japanese to retreat, and in subsequent charges, the Americans were able to gain control of the entire ridge. The 96th Division then made its way forward to the defensive zone surrounding the Kakazu area, where the fighting would be bloody and fierce. In this defensive zone, American troops would face three Japanese battalions, which were each composed of 1,200 troops.

In the north, Japanese defenses were not as strong as those in the south. As progress to the south was made, the American forces pushing north destroyed two pockets of Japanese resistance on their way to the town of Nagahama during the first week. The northern expedition then increased their advance in the hopes of coming upon Japanese units before they had time to adequately prepare a defense. Japanese troops in the area withdrew toward the Motobu Peninsula, and by April 7th, Americans forces had sealed off the peninsula from the rest of Okinawa and moved to destroy the Japanese forces there. By April 8th, the Japanese had retreated to prepared positions on the Motobu Peninsula, where American forces in that sector (the Marines of the III Amphibious Corps) were ordered to eliminate them. While the Americans encircled the Japanese positions on the Motobu Peninsula, the Japanese forces decided to engage in a guerrilla-style defensive strategy.

While the northern and southern campaigns in Okinawa pushed on, Allied naval vessels unloaded goods and equipment for the ground troops. Naval strategists were aware of the threat still posed by Japanese aircraft and naval vessels, so they placed vessels to screen the Allied transports at Okinawa. They also created an anti-submarine screen stretching from the northern coast of Okinawa to the Keramas. Finally, a radar picket lay beyond this, and then the Fast Carrier Force and British Carrier Force lay beyond this.

Along with early air attacks against naval ships, the Japanese Navy decided to utilize the remaining ships from its Combined Fleet: the battleship *Yamato*, as well as the cruiser *Yahagi* and seven destroyers. Because the *Yamato* only had enough fuel to make it to Okinawa, Japan's plan was to beach the battleship at Okinawa and then use its guns against the Allied forces off the coast.

As the *Yamato* task force moved toward Okinawa, Japanese aircraft began attacking American vessels, and during attacks on April 6th, roughly 355 of the 900 planes used were manned by kamikaze pilots. The fact that over 1/3 of the aircraft used were kamikazes reveal the great lengths Japanese military leaders were willing to take to defend the island, and during the fighting, the Americans lost three destroyers, two ammunition ships and one landing ship. The next day, kamikaze planes damaged the battleship *Maryland*, the destroyer *Bennet*, and the destroyer escort *Wesson*. The carrier *Hancock* was also hit by a kamikaze plane, and though 72 men were killed in the incident, *Hancock* was still able to recover its planes and continue operations.

As the ships dealt with Japanese planes on April 6, American reconnaissance identified the *Yamato* heading for Okinawa, and the Allied navy sought to destroy the ship before it was able to reach Okinawa and attack Allied vessels with its incredible firepower. American Rear Admiral M.L. Deyo made preparations to deal with the *Yamato* group by sending a force of six battleships, seven cruisers and 21 destroyers to form a wall between the *Yamato* group and the Allied transports.

A map showing the route of the Allied forces (red) intercepting the *Yamato* group (black).

The first attacks took place when planes from the Task Group 58 (280 in all) attacked the *Yamato* Group, and after multiple waves of aerial bombardment, the cruiser *Yahagi* was disabled, the destroyer *Hamakaze* had been sunk, and the *Yamato* had been hit by two bombs and a torpedo. Although the *Yamato* continued to move forward, its speed had been affected and its slower movement now made it an easier target for Allied bombers. Eventually, both the *Yamato* and and *Yahagi* were destroyed, killing 3,665 men in all, and with the loss of the *Yamato* group, the Japanese navy lost almost all ability to contest the Allied forces at sea. From that point forward, their only capabilities to challenge the Allied naval forces were through air attacks (Gow, p. 92).

Aerial view of the attacks on the *Yahagi*.

Aerial view of American planes attacking the *Yamato*.

Aerial view of the *Yamato* under attack.

The *Yamato* shortly after exploding on April 7.

Fighting in the South

Back on Okinawa, intelligence reports were still hazy as to Japanese positions, but the Americans understood that they would soon be facing the main body of Japanese forces. On April 7th, the 7th Division was still heading south when its western wing, made up of the 184th infantry, encountered a major Japanese position near Minami-Uebaru that was called Red Hill. Red Hill consisted of a hill with trenches and caves that were covered with mines and barbed wire. The 184th attempted a frontal assault to take the position, but they were forced to abandon it when they encountered heavy machine gun and mortar fire. A second attempt at a frontal assault included tanks, but one hit a landmine and another was blown up by a satchel-charge. Japanese heavy artillery fire drove the infantry units once again, and some more tanks were disabled in the engagement. Finally, when the 3rd battalion of the 184th moved in a flanking maneuver on the enemy's right, it caught the Japanese by surprise and allowed the Americans to take the hill.

The 184th Infantry would come across two more fortified positions over the next few days. The first, called Tomb Hill, was located northwest of Ouchi, while the second was called Triangulation Hill. While the 184th managed to take both positions, they again faced problems when trying to attack Japanese positions with tank-infantry teams. Tanks were susceptible to the heavy artillery fire from these Japanese positions, and once they were disabled and their infantry escorts driven off, the tank crews were bayoneted and the tanks were incorporated into the Japanese defensive works.

After capturing Tomb Hill and Triangulation Hill by April 8th, the 184th came upon the Shuri Fortified Zone. Meanwhile, the other half of the American forces moving southward, the 96th Division, also came across a heavily fortified area near Kakazu. Unaware that they had come upon the outer rim of a heavily fortified defensive position and believed they were only engaging in another Japanese defensive pocket. In actuality, the Japanese 32nd Army had set up their headquarters here, and their position was heavily defended with tank moats, trenches, mortars, heavy artillery support, and reinforcements that could be sent to shore up any potential breaches in their defense.

As Companies A and C of the 1st Battalion moved forward to engage with Japanese forces on the western portion of Kakazu Hill, they were able to reach the crest of the ridge without being detected, but when Japanese soldiers finally spotted them, Company A was pinned down by heavy fire. Company C attempted to reach them, but they were forced back by Japanese fire. Finally, all three companies were forced to retreat away from the hill. The surviving troops from the three companies of the 1st Battalion were so badly injured that army medical personnel deemed them all unfit for further combat duty.

The western edge of the Kakazu ridge

At the same time that the 1st Battalion began their attack from the west, Company L charged up the ridge from the other side without being spotted by the Japanese and also reached the crest. However, Company I, which was supposed to support Company L, had been delayed in initiating its attack and was pinned down by enemy fire. This isolated Company L at the top of the ridge, where they were forced to repel a Japanese attack. Company L was later able to retreat under smoke cover, but by the time this engagement ended, the 1st Battalion had been reduced to about half strength and was no longer operational. These assaults, which took place on April 9th, had failed to gain the Americans any ground, but they had managed to kill roughly 400 soldiers, thus weakening the manpower of the Japanese defense.

The Japanese 32nd Army was carrying out its plan of inflicting as much damage as possible, but at this point, military leaders in Tokyo gave the 32nd a new directive for a counteroffensive against American positions. While the leadership of the 32nd Army had conceded the two main airfields in Okinawa and had instead focused their attention on creating a strong defensive zone in the southern portion of the island, military commanders in Tokyo considered the airfields to be of strategic importance, and their orders for a counteroffensive were aimed at reclaiming the airfields. The plan that the 32nd Army created involved sending Japanese troops into close proximity with American units, thereby neutralizing American artillery, naval guns and air support because they would be reluctant to hit their own soldiers. The Japanese offensive began on April 12th, but was quickly defeated. From that point on, the 32nd Army focused its attention on defending their base in the south, with the only offensive operations being nighttime infiltrations of American camps.

By the end of fighting on the 12th, American casualties had grown to 2,900 with 451 dead, while Japanese casualties were at 5,750.

American soldiers pass a dead Japanese soldier on Okinawa, April 1945.

Fighting in the North

An American plane firebombing northern Okinawa.

During the second half of April, American troops faced heavy fighting in the south, while the units in the north surrounded Japanese positions in the Motobu Peninsula. One critical region in the north, called Ie Shima, was deemed to be important as a place where the Allies could install an early warning air defense system for units on Okinawa, as well as being a launch point for the invasion of Japan. The Japanese were aware of the strategic importance of Ie Shima, and in the early part of 1945, they ordered 2,000 soldiers and civilians to destroy the airfields and military installations there. They had also constructed defensive positions from which they hoped to repel invading soldiers.

The Japanese strategy for Ie Shima was based on trying to entice American troops to land on the lightly guarded beaches and trick American military commanders into believing the area was only lightly defended when in fact there were 2,000 Japanese soldiers stationed there. The Americans encountered not just a strong military force on Ie Shima but also resistance from civilians (including women), who attacked American soldiers with anything from modern weapons to wooden spears. As a result, American soldiers at Ie Shima were among the first to experience the "fanatical resistance" of civilians, something that would represent considerable danger for any American invasion of the Japanese mainland as well.

American soldiers in a foxhole with a Japanese orphan, April 1945.

As the Americans began their attack, Japanese forces were centered around the town of Ie, which was protected by ridges surrounding the area. The largest ridge, called the Bloody Ridge by the 77th Division, was the main natural defensive barrier. For U.S. ground forces, it was important for them to capture defensive positions on the high ground, because from those positions, Japanese troops could fire artillery at the transport ships unloading troops and equipment on the beaches. To soften up enemy positions, American planes flew bombing missions during the two days preceding the attack, and on April 16th, American ground troops commenced their attack. American troops quickly took the airfields and made progress moving inland before Japanese forces counterattacked. The 3rd Battalion, 305th Regimental Combat Team (RCT) took the brunt of this assault, as Japanese soldiers armed not only with guns but also grenades and satchel charges sought to either shoot Americans or blow themselves up in the vicinity of American troops. During the attack, one American soldier broke his arm when the leg of a Japanese trooper who had blown himself up hit him (Gow, p. 112).

Aerial view shows the town of Ie and the high ground along the eastern end of the island.

American tanks on Bloody Ridge knocked out by Japanese artillery, April 20.

The Americans faced a difficult situation when they came upon the ridges of Ie Shima. The 1st Battalion, 305th RCT attempted to secure the Bloody Ridge on April 17th but were driven back. What amounted to a stalemate at the Bloody Ridge turned when the Americans decided to approach the ridge from the south and west rather than the north. The 305th and 307th moved slowly up the ridge and were able to take the fortifications at the top of the ridge, but then they had to face a major Japanese counterattack to hold it. The Japanese sent 300 troops, along with civilians, and after marching through their own mortar fire, they got within 15 feet of the Americans before they were driven back. While the Americans suffered heavy casualties, the Japanese lost 280 soldiers.

As this battle was raging at the Bloody Ridge, the 3rd Battalion, 305th Infantry destroyed Japanese positions around the town of Ie, which opened up a path to the ridge network from the south. As the rest of the 305th approached from the south, a simultaneous attack allowed American forces to make their way up the ridges and destroy the remaining Japanese defenders. Even after being driven from the ridges, Japanese troops and civilians mounted a counterattack on April 22nd, but these attackers were defeated with no further casualties suffered by the Americans. In all, the Japanese lost 4,706 casualties, including at least 1,500 civilians who had been forcibly armed and placed in uniform. For the Americans, the 77th Division suffered 1,100 casualties. (Gow, p. 115) Although the cost had been very high, capturing Ie Shima allowed the Americans a base from which to launch support operations for ground troops still fighting on Okinawa, as well as providing them airfields from which to launch a potential attack against the Japanese home islands.

Meanwhile, Marine commanders began planning an assault on the last remaining Japanese forces in northern Okinawa (the soldiers who had retreated to Motobu Peninsula). The plan, devised on April 13th, involved having the 1st and 2nd Battalions of the 4th Marines, the 3rd Battalion of the 29th Marines, and the 1st and 2nd Battalions of the 29th Marines attack simultaneously from all directions. The various battalions maneuvered into position, and on the 16th, the Americans commenced their attack. The 3rd Battalion (29th Marines) and 2nd Battalion (4th Marines) attacked Japanese forces to the west, while the 3rd Battalion (4th Marines) pushed north. At the same time, the 29th Marines moved into position to attack the stronghold of Yae Take. All of these units were supported by artillery and aerial bombardment of Japanese positions, and by the late afternoon, the crest of Yae Take had been captured and many Japanese units had fled the area. Many were killed later when they attempted to reengage American troops.

By April 18th, Japanese troops at the Motobu Peninsula were in flight, and the 4th and 29th Marines were tasked with chasing them. The 4th Marines killed over 700 soldiers as they tried to retreat away from the peninsula, and from this point forward, the biggest danger of Japanese attacks in northern Okinawa would be from small groups engaging in guerrilla warfare.

American advances (in red) across Okinawa by April 15.

May

   With Japanese forces effectively neutralized in the north, American troops began preparing the area for support operations. But while the north had mostly been cleared of enemy soldiers, the south would continue to be a major area of operations because American units still had to breach the 32rd Army's fortifications around Shuri. In fact, the fighting around Shuri would represent the last major ground battle by American forces against the Japanese in the Pacific War.

   The Japanese defenses at Shuri represented a "tightly-held, fortified coast-to-coast defense line relying on a series of intricate and skillfully constructed underground positions. American veterans now expected accurate and heavy light mortar and machine gun fire backed by artillery, ferocious counterattacks and infiltration attempts plus excellent reverse slope defense." (Gow, p. 119) As General Hodge relayed to his troops on the eve of American attacks on the Japanese position, "It is going to be really tough, there are 65,000-70,000 fighting Japanese holed up in the south end of the island. I see no way to get them out except to blast them out yard by yard." (Gow, p. 119)

As American forces in the south prepared for their attack on Shuri on April 19th, they captured a Japanese document suggesting that the Americans never advanced at night and therefore Japanese troops did not have to be as vigilant during that time. As a result, the Americans moved some units during the night of April 18th without being seen by Japanese soldiers. However, the Americans faced a problem in that they needed to build bridges over an inlet leading up to the outer portions of the Shuri defensive positions. The 27th Engineering Division was ordered to build two 90-foot bridges, and they did so by building the bridges during the night and placing them into position at 3:00 a.m. on April 18th.

As three U.S. army divisions moved toward the Japanese 62nd Division's forward defensive line, naval vessels stationed off the coast engaged in a massive bombardment of Japanese positions. Beginning at 6:00 a.m., six battleships, six cruisers, and six destroyers shelled the 62nd's position for 20 minutes, and then they targeted the rear for 10 minutes in hopes of drawing Japanese troops back toward the forward areas of their defensive perimeter. After that, the ships started shelling the forward areas once more. Meanwhile, the 10th Army, with 27 corps and division artillery units, also began shelling the Japanese positions. Together, this was the greatest concentration of artillery used in the Pacific Theater, and it was estimated that 19,000 shells hit Japanese positions over 40 minutes of bombing (Gow, p. 121), but the grand bombardment of Japanese positions had little effect because Japanese soldiers were able to hide in underground shelters and caves.

In their initial engagement against Shuri, which occurred on April 19th, the XXIV Corps was unable to break through the Japanese forward line. Further fighting occurred between April 20th and 24th, but American troops once again found it extremely difficult to break the Japanese defense. An important problem that developed during the four days of fighting was the creation of a mile long gap between the 27th and 96th Divisions that the Americans needed to close, since American commanders feared that the Japanese could counterattack through this gap to flank both the 27th and 96th Divisions. The 165th Infantry was ordered to close the gap, but they encountered problems almost immediately when the 1st Battalion lost contact with the 2nd Battalion. Both battalions then found themselves in a heavy firefight when they made contact with a heavily fortified Japanese position that they called the "Item Pocket", which was manned by 600 soldiers as well as several hundred civilians.

The 165th faced the Japanese defenses in this area without mortar or tank support, and even though they suffered heavy casualties, they had established an unbroken line by April 26th and began an advance to the south. After securing the area west of the Item Pocket, they were joined by tank-infantry units that assaulted the Item Pocket and were able to conquer the position by the evening of the 27th.

Another position that the Japanese had heavily fortified was the area surrounding the village of Iso. At Iso, the Japanese 21st Independent Infantry Battalion was joined by the 1st Heavy Mortar Division. Two peaks jutting out of the ridge network surrounding Iso were the keys to the defense of the area; East Pinnacle rose 50 feet above the ridge and Japanese soldiers had constructed fortifications and tunnels there, while West Pinnacle was also fortified and included machine gun positions. As the 2nd and 3rd Battalions of the 27th Division's 105th Infantry began their attack, they suffered heavy casualties but were able to take East Pinnacle when two assault battalions of the 105th Infantry scaled the peak and surprised the Japanese soldiers stationed there. The West Pinnacle was also captured after the Japanese soldiers positioned there decided to wildly charge the American soldiers who had surrounded it.

The Japanese 32nd Army's leadership determined early on that its outer defense perimeter would eventually be breached, so they decided to withdraw the bulk of their troops to the second Shuri defense line. This meant that American advances after April 24th only came up against small pockets of Japanese troops instead of facing the full brunt of the Japanese defense, but the withdrawal also gave the Americans time to regroup and reshape their plans for taking southern Okinawa. With the successes in northern Okinawa, General Buckner now decided to shift III Amphibious Corps to the south, where the increase in manpower would help him in the frontal assault that he planned against the Shuri defense rings. In addition, the Americans began rotating units. The 96th Division, which had engaged in much of the fighting in southern Okinawa up to this point, was replaced on the front line by the 77th Infantry Division. After a week of rest, the 96th was then sent back to the front lines to replace the 7th Division. The 27th Division had also suffered heavy casualties and was replaced by the 1st Marine Division, which moved south from northern Okinawa.

Japanese strategists originally believed the most likely American attack would be a flanking maneuver attempting to catch the Japanese by surprise, but on April 26th, General Ushijima abandoned his defense of possible flanking maneuvers and instead met the threat of a frontal assault by redeploying these troops to help hold the second Shuri defense ring. He deployed the 44th Independent Mixed Brigade behind the 62nd Division to prevent American penetration of the western area. He then sent the 22nd Regiment of the 24th Division to relieve the 62nd Division in the east, while sending the rest of the 24th Division to the northeast, where they would act as reserves.

As each side maneuvered units into strategic locations in southern Okinawa and braced for the next attack, Allied naval forces were still stationed off the coast to provide support for the ground troops. At the same time, the navy had to protect itself from constant Japanese aerial attacks. Naval units off the coast of Okinawa became more vulnerable every day, and throughout April, as many as 20 planes attacked the fleet each day. These planes included kamikazes, divebombers, and torpedo bombers (Gow, p. 135). During the month of April, 20 Allied ships were sunk and 157 were damaged, but even with these successes, overall Japanese naval forces were losing the ability to contest the seas. The *Yamato* Task Force had been the last of the Japanese Navy's vessels capable of launching offensive maneuvers, and the Japanese had lost 1,000 planes during the month. As a result, even though the Japanese had inflicted large amounts of damage to the Allied fleet off the coast of Okinawa, they had also sustained heavy losses, which were made all the more important by the fact that Japan was having trouble replacing the pilots and warplanes that they were losing. Furthermore, by the end of April, the Allies had moved planes onto airstrips they controlled on Okinawa, and the increased number of planes meant the ships in the vicinity of Okinawa now had air cover protecting them around the clock.

American anti-aircraft fire at night from one of the Okinawan airstrips.

The Japanese High Command was aware of the staggering losses suffered by the Japanese army and navy as the battle for Okinawa continued, and they understood the enemy had superior manpower and technology. Facing those realities, the Japanese believed that losing Okinawa was only a matter of time, and they now hoped the 32nd Army could simply hold out long enough and inflict enough damage on American ground troops to discourage any attempt to invade the home islands. But even as the Japanese commanders lost faith in Okinawa's defenses, Ushijima and the 32nd were still a dangerous force, and they were even considering a counterattack on American positions.

By the end of April, American commanders had brought the III Amphibious Corps to southern Okinawa and began planning for a three-division offensive against Shuri. On the right, the 27th Division made some progress before being stopped near the town of Nakama, roughly three miles north of Shuri, but in the center, the 106th Infantry engaged in heavy fighting and was unable to advance far before their troop strength was depleted to the point that they were unable to continue the offensive. The 106th subsequently had to be relieved by the 6th Marine Division. Also in the center, the 96th Division failed to gain much ground, but they did manage to kill hundreds of Japanese soldiers in the Urasoe-Mura escarpment.

The battle lines (in red) on May 1.

An American reconnaissance plane flying over Okinawa in May.

On May 2nd, American scouts reported that the Japanese were moving their artillery further south, and with that, commanders believed that the rigid structure of the defensive positions meant the Japanese only had two choices: hold their position until the end or withdraw to the south. The Americans did not believe the Japanese had the capability to counterattack, so they were completely unprepared when the Japanese actually did mount a counterattack. At the time, the Japanese commanders had become increasingly worried about the troop losses they were sustaining. The 62nd Division, for example, was down to less than 50% of its fighting strength, and additionally, it seemed that many Japanese soldiers were suffering from a loss of morale. These two factors convinced the 32nd Army's leadership to consider mounting an attack against the Americans. Lieutenant General Isamu Cho, Ushijima's chief of staff, believed Japanese forces were being slowly eroded, and that the best course of action was to attack while they still had the manpower to do so.

As a result, on May 2nd, the Japanese officers announced the plan for their attack. They would engage in a large-scale counterattack on May 4th in coordination with an assault on Allied naval forces off the coast. The goal of the attack was to destroy the XXIV Corps on Okinawa and also to cripple the Allied fleet, an action which they believed would turn the tide of the battle. The main attacking force would be the 24th Division, which was comprised of 15,000 men. The 24th Division was supposed to lead breakthroughs of the American lines at the center and eastern sectors, and once through, other units would pour into the gaps and destroy the isolated American forces. In conjunction with the advance on the ground, suicide boats and planes would hit the Allied fleet, disrupting the supply lines to the ground forces on Okinawa and giving Japanese troops an opportunity to strangle American ground forces on the island.

On May 4th, the attack commenced, and Japanese troops were ordered to "kill one American devil for every Japanese," which was asking a lot considering that the kill ratio on Okinawa to that point had been 10 Japanese dead for every American killed. (Gow, p. 143). At the same time, the complexity of the Japanese plan helped bring about its undoing. For instance, the 26th Shipping Engineers were supposed to make an amphibious landing but missed their landing point and instead came to an area between the Yontan and Kadena airfields that was heavily defended by the Americans. All the boats were destroyed, and the men who managed to reach shore were cut down by American machine-gun fire. A small group did manage to elude the Americans, but they were killed the next day when they were engaged by American forces near Chatan. On the east coast, Japanese forces encountered similar problems; when native Okinawan boatmen tried to row several hundred troops behind the American 7th Division for an attack, they were spotted by naval ships and destroyed. In total, the Japanese lost between 500-800 men in the two botched attacks, and they also lost all their boats.

The main attack began with an artillery barrage that was perhaps the heaviest the Americans faced in the Pacific Theater. The 24th Division then surprised American forces by marching through their own mortar fire. However, after overcoming the initial element of surprise, the American 7th Division was able to hold its ground, and as Japanese troops were caught in open ground and not able to continue pushing forward, they were exposed to American artillery and gunfire that had a devastating effect on the Japanese soldiers.

At a second point, the Japanese attempted to open a breach in the American lines by pushing infantry, tanks and engineers forward, but here too the Americans stopped their forward momentum by disabling the Japanese tanks with artillery fire. This left Japanese forces unable to concentrate their forces in the spearhead maneuver that had been planned, and again, they were unable to open a gap in the American lines.

Even though reports coming back to the Japanese commanders indicated that they had been unsuccessful in breaching the American lines, Lieutenant General Tatsumi Amemiya, commander of the 24th Division, continued the attack by launching another wave of attackers at the American lines on the evening of May 4th. In this second attack, Japanese troops succeeded in opening a gap about 1,000 yards behind American lines, but they withdrew later in the evening for unknown reasons. In the early morning of May 5th, the Japanese attacked this area again with a combined force of infantry and tanks, but this time, the Americans held their lines. By the end of the engagement, the Japanese had lost 248 soldiers as well as much of their equipment.

The only real success occurred in the 77th Division's sector, where the Japanese managed to occupy Tanabaru and Tanabaru Ridge, which cut off supply lines to some of the American front line troops in that area. American commanders were very worried by this turn of events and pushed for American troops to retake Tanabaru Ridge. It took three days of fierce fighting, but eventually, the Americans regained control of the ridge, and in the process they killed another 460 Japanese soldiers.

By the evening of May 5th, it had become obvious to Japanese commanders that the offensive had failed, and in order to save face, they announced to the Japanese military leaders that they had inflicted a large amount of damage on the Americans and were now going to temporarily suspend the offensive to go revise their plans for a future engagement. In all, 5,000 troops had been lost, and the 24th Division, which spearheaded the attack, had suffered the largest number of casualties. The loss of equipment was equally important, because the Japanese lost much of their tank capabilities and had also exposed their artillery placements to American fire. On May 4th, 19 pieces of field artillery had been destroyed.

Meanwhile, the Americans had also endured heavy casualties. The 1st Marine Division had lost 352 men, while the 7th and 77th Divisions had lost 379 men. Had the Japanese offensive occurred before the Americans had rotated their forces on the front lines, they might have been able to force open the gaps they had planned, but since they were facing relatively fresh American troops, they were unable to achieve their objectives.

Once the Japanese offensive had been halted, the 10th Army began a renewed push south. In the southeast, on May 6th and 7th, the 7th Division sent patrols to sweep the area in front of them for enemy soldiers, and, after finding none, they began an attack. They took an area called Gaja Ridge with little resistance before finally being pushed back at Conical Hill, where Japanese troops mounted a strong defense and used mines that had been placed in the area to prevent tanks from supporting the American soldiers there. Over the next two days, the 7th Division made incremental progress against the Japanese 22nd Regiment of the 24th Division, which had been ordered to hold their ground for as long as possible. At the same time, the 7th Division was under pressure from American commanders to make better progress, and by May 9th, the 7th Division had pushed forward into an area called Kochi Ridge, where exhausted soldiers were finally replaced with troops from the 96th Division.

Although the Americans were making progress in their southern drive, it was taking a lot of time, and total American casualties were mounting, reaching 20,000 by early May. General Buckner, who was becoming frustrated by the Japanese defense, decided to launch an all-out attack on Japanese positions that would begin on May 11th. This general offensive involved two corps that would align themselves across the island; the American units involved included the 6th Marine Division and 1st Marine Division of the III Amphibious Corps and the 77th Division and 96th Division of the XXIV Army Corps. The 27th Division was given the responsibility to control northern Okinawa, while the battle-weary 7th Division was allowed to rest.

General Buckner's ultimate goal was to use the two corps to envelop the Shuri defenses along the west and east while attacking heavily through the middle of the Japanese position. Buckner's staff believed the Japanese were weaker along their right flank, so they placed their freshest troops there in the belief that they could break through the Japanese lines. However, because Ushijima had previously removed units guarding the coastal areas and redeployed them facing the American ground troops, the Japanese defenses were now strengthened beyond what American planners had assumed.

The battle lines (in red) in mid-May

Even though the Americans had planned on a coordinated attack involving their western, eastern, and central units, things devolved quickly into uncoordinated battles in all three sectors. In the west, American forces were making slow progress as they had to construct and cross bridges while also getting their heavy equipment across, all while facing heavy fire from Japanese troops. The most difficult area that the troops in the west had to face was at Sugar Loaf Hill, a three-hill complex that was covered by artillery positions at Shuri. The fighting at Sugar Loaf Hill was extremely intense, and the 2nd Battalion suffered 400 casualties over a three day period. The 6th Marine Division also suffered heavy casualties, but American troops were finally able to take the hill on May 18th after four days of heavy fighting. After that, American troops were quickly confronted with another strong defensive position at Horseshoe and Crescent Hill.

At Horseshoe and Crescent Hill, American troops not only had to take another well-defended Japanese position, but Japanese troops counterattacked, forcing the Americans to call on battle-weary reserve troops to help stem the tide.

A demolition crew from the 6th Marine Division blowing up a Japanese cave in May.

On the left, the 77th Division faced a tough defensive position at Chocolate Drop Hill. Not only was the hill heavily fortified, the ground leading up to the hill was completely open and had no cover that could shield American infantry units from artillery and small-arms fire as they moved toward this position. Even worse, portions of the ground were marshy, and when it began to rain, tanks were unable to provide support for infantry units storming the hill. It took the 77th Division a number of days before they were able to take the hill, and as on the right, once they captured Chocolate Drop Hill on May 20th, they were immediately faced with more fortified positions in Flattop Hill and Dick Hills. These two positions were right on the inner edge of the Shuri Defense Zone, and Japanese soldiers stationed at these two areas held out for 10 days before they were overcome by a combined force of the 77th an 96th Divisions.

The breakthrough of the Shuri Defense Zone finally occurred on this left side of the American attack, and it involved the Tenth Army, which attacked Conical Hill, a 476 foot high hill that was a key defensive position. In addition to its mortar and artillery placements, Conical Hill was manned by the Japanese 89th Regiment of the 24th Division, with support from the 27th Independent Battalion. American commanders launched a frontal assault against Conical Hill with the 96th Division, which the Japanese expected, but the Japanese did not expect two American platoons to concentrate their efforts against an area that had strong natural defenses but was weak in terms of manpower. Focusing on this weak spot ultimately allowed the 96th to take the hill.

Once the 96th Division had taken Conical Hill, the American forces in that area had created a narrow path through the Japanese defenses between Conical Hill and the coast, where American naval vessels were positioned. The 7th Division, back in action after receiving a rest period, was ordered to move through the path created by the 96th Division. Japanese forces were not ready for the suddenness of the American attack, which began on the night of May 19th and commenced without tank support. The 184th Infantry made the initial push into the Japanese lines, and as they moved to protect the western flank, the 32nd Infantry continued the push forward to cut Shuri off from the south.

The 32nd Infantry's progress was slowed as the weather turned, and without tank support, they faced a succession of Japanese counterattacks alone. From May 23-26, the 32nd Infantry made little progress, and for American commanders, it seemed as though the Japanese were planning on holding out and fighting until the last man. What they did not realize was that Japanese leaders had planned a coordinated retreat from their positions. The Japanese 32nd Army had been in contact with their superiors in Tokyo and told them that they had engaged their last reserves. From this point forward, the 32nd Army would have to either engage the enemy in guerrilla warfare or hold out until the end at Shuri, after which the Americans would be able to plan their assault of the Japanese mainland unimpeded.

With no reinforcements from Japan forthcoming, the 32nd Army's commanding officer, Ushijima, decided that fighting until the end at Shuri was not the optimal decision. Given that a number of his 50,000 men were unarmed, packing his men into the small area of Shuri could cause chaos, and standing until the last man at Shuri would shorten the amount of time military planners in Tokyo would have to prepare for an American assault of the home islands. Instead, Ushijima decided on a retreat to prepared positions on the Kan Peninsula. As the retreat began, Ushijima left a few units behind at Shuri to engage the Americans and delay them beginning a pursuit of Japanese forces.

American units saw Japanese movements as early as May 22nd, but at this time they assumed these were civilians and disregarded their importance. It was not until a few days later, on May 26th, that the Americans finally understood a withdrawal was in progress. On that day, they saw

3,000 troops and 100 trucks moving south. This meant that only a skeleton force was left at Shuri, and American units commenced to storm Shuri positions, taking Shuri Castle by the end of the month. With Shuri under American control, they now moved to the last Japanese position at the southern tip of Okinawa.

U.S. Marine Lieutenant Colonel R.P. Ross, Jr. placing the American flag on a parapet of Shuri castle at the end of May.

The End of the Battle and Its Aftermath

At the end of May, American forces had been on Okinawa for two months, and they had killed over 62,000 Japanese soldiers, with another 9,500 estimated as killed. About 8,000 of these deaths had occurred in northern Okinawa, with the rest occurring in southern Okinawa. The Americans had also suffered heavy casualties, with the III Amphibious Corps and XXIV Corps suffering 26,044 casualties. The Marines had suffered 6,315 casualties, while the army had 7,762 casualties, but even with these casualties, the ratio of Americans killed to Japanese killed was still roughly 1:10 (Gow, p.166-167). Added to the casualty numbers were issues of exhaustion; over 61 days of fighting, the 96th Division had fought for 50 days, the 7th Division had fought for

49 days, and the 77th Division fought for 32 days.

Even though the Americans saw the Japanese retreat, they believed it was not an organized withdrawal but actually the end of organized resistance. General Buckner believed there was nothing left to do but mop up the last pockets of Japanese resistance. However, the Japanese forces that had withdrawn from Shuri were still organized, even though they now split into two groups. The 32nd Army comprised the bulk of the forces, and they had cooperated during the defense of Shuri with the remnants of the Okinawa Naval Base Force, which was under the command of Rear Admiral Minoru Ota.

During the retreat, the Naval Base Force's 2,000 men moved to the southwestern area of Oroku, but as the 4th Marines moved to seal off and then destroy the Naval Base Force, they faced off against a mixed Japanese unit that included conscripted Okinawans, administrative troops, and construction and submarine crews. Few of these men had experience in ground combat, and as the 900 American troops and 24 tanks moved against the Naval Base Force on June 4th, they were able to quickly move in against little resistance. However, after that first day, the American soldiers moved within range of the Naval Base Force's machine guns and 40 mm cannons, and the 4th Marines were without tank support because they had to cross marshy ground. By June 7th, the Japanese forces here had blocked the American advance, but the 4th Marines were eventually joined by the 29th Marines from the west, the 4th Marines from the south, and the 22nd Marines from the southeast. With these reinforcements and the possibility of multiple points of attack, the Japanese Naval Base Force was surrounded and slowly pushed together into an area near the town of Tomigusuki. On June 11th, the Americans began their attack on this final position, and by the next day, nearly all of the Japanese soldiers had either been killed in the fighting or had committed suicide, with the exception of a group of 159 who surrendered. This turned out to be the largest surrender of Japanese forces on Okinawa.

A group of Japanese prisoners who surrendered rather than commit suicide.

While the Naval Base Force moved to its position on Oroku, the 32nd Army retreated to prepared positions at Yuza-Dake and Yaeju-Dake. These positions were located on ridges, with the ground leading up to them pocked with hills from which small bands of Japanese soldiers could harass and delay American troops. At this point, Ushijima's 32nd Army consisted of roughly 11,000 men, and they were ordered to fight to the death. The bulk of this force consisted of the 24th Division, which was deployed along the west from Yaeju-Dake to the town of Itoman. Ushijima held the 62nd Division back as reserves, and in the east, he deployed the 44th Independent Mixed Brigade. While Ushijima still had a core of veteran soldiers, many of his remaining men had been poorly trained and were not likely to put up much of a fight against the Americans. Moreover, the 32nd Army had little artillery and mortar support this time, which would obviously hamper their efforts at holding off American attacks.

On June 1st, American forces moving toward Ushijima's positions attempted to close the gap quickly, but the marshy, muddy terrain was difficult for the soldiers to move on, and they also experienced delays while moving supplies to the frontline troops. As they came upon pockets of Japanese resistance, the defenders also slowed their progress. When the first American units finally reached the Japanese positions, on June 6th, the 381st Infantry was driven back at Yaeju-Dake, but they were eventually able to take the lower section of the ridges. The Americans next planned to attack from the west against a strongly defended hill area that they called the "Big Apple."

As the 381st Infantry moved up toward the Big Apple, they were caught in machine gun and 20mm fire and were forced off the lower ridges they had previously taken, so the Americans took a different approach the next day. This time, they called in airstrikes against the Japanese positions and also fired artillery barrages against it. The 381st were able to move higher up the ridges by utilizing smoke shells to screen an advance, aided in this effort by the fact the Japanese soldiers thought the smoke was a cover for a retreat. When they began showing themselves along their position, many were killed by artillery fire.

Although the 381st continued to make progress, by June 12th, American commanders realized that the terrain on Big Apple made it nearly impossible for these troops to continue to push forward in a timely manner. Instead, they shifted their attention to the advance by the 7th Division, which was moving along the right flank. The 7th Division's task since the beginning of June had been to move southward and eliminate any threats along the Chinen Peninsula. They spent the first week of June gathering roughly 10,000 civilian prisoners at Chinen, and then on June 8th, they moved into position for an attack on Yaeju-Dake. Since the paths leading up Yaeju-Dake were in open view of Japanese soldiers, the 7th Division decided to attack at night, and a heavy fog that rolled into the area further shielded their movements from the Japanese.

Once again, the Japanese did not believe the Americans would attack at night, so they actually withdrew from the high ground that night to avoid artillery fire and planned to return early the next morning before American troops began their movements for the day. Instead, when the Japanese troops returned to their positions the next morning, they found American soldiers manning their posts. Many of the Japanese soldiers were killed in the morning's engagement, and by the time it had finished, the Americans had taken a key defensive position. Further American advances occurred in the southeast, where the 96th Division engaged the Japanese 44th Independent Mixed Brigade, and by June 12th, the Mixed Brigade had suffered enough casualties that their lines were beginning to give way. As the 44th Mixed Brigade lost its cohesiveness in the face of the American assault, Ushijima committed his reserves to shore up the southeastern defenses, but even with the reserves, the Japanese had insufficient manpower to hold the line. On June 12th, the 96th Division entered the town of Yuza, and by June 16th, Yuza Peak also fell into American hands, representing another major blow to the Japanese defense.

Men from the 96ᵗʰ Division look for hidden Japanese soldiers on Yaeju-Dake.

While the 7ᵗʰ Division was holding its position and the 96ᵗʰ Division continued its push forward, the third part of the plan involved the 1ˢᵗ and 7ᵗʰ Marines near Kunishi Ridge. Like the 96ᵗʰ Division, the 1ˢᵗ and 7ᵗʰ Marines decided on a nighttime attack that began shortly after midnight on June 12ᵗʰ, but this attack, which utilized both tanks and infantry, was quickly met by Japanese machine gun and artillery fire that pushed both the soldiers and tanks back. The Japanese positions at Kunishi Ridge proved so strong that the Marines were unable to overcome the defenses even after attacking over the next several days. The Marines suffered heavy casualties from Japanese machine gun and mortar fire, and it was only after the Americans called in a series of airstrikes that the Japanese defenses were weakened to the point that they could be taken. On the 16ᵗʰ, the 1ˢᵗ and 7ᵗʰ Marines were reinforced with the 22ⁿᵈ Marines, and it was only at this point that they were able to take the ridge and deal another blow to the Japanese 32ⁿᵈ Army.

By June 17ᵗʰ, the Americans had breached the final Japanese positions, and the 32ⁿᵈ Army had finally lost its ability to hold out. As the 32ⁿᵈ Army lost its cohesiveness, the ensuing chaos allowed the Americans to chase random groups of Japanese soldiers and kill them. The one portion of the 32ⁿᵈ Army that remained intact, the 24ᵗʰ Division, withdrew to its former command post at Medeera and held out for four days before being overrun by American troops.

Even after Medeera was taken, Ushijima ordered the last of his troops to engage in guerrilla tactics against the Americans. Many did continue fighting until the end, but roughly 3,000 of them eventually surrendered over the rest of the month, as did 1,000 Okinawan labor troops. For General Ushijima and his second in command, Lieutenant General Cho, surrender was not an option even though General Buckner offered them the chance to surrender. Instead, Ushijima and Cho decided to commit seppuku, a ritual disembowelment that was a part of the Japanese samurai and Imperial Japanese Army traditions. Ironically, Ushijima committed suicide just 4 days after Buckner himself had been mortally wounded during the mop up by a Japanese artillery shell. Buckner had often drawn enemy fire by wearing a helmet with his three stars visible, but he was wearing an unmarked helmet when he was hit on June 18.

A picture of Buckner (far right) taken on June 18, shortly before he was killed.

On June 22, the Battle of Okinawa officially concluded as American troops finally controlled the entire island, but Okinawa has remained an endless source of both fascination and controversy. One of the most notable aspects of the battle was the Japanese's determination to fight to the death, but they also forced civilians into fighting and even forced civilians to commit mass suicide when the end was near. A recent documentary has asserted "there were two types of orders for 'honorable deaths' - one for residents to kill each other and the other for the military to kill all residents." As a result, it's believed that over 100,000 civilians may have been killed, a number made all the more difficult to estimate due to the fact that an untold number evacuated into caves and were entombed in them when American soldiers sealed them as they advanced in order to protect themselves. American troops also used flamethrowers to smoke the Japanese out of caves, and in the process, it was impossible to distinguish civilians from soldiers.

An American Marine using a flamethrower on a Japanese cave.

Most importantly, the Battle of Okinawa was so ruthless that it convinced Allied leaders that the invasion of Japan would be an absolute bloodbath for all sides. American military officials estimated that there would be upwards of a million Allied casualties if they had to invade the Japanese mainland, and if they were successful, Japan would suffer tens of millions of casualties in the process. As the Battle of Okinawa was about to finish, America's secret Manhattan Project was on the brink of its final goal: a successful detonation of a nuclear device. On July 16, 1945, the first detonation of a nuclear device took place in Alamogordo, New Mexico.

The Atomic Bombs

Before World War I, research in atomic theory was concentrated solely in Europe. The United States clung to old fashioned physics while the Europeans moved on to more sophisticated topics. Only after the war did the United States embark into the realm of atomic research, first in California, at Berkeley.

Ernest Lawrence, a Berkeley physics professor, began toying with generating high energy through particle acceleration. Because a linear accelerator would have to be miles long to generate enough energy, Lawrence opted for a spiral model, which he dubbed a cyclotron. Throughout the 1920s and into the 1930s, Lawrence accelerated atoms faster and faster, increasing the amount of energy (measured in electron volts) he was able to produce.

Ernest Lawrence

Lawrence's experiments received a boost in the early 1930s from events taking place in Europe. With Adolf Hitler's rise to power in Nazi Germany, Jews were facing violent persecution at a time when many of them held positions of high prestige in German universities. Nations around the world offered to give the fleeing Jews a new home, including the United States, which recruited many Jews to its universities. Among them was Albert Einstein, who arrived in Princeton, New Jersey, in 1932, and Leó Szilárd, who came to Columbia University in 1938. Others escaped Europe because of the rise of fascist dictatorships; Enrico Fermi fled to the United States during the rise of Benito Mussolini. This flood of scientists into the United States helped propel the country's interest in atomic physics.

Albert Einstein

On the eve of the outbreak of World War II in Europe, Albert Einstein and Leó Szilárd, both European Jews who had immigrated to the United States, sent an urgent letter to President Franklin Roosevelt. Szilárd had been working alongside Enrico Fermi to develop a nuclear chain reaction using uranium to generate vast amounts of power, and he hoped to convince the President to provide more funding and resources to his research.

The now-famous Einstein-Szilárd Letter, written by Szilárd but signed only by Einstein, asserted that "it appears almost certain that this [the creation of nuclear power] could be achieved in the immediate future." It then goes on to discuss the potential of converting this energy source into a bomb, though they cautioned that such a weapon might "be too heavy for transportation by air."

Ominously, the letter discussed an important ingredient in building nuclear technology, access to uranium ore. The United States had only moderate quantities of the ore, though Canada and the Belgian Congo were deemed to have bounties of uranium. Another location, Czechoslovakia, was particularly rich in uranium deposits. However, the two informed President Roosevelt that the German annexation of Czechoslovakia had led the Nazis to stop all sale of uranium from Czechoslovakian mines. They correctly suggested that Germany was probably using the uranium to develop nuclear technology of its own, and that it was important for the United States to outpace Germany in the race to develop nuclear energy.

Though the letter was written in August 1939, about a month before Germany's invasion of Poland and the outbreak of World War II, Roosevelt did not receive the letter until October 11th, 1939. Perhaps this was for the best. With war now raging in Europe, Szilárd's suggestions about a German arms race were all the more potent.

One of Roosevelt's close confidants, Alexander Sachs, presented the letter to the President. He did so by also recalling a story about an American inventor who offered to build steam ship technology for the French Emperor Napoleon. Napoleon was short sighted and rejected the American's offer. The American later took his offer to England, where it was accepted. England, of course, went on to win to win the Napoleonic Wars, and Napoleon met his Waterloo. Would Roosevelt also suffer from such shortsightedness?

With that, Roosevelt was convinced, though hesitant. He called on Lyman Briggs, the Director of the Bureau of Standards, to set up a committee to investigate the uranium issue. The Advisory Committee on Uranium began meeting on October 21st, with Szilárd in attendance. By the end of the meeting, a paltry $6,000 was given to the scientists to further their studies. While the President had committed funds to nuclear research, his generosity was clearly quite limited.

Meanwhile, across the pond, Great Britain was considering nuclear weaponry amid the urgency of a continental war. British scientists Otto Frisch and Rudolf Peierls, both Jewish immigrants from Austria and Germany, authored a letter very similar to that delivered by Einstein and Szilárd.

Both were working at the University of Birmingham when they made a critical discovery. The two had found that, contrary to existing beliefs, a nuclear bomb would require only a tiny bit of uranium – about one kilogram, or 2.2 pounds. Einstein and Szilárd had cautioned that the construction of a bomb rested on the idea that the weapon's weight would be too much to transport by air. On the contrary, Frisch and Peierls' discovery made clear that a bomb could be delivered by air.

The two penned a memorandum and sent it to Henry Tizard, head of the Scientific Survey of Air Defense. Still undecided, he formed a committee to investigate the idea, much as Roosevelt had done in the United States. The MAUD (Military Application of Uranium Detonation) Committee was formed in April 1940, just months after the American Advisory Committee on Uranium had been formed. The United Kingdom had now joined the United States, and possibly Nazi Germany, in the quest to create a nuclear bomb.

Unlike the Americans, however, the British experiments with nuclear weaponry initially advanced much more quickly, no doubt because of the urgency of war. By mid-1940, the Nazis were on the verge of overrunning France, and with the Nazis and Soviets having a nonaggression pact, the Axis were about to be unopposed on the European continent. Britain had to worry about the Nazis turning the full force of their military against them. Naturally, the discovery that a bomb could be produced with potentially decisive effects on the war increased political support for research, reaching all the way up to the highest levels. Even Prime Minister Winston Churchill was offering his seal of approval.

Although weaponry innovations were slow back in the United States, researchers nonetheless made advances in nuclear technology. Most important among these was Glenn Seaborg's discovery of plutonium in March 1941. He had isolated a gram of element 94 and named it plutonium after the recently-discovered planet, Pluto. This discovery yielded another fissionable material in addition to uranium, but political interest in the United States was still tepid at best. The British, however, had hopes of working with the Americans to speed up bomb production. With the Battle of Britain on the verge of reaching its climax, British resources were limited, and safe spaces for research were equally sparse. Hoping to spur American interest, MAUD sent a report detailing its discovery of the feasibility of a nuclear bomb to the American committee headed by Lyman Briggs.

To MAUD's surprise and consternation, the memorandum seemed to have gone unnoticed within the American nuclear community. In August 1941, Australian physicist Mark Oliphant flew to Berkeley, where he met with the American atomic researchers. Oliphant had been working on the British nuclear research with the MAUD Committee, and he came to the U.S.

hoping to ignite increased research efforts in the country. Most importantly, Oliphant met with Ernest Lawrence and managed to convince him of the potential for an atomic bomb. Until then, Berkeley researchers, including Lawrence, had been focused primarily on harnessing nuclear physics as a source of energy, not weaponry.

Convincing Lawrence was a critical moment in the developed of British-American cooperation on the nuclear project. Once Lawrence was convinced, the Berkeley professor spread the word to his fellow American scientists. In particular, Lawrence spoke with Arthur Compton, a leading scientist in the government agency, the Office of Scientific Research and Development (OSRD). The agency was charged with developing scientifically-advanced weapons, though nuclear weaponry was not yet on its agenda. Compton spoke with the Office's leader, MIT professor Vannevar Bush, and convinced him to approve a unit devoted to nuclear research.

By October 9, 1941, this scientific chain, stretching from Australia to Berkeley, had now reached the President of the United States. From the MAUD Committee to Oliphant, then on to Lawrence and Compton, the news of nuclear weaponry had finally reached Bush, a high-level U.S. government official. Before funding and cooperation could be secured, Bush needed to speak directly with President Roosevelt.

That day, Roosevelt shifted his position on nuclear weapons from reluctant to assertive, and he gave the official go-ahead for secret nuclear weapons research, agreeing to collaborate with the British government at the highest levels. Two days later, the President sent a message to Prime Minister Winston Churchill suggesting the two nations work together on the matter. Full cooperation was not yet at its highest levels, however; the British remained uncertain that the Americans were up to the job.

In October, the President had authorized the Army to take over the management of the project, which was still in its baby stages. With this authorization, research into nuclear weaponry catapulted from a snail's pace to greater urgency, with physicists from around the nation now working toward one coordinated effort. Einstein, Fermi, Szilárd, and Lawrence, along with the help of British scientists, were now working under the administrative leaders Briggs and Bush. It was a literal "dream team" of physicists.

Still, events in October hadn't quite brought nuclear bomb manufacturing to fruition. Roosevelt only authorized funds and organization for *research*, stressing that the production stage could not proceed without further presidential authorization. The President wanted a first report from the scientists about the projected costs and timeline of the program.

On a casual Saturday, December 6, 1941, President Roosevelt signed an Executive Order authorizing the creation of the Manhattan Engineering District to coordinate the manufacture of an atomic bomb and giving the program $2 billion. At the time, the act was of questionable legality; Congress had legislated neutrality in the European war, and the Manhattan District opened the doors to British-American weaponry cooperation. When Roosevelt implemented the Lend-Lease program that facilitated arms sales to the British earlier in the war, isolationists were furious, and the America First Committee lobbied strongly against intervention of any sort into the war. Thus, this Executive Order was given in secret, and the President went on to spend the rest of his Saturday relaxing.

The very next day, Roosevelt's relaxation was over for good, and the legality of the Executive Order became a moot point following the attack on Pearl Harbor. The nation was now engaged in an unprecedented battle, and the importance of the Manhattan Engineering District elevated overnight. American nuclear research was about to speed ahead frenetically.

With the creation of the Manhattan District, the central problem associated with nuclear research switched from too little interest to too little time. The Allies and the U.S. had faced setbacks of all sorts entering 1942, and the outcome of the war in Europe and in the Pacific was very much in doubt. The situation remained precarious and uncertain.

Vannevar Bush

On December 18, less than two weeks after President Roosevelt's Executive Order, Vannevar Bush and his co-leader Arthur Compton created the S-1 Uranium Committee to divvy up research projects on nuclear energy. Ernest Lawrence was to research electromagnetic enrichment techniques while Harold Urey was to direct research into gaseous diffusion for uranium enrichment. Together, these top leaders coordinated with research scientists from across the country to create a unified and efficient nationwide effort. The entire relevant intellectual resources of the United States were now being put to use in creating a nuclear bomb.

Meanwhile, President Roosevelt was trying to coordinate research efforts with the British at a higher level. Despite early desires for intervention from British scientists, the lag in American research had put a damper on British hopes for transatlantic cooperation. Despite discussions between Roosevelt and Churchill, the British government was now convinced that the United States was not up to the job of creating a nuclear bomb, given the country's slowness in the early years of British development. The British and Americans thus continued to operate independent programs that were mostly uncoordinated, even though the country's scientists shared information and discoveries with each other as research progressed.

By the summer of 1942, American research into a nuclear weapon had advanced considerably. Lawrence had found enormous success with electromagnetic enrichment of uranium-235, leading American scientists to conclude that the amount of enrichment needed would be even less than previously thought. However, researchers were running into problems elsewhere. Isotope separation processes at Columbia and gaseous diffusion efforts were encountering enormous stumbling blocks.

With the urgency of war providing pressure, Vannevar Bush, as the administrative head of the project, felt that the production stages could wait no longer. Research was important, but having the infrastructure in place to build the bomb when the time was ripe was equally critical. He authorized the S-1 Committee to begin offering projections for the infrastructure that would be needed to actually build the bomb, irrespective of costs.

To initiate production, the Army Corps of Engineers became directly involved. That summer, the transition from S-1 control to Army control was complete, with Colonel James C. Marshall in control of the Manhattan Engineering District. But Marshall was an army man, not an engineer, and knew nothing about theoretical physics. Bush thought he was inadequate for the job of coordinating the creation of a nuclear bomb, so a reshuffling of administrative leadership took place in September, with Brigadier General Leslie Groves replacing Marshall as head of the Manhattan District. Unlike Marshall, Groves was an engineer with the perfect credentials for handling the project. With Groves as the military head, he appointed a man named J. Robert Oppenheimer as the project's scientific leader.

Oppenheimer

Oppenheimer's appointment surprised many. While he had made significant insights into fast neutron calculations, Oppenheimer did not have a Nobel Prize, as many other lead scientists (including Lawrence) did. Furthermore, Oppenheimer lacked administrative experience, and his associations with the military were loose at best. Some suggested he was a communist. Regardless, Groves saw great intellect in Oppenheimer and considered him the perfect fit for the position.

Together, Oppenheimer and Groves began selecting sites to build infrastructure for producing the nuclear bomb. At this point, the Manhattan Project was headquartered in New York, near Columbia University, but the construction of the bomb was anticipated to be a nationwide effort. Selecting proper sites for construction was of crucial importance.

In September, before selecting Oppenheimer as Scientific Director, Groves chose a site in Tennessee for "Site X." Site X was located in Oak Ridge, Tennessee, and would come to include four separate research laboratories by the end of the Manhattan Project. In November, both Groves and Oppenheimer sought out "Site Y," and ultimately decided on Los Alamos, New Mexico, as the ideal location.

Workers at Oak Ridge

Each of these sites was selected in part for their isolation from major population centers. The Manhattan Project was a secret and needed to be removed from public interest. The U.S. Army Corps of Engineers went about creating literally new cities to house the facilities' workers, while the airspace over the facilities was heavily guarded and closed off. In Oak Ridge, a once sparsely inhabited valley saw its population jump from 3,000 in 1942 to 75,000 by the end of the war. Because of the sensitivity of the research being conducted, the sites also needed to be distant from international borders. Unsure of what their research would yield, Groves and Oppenheimer did not want a nuclear meltdown to take place in a location that could leak across international borders.

With these two initial sites of production selected, construction of laboratories quickly began at both locations. In the meantime, work continued at universities, much as it had before the centralized takeover of American nuclear research. During this time period, the most important breakthrough in nuclear science came from the laboratories of Enrico Fermi, in collaboration with Leo Szilárd, at the University of Chicago. There, the two created the first man-made nuclear reactor, known as Chicago Pile-1.

Chicago Pile-1 went into action successfully on December 2nd, 1942. The nuclear reactor, unlike almost all nuclear reactors since, did *not* have any cooling system or radiation shield. Fermi thought this was unnecessary and predicted that a self-sustaining nuclear chain reaction faced little threat of melting down. This was, of course, dangerously incorrect. In hindsight, Fermi's first controlled reaction put the city of Chicago in enormous danger. Luckily, after 28 minutes of operating Chicago Pile-1, Fermi closed down the reactor and all was fine. Had it spun out of control, however, a nuclear meltdown would have destroyed one of the nation's most densely populated cities, and a disaster would have certainly eliminated any public support or political will to continue the Manhattan Project.

In conveying to his colleagues around the country that the project was a success, the scientist simply stated that "the Italian navigator has landed in the New World." Secret codes like this ensured that the Manhattan Project remained known by only the nation's most elite scientists. It was quickly, however, becoming a national effort encompassing thousands of employees. By the end of the war, the Manhattan Project employed nearly 150,000 people.

At last the Americans were making significant headway in the production of nuclear weapons. President Roosevelt had given his seal of approval, but the British had soured on the idea of conducting a joint British-American effort. With more credibility now supporting the country's project, Roosevelt was ready to attempt closer transatlantic cooperation once again.

President Roosevelt and Prime Minister Churchill met in Quebec City, Canada, in August 1943 to discuss joint cooperation. While fortunes in Roosevelt's country had changed for the better between 1941 and 1943, progress had stalled in Britain. The British and their Empire were now under continual military assault, and all of their resources were being poured into fighting Nazi Germany. Building a nuclear bomb was important, but marshaling resources toward a bomb that existed only in scientists' imaginations was removed from the forefront in the interest of battling the Luftwaffe in Europe. Moreover, the British were having trouble moving forward on the project.

On August 19, 1943, President Roosevelt and Prime Minister Churchill signed the Quebec Agreement, a formal statement that laid out the terms of transatlantic cooperation on nuclear weapons research. The agreement not only allowed the British "Tube Alloys" program to join the Manhattan Project, but it also designated how the two nations and Canada would use nuclear weapons in the future. Specifically, the three nations agreed to never use nuclear weapons against each other, never to use them against another country without the consent of all three nations, and never to give the research to another nation without unanimous agreement among the three countries.

With the Quebec Agreement in hand, British scientists came to the United States to join American researchers working on the Manhattan Project. In reality, the two groups had been communicating throughout their respective projects, but the Quebec Agreement allowed them to do so officially. Separated from Japan and Germany by oceans, the U.S. was a much safer place to work on the project anyway, ensuring that the Project could remain a secret. And with more rural land with which to work, the United States also provided better space for conducting nuclear tests than the United Kingdom anyway.

With the addition of British scientists, the Manhattan Project expanded rapidly throughout 1943 and 1944. Construction on sites began not only at Oak Ridge and Los Alamos, but elsewhere across the country. The three most important sites were Oak Ridge and Los Alamos, and another site in Washington called the Hanford site. Oak Ridge served to enrich uranium, Hanford enriched plutonium and Los Alamos was the research site used for assembly of the bomb itself. The Manhattan Project, however, was not limited to these three sites. It expanded into dozens of locations across the United States and Canada at the Project's peak. Each site served a unique purpose, and all were under the central command of the Army Corps of Engineers, led by General Groves and Oppenheimer.

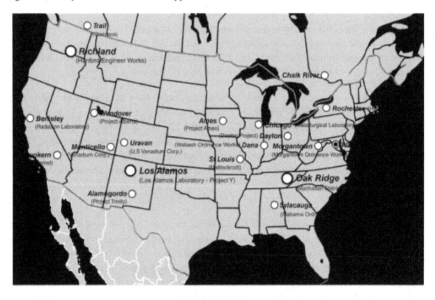

Sites where work was conducted on the Manhattan Project

In the fall of 1943, the production phase of nuclear weaponry moved on to the delivery aspect of the project. While scientists were working on the physics of a nuclear reaction, engineers needed to find a way to deliver nuclear energy in a manageable bomb format. In October of 1943, groups of Army engineers in Los Alamos and a site at the Wendover Army Airfield in Utah got to work designing the bomb itself. This project became known as Project Alberta, known colloquially as "Project A."

Project A not only designed the shape and size of the bomb, it also created measures to ensure that the bomb did not detonate prematurely or become vulnerable to induced detonation from a Japanese attack. The engineers also created devices to time the explosion and test the effects of high altitudes on nuclear reactions.

Project Alberta was a final stage in the creation of the nuclear bomb. For the first time, sites in

Japan were now being targeted for nuclear delivery, and the design of the bombs took these targets into account.

1944 brought enormous progress with the construction of the nuclear bomb, though not without some initial failures. First among these setbacks was the discovery in April that the "gun-type" fission weapon would probably not work. A man named Emilio Segrè, another Jewish-American who escaped oppression in fascist Europe, worked with enriched plutonium at Los Alamos. He discovered that plutonium was unsuitable to the "Thin Man" nuclear bomb prototype proposed by scientists at Oak Ridge. "Thin Man" proposed using fissionable plutonium to explode a bomb via a gun-like contraption within the bomb itself. Segrè discovered, however, that the fission rate of plutonium was too high and was unsuitable to this model.

Segrè

Two other models were also in development: another gun-type bomb using uranium, called "Little Boy," and an implosion-based bomb called "Fat Man". "Thin Man" was discarded after Segrè's discovery, and priority was thereafter given to the other two types of bomb. Lead-scientist Oppenheimer reviewed Segrè's discoveries and made the call to suspend development on the plutonium gun-type bomb.

By the middle of the summer of 1944, the Manhattan Project had developed the two prototypes that would eventually form the bombs dropped on Hiroshima and Nagasaki.

The design for Little Boy

The design for Fat Man

Franklin D. Roosevelt had been disabled for much of his adult life, but it still came as a surprise when he suffered a hemorrhage and abruptly died in April 1945. Vice President Harry Truman succeeded him. Incredibly, the Manhattan Project had been so secretive that the Vice President-turned-President did not even know of its existence. Following his first Cabinet meeting on his first day as President, Secretary of War Henry Stimson informed the President of the Project.

Despite the glaring oversight of failing to brief the Vice President, the Manhattan Project was unfazed by Roosevelt's death and continued undisrupted. The war itself was also mostly undisturbed by Roosevelt's death. Months earlier, with the Soviets racing toward Berlin from the east and the British and Americans pushing toward Germany from the west, Roosevelt had met with Churchill and Stalin at the Yalta Conference to plan out a postwar Europe. A month after the President's death, victory was achieved in Europe.

Construction of the bomb, however, did not stop with victory in Europe. There was widespread jubilation when Germany surrendered, but the Japanese were showing no sign of surrendering. In May 1945 the Americans and Japanese were engaged in an extremely deadly campaign at Okinawa, an island close enough to use for air attacks on the Japanese mainland. Facing kamikaze attacks and fanatic Japanese soldiers, the Allies suffered 50,000 casualties, leading American military officials to estimate upwards of a million Allied casualties if they had to invade the Japanese mainland. Besides, the nuclear bombs being constructed in Los Alamos were always intended to be used in Japan, and so the end of the war in Europe did not make the bombs any less necessary.

Under a new President, the Manhattan Project continued unabated. When Truman came to office, the Manhattan Project was on the brink of its final goal, a successful detonation of a nuclear device, which would come in a matter of months. At that point, President Truman would be left to make a fateful decision about using the most destructive weapon ever created.

The bomb was not yet officially complete, nor had it been tested, before President Truman and his advisors were being pelted by letters from scientists raising ethical objections to the use of the nuclear bomb. It was not making Truman's decision any less difficult.

The first of such letters came in June 1945 from James Franck, yet another Jewish escapee from Central Europe who came to the United States and worked on nuclear research. In his letter, Franck offered apt advice on the threat of a nuclear arms race should the U.S. use the weapon. He suggested that the weapon would be so powerful and so devastating that nations around the world would race to gain access to the technology themselves. Franck's solution was to either keep the nuclear bomb secret indefinitely or to test it in a barren desert before the United Nations, to show Japan and the world its devastating destructiveness. The letter was signed by Franck and other notable nuclear scientists, including Leo Szilárd and Glenn Seaborg, both early proponents of and contributors to the Manhattan Project. The letter was received and taken into account by a nuclear arms committee appointed by President Truman.

Franck

A second important letter came in July, less than a month before the nuclear detonations over Hiroshima and Nagasaki. Penned by Leo Szilárd, the document was signed by an additional 69 physicists and researchers. It explicitly opposed using the weapon against Japan unless that nation was offered surrender terms beforehand and rejected them. All 70 petitioners lost their jobs in the Manhattan Project, though the letter was received by the same committee that reviewed the Franck Letter.

In between the two petitions, the American nuclear bomb had finally come to fruition. On July 16, 1945, the first detonation of a nuclear device took place in Alamogordo, New Mexico.

The first bomb was nicknamed the "gadget," to avoid espionage attempts to discover that it was, indeed, a bomb. In some sense, the device detonated in July was not really a "bomb" anyway; it was not a deployable device, though it one that could be detonated.

The Trinity Test device was a "Fat Man" implosion type of nuclear device that relied on plutonium, not uranium. It featured a rounded capsule filled with a plutonium center surrounded by explosives. The explosives detonated simultaneously inward, forcing dense pressure onto the plutonium. This resulted in a nuclear explosion.

To conduct the actual test, a 100-foot tower was built, to which the bomb was hoisted at the top. Because the Trinity site was a huge desert, physicists scattered around the tower at no less than 10 mile distances, and everyone wore ultraviolet lenses to protect their eyes from damage.

At 5:10 p.m., the 20-minute countdown began. No one *really* knew what would become of the detonation; some speculated that the bomb would ignite the atmosphere of the entire planet, killing all life on earth. That, however, was among the more extreme predictions. Other less extreme but still horrifying predictions guessed that all of New Mexico would be incinerated.

After waiting 20 minutes, however, all these fears were put to rest, when the world's first mushroom cloud was detonated over the desert sky. For a few seconds, all of the mountains within view of the detonation were reportedly brightly lit up, and the earth trembled.

The Trinity Test

With this success, word reached President Truman, who was then attending an Allied Conference in Potsdam. There, he presented the news to Soviet leader Josef Stalin. Stalin feigned surprise; espionage missions had revealed American nuclear research to the Soviets before it had even reached then-Vice President Harry Truman.

The physicists present at the detonation inspected the site a few weeks later. Little did they know that nuclear fallout had infected some parts of New Mexico, though no densely populated regions were affected. Upon inspection, they found sand that had been turned to glass by the enormous force of the world's first nuclear explosion.

Oppenheimer and Graves inspect the detonation site

The blast site

Before making his decision to use the bomb, Truman considered some of the ethical advice submitted by American physicists. In particular, he took the idea of informing the Japanese beforehand to heart. At the Potsdam Conference on July 26th, Truman, the United Kingdom and China issued the Potsdam Declaration, giving the Japanese an ultimatum to surrender or suffer "prompt and utter destruction."

Japan chose to ignore the ultimatum, and ultimately Truman chose to use the bombs. Truman took the scientists' concerns into account, but the deadly experience of Okinawa made clear that hundreds of thousands of Americans would be casualties in a conventional invasion of the mainland of Japan. Moreover, the fanatical manner in which Japanese soldiers and civilians held out on Okinawa indicated that the Japanese would suffer more casualties during an invasion than they would if the bombs were used. Pursuant to the Quebec Agreement, Canada and Great Britain consented to the use of the bomb. As a result, Truman authorized its use on two sites in Japan.

President Truman Ordering the Bomb to Be Dropped

Once Truman gave the go ahead to use the bomb, there was still a matter of picking out sites. Though largely forgotten today, the U.S. listed sites in Japan that had the most military value when choosing where to hit. Moreover, the Americans had to deal with weather conditions, which doomed Nagasaki on August 9.

The primary target for the use of the first bomb was the city of Hiroshima, located in south-central Japan and the largest in the Hiroshima Prefecture. The 509th Composite Group of the U.S. Air Force was created to deploy nuclear weapons, thus given the mission to hit Hiroshima. Lieutenant Colonel Paul Tibbets was selected for the mission well beforehand, and had been training at the remote Wendover Army Air Field in Utah. In the days leading up to the use of the bomb, the Air Force dropped leaflets telling residents of Hiroshima to flee, a warning about half the residents heeded.

On August 6, three planes set off from the island of Tinian to make the 6 hour flight to Hiroshima. Tibbets led the mission, flying the *Enola Gay*, a plane named after his mother that carried the nuclear "Little Boy" uranium gun-type nuclear bomb. Two other planes, *The Great Artiste* and *Necessary Evil* accompanied the mission. All three planes were B-29's.

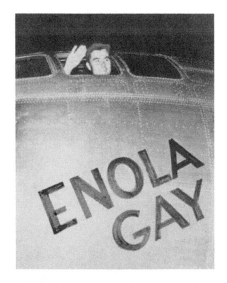

Tibbets about to take off in the *Enola Gay*

At approximately 8:15 a.m. on August 6th, 1945, the bomb was dropped from the *Enola Gay*, almost exactly as planned. The bomb missed its precise target by 800 feet, an insignificant distance given the bomb's destructiveness.

With the detonation of "Little Boy," the destruction of Hiroshima was far from "little." Japanese officials estimated that approximately 70% of the city's buildings were completely destroyed and another 5-10% were severely damaged. 80,000 people were killed instantly, and another 70,000 severely injured. The entire world had witnessed the devastation of the world's most powerful weapon.

Wreckage in Hiroshima after the Bomb

Hiroshima would not be the only Japanese city to be destroyed by an American atomic bomb. President Truman reiterated his plea for an unconditional surrender after Hiroshima, cautioning that failure to do so would result in an additional "rain of ruin from the air, the like of which has never been seen on this earth." Making matters worse for Japan, the Soviet Union broke its Soviet-Japanese Neutrality Pact and declared war on Japan on August 9, as part of an agreement the Soviets had reached with the Allies.

Still, Japan refused to surrender. Instead, the Japanese government instituted martial law within the country to prevent anyone from surrendering. As such, Truman's "rain of ruin" continued. The second site targeted was the city of Kokura, in Southern Japan. This time, a plane called the *Bockstar* was to deliver the bomb, piloted by Major Charles Sweeney.

Luckily for the residents of Kokura, its name would remain irrelevant in the narrative of World War II. The nuclear bombing required the pilot to be able to see the ground, but Kokura was obscured by dense cloud cover on the date of the bombing. Thus, Sweeney made the call to divert to the secondary target, a city farther south called Nagasaki.

There, too, the city was covered in clouds, but a very brief break in the cloud cover at about 11:00 a.m. on August 9 allowed *Bockstar* to drop the "Fat Man" plutonium implosion-type bomb it was carrying. The bomb landed significantly north of its intended epicenter, about two miles to the north and west, in Nagasaki's industrial district. As such, Nagasaki was not as badly destroyed as Hiroshima, but over 40,000 people were still killed.

On August 14th, 1945, five days after the bombing of Nagasaki, Japan's Emperor Hirohito offered a capitulation and unconditional surrender. Despite some initial protest from Japanese militarists, the war was now definitely over. Hirohito cited the unprecedented nuclear attack as the primary reason for surrender, though the Soviet invasion was also a significant factor.

World War II was now officially over on both fronts. On August 28, the Supreme Allied occupation of Japan began, and the official surrender ceremony was completed on the USS *Missouri* on September 2. Interestingly, the official end of the state of war between the U.S. and Japan, however, did not come until 1952, with the Treaty of San Francisco being signed on April 28 of that year.

With the bombings of Hiroshima and Nagasaki marking the end of World War II, the Manhattan Project went from top secret to public knowledge. Just a year after the war's end, Congress began debating what to do with its newly-found nuclear arsenal and how to control the deadly technology.

An important component of the post-war discussion of atomic energy involved the military's lone control over nuclear technology during the war. Was this politically justified? Even after the war, the U.S. military alone had access to the secrets of nuclear technology and controlled the nation's arsenal, without any oversight by Congress. Amazingly, the U.S. Congress was largely unaware of the Manhattan Project during most of its history. For many Americans, this represented a major violation to the nation's concept of a civilian-controlled military.

Out of this came the Atomic Energy Act of 1946, proposed by Senator Brien McMahon of Connecticut. It passed the Senate unanimously and also passed overwhelmingly in the House. It was signed by President Truman on August 1, 1946, going into effect on January 1, 1947. The Atomic Energy Act created the United States Atomic Energy Commission to ensure that future developments in nuclear technology were overseen by Congress. The law also restricted the ability of the United States to share nuclear knowledge with other nations, a proviso that offended Great Britain and Canada, who had contributed to the Manhattan Project and had shared information with the U.S. during the war. As a result of the Atomic Energy Act, both nations were forced to decide whether or not to pursue their own separate nuclear energy programs. Congress had essentially voided the Quebec Agreement; because it was signed by Roosevelt in secret, it was not legally binding.

A raging debate over the ethics of the attacks on Hiroshima and Nagasaki lasts to this day. Were the nuclear attacks on those cities justified? Proponents of the bombings say that, had the U.S. not dropped the bombs, more Japanese and American citizens would have eventually died during continued fighting between the two countries. To this, critics insist the U.S. could have achieved victory on its own terms without killing as many innocent civilians. But it remains unclear how that could have happened. The U.S. obviously could not have achieved victory faster without using the nuclear bomb, which ended the war within a week of its use on Hiroshima. There's no question that a combined naval and military assault on Japan would have taken much longer. And the suggestions that the U.S. demonstrate the bomb's deadliness to Japan beforehand seems to fall flat, considering Japan rejected surrender terms and still refused to surrender after the bombing of Hiroshima.

In the end, the debate comes down to one of speculation. It's impossible to know how intense Japanese-American fighting would have been without the nuclear bomb, and how many people would have been killed as a result.

Another lasting issue that came out of the Manhattan Project involves the global nuclear arms race it ignited. On this, the Project's legacy is much more certain. Much as the Franck letter forewarned, the bombings of Hiroshima and Nagasaki *did* ignite a multi-decade arms race between the Soviet Union and the United States. Arms races sprung up elsewhere in the world, notably between India and Pakistan, and nations around the world vie to gain access to nuclear weapons \ today. The nuclear attacks on Japan solidified the idea that ownership of nuclear technology permanently insulated a nation from external attack. No nation would threaten to attack the United States out of fear of nuclear retaliation. Countries like Iran hope to gain that sort of invincibility today, while its enemies fear the consequences of letting antagonistic regimes get hold of such deadly weapons.

While the Manhattan Project undoubtedly spurred an arms race, the consequences of that race are more hotly debated. Is a global nuclear arms race necessarily a bad thing? After the World War, two global superpowers, the Soviet Union and the United States, avoided war for decades, despite unprecedented hostilities. Nuclear weapons are given significant credit for this lasting state of peace. The weapons served as a significant deterrent; neither nation could conceivably go to war with the other without risking nuclear annihilation. Similar peace has been kept elsewhere in the world because of the strategic balance created by opposing sides holding nuclear weapons.

Finally, it's important to remember the legacy of the Manhattan Project is not limited merely to political issues of war and peace. Having broken enormous ground in the science of atomic energy, the Manhattan Project has given the world a new and powerful source of energy. While the risks of nuclear power are many, the reality is that few meltdowns have occurred and nuclear energy remains a clean and promising way of powering an information-age society. At its start, the Manhattan Project in the United States was devoted more to this use of uranium and plutonium. In the end, domestic energy serves as one of the brightest contributions the Manhattan Project offered to global society.

Online Resources

Other World War II titles by Charles River Editors

Bibliography

Appleman, Roy Edgar; Burns, James M.; Gugeler, Russel A.; Stevens, John (1948). Okinawa: The Last Battle. Washington DC: United States Army Center of Military History. ISBN 1-4102-2206-3. full text online

Astor, Gerald (1996). Operation Iceberg: The Invasion and Conquest of Okinawa in World War II. Dell. ISBN 0-440-22178-1.

Buckner, Simon Bolivar, Jr. and Joseph Stilwell. Seven Stars: The Okinawa Battle Diaries of Simon Bolivar Buckner, Jr. and Joseph Stilwell ed. by Nicholas Evan Sarantakes (2004)

Caidin, Martin (1960). A Torch to the Enemy: The Fire Raid on Tokyo. Balantine Books. ISBN 0-553-29926-3. D767.25.T6 C35.

Coffey, Thomas M. (1987). Iron Eagle: The Turbulent Life of General Curtis LeMay. Random House Value Publishing. ISBN 0-517-55188-8.

DeGroot, Gerard J. The Bomb: A Life. Cambridge: Harvard University Press, 2005.

Boston: Little, Brown and Company, 1967.

Feifer, George (2001). The Battle of Okinawa: The Blood and the Bomb. The Lyons Press. ISBN 1-58574-215-5.

Fisch Jr., Arnold G. Ryukyus. World War II Campaign Brochures. Washington D.C.: United States Army Center of Military History. ISBN 0-16-048032-9. CMH Pub 72-35.

Frank, Benis. Okinawa: Touchstone to Victory. New York, NY: Ballantine Books Inc., 1969.

Frank, Richard B. (2001). Downfall: The End of the Imperial Japanese Empire. Penguin. ISBN 0-14-100146-1.

Gandt, Robert (2010). The Twilight Warriors. Broadway Books. ISBN 978-0-7679-3241-7.

Gow, Ian. Okinawa 1945: Gateway to Japan. Garden City, NY: Doubleday & Company, Inc., 1985.

Grayling, A. C. (2007). Among the Dead Cities: The History and Moral Legacy of the WWII Bombing of Civilians in Germany and Japan. New York: Walker Publishing Company Inc. ISBN 0-8027-1565-6.

Groueff, Stephane. Manhattan Project: The Untold Story of the Making of the Atomic Bomb.

Hallas, James H. (2006). Killing Ground on Okinawa: The Battle for Sugar Loaf Hill. Potomac Books. ISBN 1-59797-063-8.

Hastings, Max (2007). Retribution – The Battle for Japan, 1944–45. New York: Alfred A. Knopf. ISBN 978-0-307-26351-3.

Lacey, Laura Homan (2005). Stay Off The Skyline: The Sixth Marine Division on Okinawa— An Oral History. Potomac Books. ISBN 1-57488-952-4.

Leckie, Robert. Okinawa: The Last Battle of World War II. New York: Penguin Books, 1996.

Manchester, William (1980). Goodbye, Darkness: A Memoir of the Pacific War. Boston, Toronto: Little, Brown and Co. ISBN 0-316-54501-5.

Morison, Samuel Eliot (2002 (reissue)). Victory in the Pacific, 1945, vol. 14 of History of United States Naval Operations in World War II. Champaign, Illinois, USA: University of Illinois Press. ISBN 0-252-07065-8.

Nichols, Charles Sidney; Henry I. Shaw Jr. (1989). Okinawa: Victory in the Pacific. Battery

Press. ASIN B00071UAT8.

Rottman, Gordon (2002). Okinawa 1945: The last Battle. Osprey Publishing. ISBN 1-84176-546-5.

Sledge, E. B.; Paul Fussell (1990). With the Old Breed: At Peleliu and Okinawa. Oxford University Press. ISBN 0-19-506714-2., famous Marine memoir

Sloan, Bill (2007). The Ultimate Battle: Okinawa 1945—The Last Epic Struggle of World War II. Simon & Schuster. ISBN 0-7432-9246-4.

Yahara, Hiromichi (2001). The Battle for Okinawa. John Wiley & Sons. ISBN 0-471-18080-7.- Firsthand account of the battle by a surviving Japanese officer.

Zaloga, Steven J. Japanese Tanks 1939–45. Osprey, 2007. ISBN 978-1-84603-091-8.

Made in the
USA
Middletown, DE